GOOD HOUSEKEEPING

BEST RECIPES

GOOD HOUSEKEEPING

BEST RECIPES

Good Housekeeping
Institute

EBURY PRESS
LONDON

Published by Ebury Press
National Magazine House
72 Broadwick Street
London W1V 2BP

First impression 1984

ISBN 0 85223 381 7

Designed by Harry Green

Colour photographs by
Bryce Atwell, Alan Duns, Laurie Evans, Melvin Grey, Robert Golden,
Christine Hanscomb, Paul Kemp, Frederick Mancini,
Philip Pace, Bill Richmond, Paul Williams.

Jacket photograph by Paul Kemp shows Boned Stuffed
Poussin (page 54) and Iced Strawberry Soufflé (page 76).
Title page photograph shows Roast Pheasant (page 56).

Filmset by Advanced Filmsetters (Glasgow) Ltd
Printed and bound in Italy by New Interlitho S.p.a. Milan

CONTENTS

CHAPTER ONE

SOUPS AND STARTERS

TARRAGON EGG TARTLETS
Serves 4

75 g (3 oz) shortcrust pastry (see Aubergine Samosas, page 14)	4 eggs
	60 ml (4 tbsp) single cream
	few sprigs fresh tarragon
1 pimento cap	or 1.25 ml ($\frac{1}{4}$ level tsp)
salt and milled pepper	dried tarragon
pinch sugar	2.5 ml ($\frac{1}{2}$ tsp) lemon juice

On a lightly-floured surface, thinly roll out the shortcrust pastry. Cut or stamp out four 10-cm (4-inch) rounds. Line four 7.5-cm (3-inch) tartlet tins. Chill for 30 minutes.

Bake the tartlets blind at 190°C (375°F) mark 5 for 15–20 minutes. Turn out to cool on a wire rack. Finely chop the pimento cap. Season with salt, pepper and sugar.

Not more than 30 minutes before serving, softly poach the eggs. Drain and place on greaseproof paper. Trim neatly and cover with damp greaseproof paper.

To serve, spread the pimento in the base of each tartlet. Place an egg in each. Stand the tartlets on a baking sheet, cover with the damp greaseproof paper. Warm gently at 180°C (350°F) mark 4 for about 3 minutes.

Meanwhile gently warm the single cream with a small sprig of tarragon, salt, pepper and lemon juice. Spoon around the warmed tartlets and garnish with sprigs of tarragon.

Not suitable for freezing.

WATERCRESS & ORANGE SOUP
Serves 6

2 large bunches watercress	1.1 litres (2 pints) chicken stock
175 g (6 oz) onion, skinned and chopped	1 medium orange
50 g (2 oz) butter or margarine	3 slices white bread
45 ml (3 level tbsp) flour	142-ml (5-fl oz) carton single cream (optional)
salt and milled pepper	croûtons to garnish

Trim the watercress, wash and drain well then finely chop.

Melt the fat in a large saucepan, add the watercress and onion. Cover the pan and cook gently for 10–15 minutes or until the vegetables are almost tender. Off the heat, stir in the flour followed by the stock and seasoning. Bring slowly up to the boil stirring all the time. Cover the pan and simmer gently for 30 minutes. Stir in the finely grated orange rind and 45 ml (3 tbsp) orange juice. Cool a little, then purée the soup in an electric blender.

Meanwhile cut the bread into small cubes and grill until golden.

Reheat the soup and stir in the cream or serve the soup well chilled.

Garnish with the croûtons.

To freeze Cool, pack and freeze the soup after blending. To use, thaw overnight at cool room temperature, complete as above.

Tarragon and egg tartlet is the perfect starter for an elegant dinner party

PURÉE OF PARSNIP SOUP
Serves 6

40 g (1½ oz) butter or margarine
125 g (4 oz) onion, skinned and sliced
700 g (1½ lb) parsnips, peeled and finely diced
salt and milled pepper

5 ml (1 level tsp) curry powder
2.5 ml (½ level tsp) ground cumin
1.4 litres (2½ pints) light stock

Heat the butter in the base of a large pan and fry the onion and parsnip together for about 3 minutes. Stir in the curry powder and cumin and fry for a further 2 minutes.

Add the stock, bring to the boil, reduce heat and simmer covered for about 45 minutes or until the vegetables are tender.

Cool slightly, then use a perforated draining spoon to place the vegetables in a blender, add a little stock, purée until smooth. Return to the pan. Adjust the seasoning and reheat to serving temperature.

To freeze Cool and pack. To use, reheat slowly from frozen adding a little stock to the pan.

SMOKED FISH CHOWDER
Serves 4 as a meal soup, 6 as a starter

450 g (1 lb) smoked haddock fillet
225 g (8 oz) potatoes, peeled
175 g (6 oz) onion, skinned and sliced
50 g (2 oz) butter

30 ml (2 level tbsp) flour
175 g (6 oz) carrot, pared
142-ml (5-fl oz) carton single cream
salt and milled pepper
chopped parsley

Simmer the fish in 1.1 litres (2 pints) water for 10 minutes until tender. Drain, reserving the liquid. Flake coarsely, discarding skin and any bones.

Cut the potatoes into 1-cm (½-inch) cubes. Sauté the onion in the butter until soft, then stir in the flour. Gradually add the strained fish stock and bring to the boil, stirring. Add the potatoes and coarsely grate in the carrot. Simmer for about 10 minutes until the vegetables are tender.

Stir in the cream and flaked fish. Season well and heat to serving temperature. Do not boil. Garnish with lots of chopped parsley.

Not suitable for freezing.

CREAM OF SKATE SOUP
Serves 6

450 g (1 lb) skate
125 g (4 oz) onion, skinned and thinly sliced
125 g (4 oz) celery, washed and sliced
45 ml (3 tbsp) lemon juice
2 bayleaves

salt and milled pepper
300 ml (½ pint) milk
142-ml (5-fl oz) carton soured cream
25 g (1 oz) lump fish roe (caviar-style)
chives

Rinse the skate and place in a medium-sized saucepan with the onion and sliced celery. Pour over 600 ml (1 pint) water with 30 ml (2 tbsp) lemon juice, bayleaves and seasoning.

Bring slowly to the boil, cover the pan and simmer gently until the fish begins to flake away from the bone. Flake the fish, discard skin and bone. In an electric blender, purée the pan ingredients (discarding bayleaf) with the fish and milk until smooth. Adjust seasoning, add remaining lemon juice if necessary.

Chill well before serving with stirred soured cream and caviar swirled through each portion. Garnish with snipped chives.

To freeze Pack and freeze without soured cream and caviar. To use, thaw at cool room temperature overnight; chill before serving.

POTATO BROTH
Serves 4-6

50 g (2 oz) butter or margarine
15 ml (1 tbsp) oil
450 g (1 lb) chicken drumsticks
700 g (1½ lb) old potatoes
125 g (4 oz) each celery, carrot, onion, chopped

125 g (4 oz) button mushrooms, halved
75 g (3 oz) streaky bacon, chopped
1 bayleaf
salt and milled pepper
60 ml (4 tbsp) double cream

Heat the fat and oil in a large saucepan. Sauté the chicken drumsticks until well browned.

Meanwhile peel and coarsely grate the potatoes. Add the vegetables and bacon to the pan. Sauté for a further 2–3 minutes until browned also. Stir in 1.1 litres (2 pints) water, the bayleaf and seasoning. Bring to the boil. Cover and simmer for 30–35 minutes or until the vegetables and chicken are cooked.

Remove the chicken drumsticks and discard the skin. Scrape off all the flesh and cut into small pieces. Stir the chicken flesh back into the soup with the cream. Adjust seasoning. Reheat gently to serve.

Not suitable for freezing.

CHILLED LETTUCE & PEA SOUP
Serves 4

2 round lettuce
50 g (2 oz) butter
125 g (4 oz) onion, skinned
    and finely sliced
15 ml (1 level tbsp) flour
900 ml (1½ pints) milk

225 g (8 oz) fresh shelled
    or frozen peas
salt and milled pepper
142-ml (5-fl oz) carton
    single cream

Prepare the lettuces, and break up the leaves. Melt the butter in a medium-sized saucepan, add the lettuce and onion, cover and cook gently until the vegetables are soft.

Stir in the flour and milk and bring to the boil. Add the peas, season well and simmer, covered, for 30 minutes stirring occasionally. Cool slightly. Purée the pan ingredients in a blender and pour into a bowl, adjust seasoning, and chill well. Serve with the cream swirled through.

To freeze Pack and freeze. To use, thaw at cool room temperature overnight.

CELERY & STILTON SOUP
Serves 4 as a main course, 6 as a starter

175 g (6 oz) celery,
    trimmed
40 g (1½ oz) butter or
    margarine
45 ml (3 level tbsp) plain
    flour

300 ml (½ pint) milk
600 ml (1 pint) light stock,
    preferably unseasoned
225 g (8 oz) Stilton,
    grated
salt and milled pepper

Finely chop the celery and fry gently without colouring for 5 minutes in the heated butter. Stir in the plain flour and cook for 2 minutes. Add the milk and stock and bring to the boil. Cover and simmer for 15 minutes or until celery is tender.

Gradually add the Stilton and stir in until melted. Add seasoning and reheat gently to serving temperature.

Not suitable for freezing.

CHICKEN LIVER PÂTÉ WITH GREEN PEPPERCORNS
Serves 6

125 g (4 oz) butter
125 g (4 oz) onion, skinned
    and chopped
450 g (1 lb) chicken livers
1 clove garlic, skinned and
    crushed
milled pepper

2.5 ml (½ level tsp) dried
    marjoram
7.5 ml (1½ level tsp) salt
5 ml (1 tsp) lemon juice
15 ml (1 tbsp) sherry
10 ml (2 level tsp) chopped
    green peppercorns

Melt half the butter in a frying pan and add onion. Fry without colouring until onion has softened. Add the remaining ingredients except the butter and peppercorns. Cook over a gentle heat for about 10 minutes or until the livers firm and change colour.

Purée in an electric blender until smooth or push through a metal sieve. Stir in the peppercorns. Adjust the seasoning, turn into a serving dish. The mixture should come to just below rim. Refrigerate until firm, at least 2 hours.

Melt remaining butter, skim and spoon over pâté. Refrigerate to set. Leave at room temperature for 30 minutes before serving.

To freeze Pack and freeze before adding extra butter. To use, unwrap, seal with butter. Thaw at cool room temperature overnight. Complete as above.

SARDINE SAVOURIES
Serves 6

two 120-g (4¼-oz) cans
    sardine in oil
grated rind and juice of
    1 lemon
125 g (4 oz) fresh brown
    breadcrumbs
salt and milled pepper

15 ml (1 level tbsp)
    chopped parsley
125 g (4 oz) shortcrust
    pastry (See Aubergine
    Samosas, page 14)
beaten egg to glaze

Place the sardines, with their oil, in a bowl. Add the grated lemon rind and 10 ml (2 tsp) lemon juice. Stir in the breadcrumbs and parsley until the mixture is thoroughly combined. Season.

On a lightly-floured surface roll the pastry out to a 25.5 × 30.5-cm (8 × 12-inch) rectangle. Spread the sardine mixture evenly over the pastry. Roll up from the longest edge.

Slice the roll diagonally at 5-cm (2-inch) intervals into six pieces. Place on a baking sheet, seam side down, and glaze with the beaten egg. Bake at 200°C (400°F) mark 6 for 20–25 minutes or until golden brown. Serve hot with lemon wedges.

To freeze Pack and freeze unglazed before cooking. To use, glaze and cook from frozen as above for about 40 minutes. Cover if necessary towards end of cooking time.

SMOKED TROUT MILLE-FEUILLE
Serves 6

125 g (4 oz) rough puff
   pastry made with 125 g
   (4 oz) plain flour;
   pinch of salt; 40 g
   (1½ oz) butter or block
   margarine; 40 g (1½ oz)
   lard; 75 ml (⅛ pt)
   water; squeeze lemon
   juice
15 ml (1 level tbsp) black
   peppercorns
beaten egg to glaze
30 ml (2 level tbsp) capers

198-g (7-oz) can
   sweetcorn kernels
1 small smoked trout,
   about 225 g (8 oz)
142-ml (5-fl oz) carton
   soured cream
5 ml (1 tsp) lemon juice
salt and milled pepper
10 ml (2 level tsp)
   powdered gelatine
lemon wedges to
   accompany

Sift the flour and salt. Cut the fat into cubes and add to the flour. Add the water and lemon juice and mix in with a round-bladed knife, taking care not to break up the fat. Draw the mixture into a ball. Turn on to a lightly-floured surface and knead gently for a few seconds. Roll into a rectangle three times as long as it is wide. Fold bottom third up and top third down over pastry. Seal edges lightly with a rolling pin, turn through 90° and repeat three times more, wrapping and chilling well between each rolling. Wrap and refrigerate for at least 30 minutes.

On a lightly-floured surface, thinly roll out the pastry to a rectangle 30.5 × 23 cm (12 × 9 inch). Cut into three 10-cm (4-inch) wide strips. Place strips on a wetted baking sheet. Prick all over with a fork. Chill for 10 minutes.

Crush the peppercorns with a pestle and mortar or rolling pin. Glaze the pastry strips with beaten egg. Sprinkle the peppercorns over one of the strips. Bake at 200°C (400°F) mark 6 for 12–15 minutes or until golden and crisp. Cool on a wire rack.

Roughly chop the capers and drained sweetcorn, flake the trout. Mix with soured cream and lemon juice. Season.

Sprinkle the gelatine over 30 ml (2 tbsp) water. Leave to soak for 2–3 minutes. Dissolve over a low heat, stir into the fish mixture. Chill until beginning to set. Layer the pastry and fish mixture, topping with the peppered pastry strip. Chill again until just set, at least 30 minutes. Prepare not more than 2 hours before serving. Serve thickly sliced with lemon wedges.

Not suitable for freezing.

VEGETABLE SOUP WITH BACON
Serves 4

175 g (6 oz) smoked
   streaky bacon, chopped
350 g (12 oz) carrot,
   pared and diced
225 g (8 oz) turnip, peeled
   and diced
175 g (6 oz) onion, skinned
   and chopped
225 g (8 oz) celery,
   washed and diced
2.5 ml (½ level tsp) dried
   thyme
1 bayleaf

1.25 ml (¼ level tsp) dried
   basil
1 clove garlic
5 ml (1 level tsp) tomato
   paste
1.7 litres (3 pints) chicken
   stock
salt and milled pepper
125 g (4 oz) pasta tubes
4 slices bread
50 g (2 oz) Edam cheese,
   coarsely grated
chopped parsley

Place the bacon, vegetables, thyme, basil, bayleaf and crushed garlic in a large saucepan. Stir over a low heat for 2–3 minutes. Stir in the tomato paste, chicken stock and seasoning. Bring to the boil, simmer for 25–30 minutes. Stir in pasta tubes. Cover and simmer for a further 12–15 minutes or until pasta is tender. Adjust seasoning.

Toast the bread lightly on one side. Press a little cheese on to the untoasted side. Grill until golden. Cut into small triangles.

Transfer the soup to a serving dish. Serve immediately, garnished with parsley and toasted cheese triangles.

To freeze Freeze without the pasta or toast. To use, thaw at cool room temperature overnight. Finish as above.

CHICKEN & CUCUMBER MOUSSE
Serves 8

1.4 kg (3 lb) oven ready
   chicken
slices carrot and onion for
   flavouring
15 ml (1 level tbsp) fresh
   chopped tarragon or
   5 ml (1 level tsp) dried
salt and milled pepper
10 ml (2 level tsp)
   powdered gelatine

small cucumber—about
   275 g (10 oz) total
   weight
25 g (1 oz) margarine
30 ml (2 level tbsp) flour
30 ml (2 tbsp) lemon juice
142-ml (5-fl oz) carton
   whipping cream
1 egg white
sprigs tarragon

Cover the chicken, flavouring vegetables, herbs and seasoning with water and poach for about 45 minutes. Mince the chicken flesh. Boil down the cooking liquor to 400 ml (¾ pint).

Soak the gelatine in 30 ml (2 tbsp) water. Peel and finely dice three-quarters of the cucumber, sprinkle with salt and leave for 30 minutes, rinse, and dry with kitchen paper.

Make a sauce from the fat, flour and strained stock. Stir in the gelatine until dissolved. Beat in the chicken and leave to cool. When cold, add the diced cucumber, lemon juice, 7.5 ml (1½ level tsp) salt and plenty of pepper. Fold in the lightly whipped cream and stiffly-whisked egg white.

Spoon into a 1.7-litre (3-pint) serving dish, cover and refrigerate to set. Serve cold, decorated with cucumber slices and tarragon sprigs.

Not suitable for freezing.

Sweetcorn and capers bring colour and bite to Smoked trout mille feuille

SMOKED MACKEREL PÂTÉ
Serves 4

225 g (8 oz) smoked
   mackerel
10 ml (2 tsp) lemon juice
1 clove garlic, skinned and
   crushed

226-g (8-oz) tub plain
   cottage cheese
175 g (6 oz) butter
salt and milled pepper
bayleaf and peppercorns

Skin the smoked mackerel. Place the flesh in a bowl with the lemon and garlic. Sieve the cottage cheese into the bowl. Beat well until thoroughly combined. Finally beat in 125 g (4 oz) softened butter. Season.

Turn into one serving dish or individual pots. Melt the remaining 50 g (2 oz) butter and spoon over the surface of the pâté. Garnish with bayleaves and peppercorns. Chill well before serving.

To freeze Freeze without the melted butter. To use, thaw at cool room temperature for about 8 hours.

SMOKED TROUT MOUSSE
Serves 6

A beautifully light mousse with a slightly chunky texture—for a smooth consistency, purée the trout in a blender. Serve with melba toast.

300 ml (½ pint) milk
slices carrot, onion, celery,
   bayleaf, peppercorns for
   flavouring
1 large smoked trout —
   about 225 g (8 oz)
7.5 ml (1½ level tsp)
   powdered gelatine
30 ml (2 level tbsp) plain
   flour

25 g (1 oz) butter
15 ml (1 level tbsp)
   horseradish sauce
30 ml (2 tbsp) lemon juice
75 ml (5 tbsp) double
   cream
salt and milled pepper
2 egg whites
watercress sprigs or
   cucumber for garnish

Place the milk in a medium-sized saucepan with the flavouring ingredients, bring to the boil, take off the heat. Cover and leave to infuse for 10 minutes. Meanwhile skin the smoked trout and flake the flesh finely, discarding any bones. Keep the flesh covered with clingfilm.

Spoon 30 ml (2 tbsp) water into a small basin and sprinkle over the gelatine; leave to swell up. Strain the boiled milk into a jug. Melt the butter in a pan, blend in the flour and cook for 2 minutes. Stir in the milk and bring to the boil, stirring all the time, bubble gently for 2 minutes. Pour the sauce into a mixing bowl and while hot, stir in the soaked gelatine until dissolved. Cool.

Mix the flaked fish into the sauce with the horseradish and strained lemon juice. Lightly whip the cream and stir into the fish mixture, adjust seasoning. Lastly fold in the stiffly whisked egg whites and spoon into six 150-ml (¼-pint) individual soufflé dishes, cover and chill until lightly set. Garnish with watercress or thinly sliced cucumber.

Not suitable for freezing.

POTTED PRAWN SPREAD
Serves 8

175 g (6 oz) peeled prawns
75 g (3 oz) butter, softened
10 ml (2 tsp) lemon juice
salt and milled pepper

20 ml (4 tsp) chopped
   parsley
2 lemon slices
toast to accompany

Finely chop the prawns, reserving two for garnish. Beat into 50 g (2 oz) of the butter with the lemon juice, parsley and seasoning to taste. Spoon into two small pots and level the surface. Garnish with lemon slices and reserved prawns.

Melt the remaining butter and pour over the prawn mixture. Refrigerate to set.

Store for up to three days in the refrigerator. Serve with triangles of hot toast.

To freeze Pack and freeze using fresh prawns only. To use, thaw at cool room temperature overnight.

FLORIDA CHICORY SALAD
Serves 6

A greenish tinge at the top of chicory heads (not to be confused with curly endive) usually means they'll taste bitter. Go for those tinged with yellow.

1 small grapefruit
2 oranges
225 g (½ lb) tomatoes
225 g (½ lb) chicory
30 ml (2 tbsp) vegetable oil
15 ml (1 tbsp) lemon juice

10 ml (2 level tsp) soft
   light brown sugar
salt and milled pepper
45 ml (3 tbsp) chopped
   parsley
herb bread to accompany

Using a serrated knife, cut away all the peel and pith from the grapefruit and oranges and divide the flesh into segments, discarding the membrane and pips. Prepare over a bowl to catch any juice, then add the segments to the bowl.

Skin and quarter the tomatoes, push out the seeds and juice into a nylon sieve held over the bowl and the juice will drop through into it. Discard the seeds. If large, slice the tomato quarters down into eighths and add to the bowl.

Trim off the root and wash the chicory, removing any outer damaged leaves. Slice diagonally into 1-cm (½-inch) pieces. Open out the slices, add to the tomato, grapefruit and orange segments.

Whisk the oil, lemon juice, sugar, seasoning and parsley well together and stir through the fruit and vegetable mixture. Adjust seasoning. If the fruit is very acidic, it may be necessary to add more sugar. Cover the bowl and chill well. Serve with a loaf of hot herb bread.

Not suitable for freezing.

AVOCADO & KIWIFRUIT VINAIGRETTE
— Serves 6 —

Use half olive oil, half sunflower oil for a lighter dressing.

1 egg
120 ml (8 tbsp) olive oil
45 ml (3 tbsp) white wine
* vinegar*
3 kiwifruit
30 ml (2 tbsp) chopped
* parsley*
2 small ripe avocados
salt and milled pepper
watercress sprigs to garnish

Boil the egg for 6 minutes only. Meanwhile, whisk together the oil, vinegar, parsley and seasonings in a medium-sized bowl. Run cold water over the soft boiled egg to cool, then carefully shell. Scoop out the yolk into the dressing and add the finely chopped egg white, whisking well.

Skin the kiwifruit and slice the fruit into rings, discarding the ends. Stir into the dressing, cover and refrigerate for at least 2 hours.

Halve, peel and slice the avocados and arrange on individual serving plates with the drained kiwifruit. Spoon the dressing over the avocados and kiwifruit and garnish with watercress sprigs. Serve with crusty French bread.

Not suitable for freezing.

CREAM CHEESE TARTLETS
— Makes 12 tartlets —

50 g (2 oz) butter or block
* margarine*
25 g (1 oz) lard
125 g (4 oz) plain flour
1 egg, beaten
105 ml (7 tbsp) single
* cream*
85-g (3-oz) packet soft
* cheese with chopped*
* chives*
50 g (2 oz) smoked salmon
* trimmings*
milled pepper
grated Parmesan cheese

Rub the fats into the flour until the mixture resembles fine breadcrumbs. Bind to a firm dough with 30 ml (2 tbsp) water; knead lightly until just smooth. Roll out and use to line twelve deep patty tins. Bake the pastry blind until set but not browned.

Gradually beat the egg and cream into the cheese until smooth. Snip the smoked salmon into small pieces and add to the egg mixture with milled pepper, but no salt. Spoon into the tartlet cases and sprinkle with Parmesan cheese.

Bake at 180°C (350°F) mark 4 for about 18 minutes or until the custard mixture is just set. Serve warm or cold (the custard will crack slightly when cool).

Not suitable for freezing.

VEAL, WINE & APRICOT PÂTÉ
— Serves 6 —

700 g (1½ lb) pie veal
25 g (1 oz) dried apricots
100 ml (4 fl oz) dry white
* wine*
225 g (8 oz) pork fat
half a small bunch of
* watercress, washed and*
* trimmed*
2 eggs
2 cloves garlic, skinned and
* crushed*
50 g (2 oz) fresh white
* breadcrumbs*
2.5 ml (½ level tsp) ground
* allspice*
7.5 ml (1½ level tsp) salt
milled pepper

Roughly cut up the pie veal and place with apricots in a shallow dish. Pour over the wine. Leave covered overnight in the refrigerator.

Drain, reserve marinade. Finely mince the veal and apricots with the pork fat. Chop half the watercress, reserve rest for garnish.

In a large mixing bowl combine all the ingredients, including marinade. Mix well. Spoon the mixture into a 1.4-litre (2½-pint) loaf tin, press down well. Cover with foil. Half fill a roasting tin with boiling water and place the loaf tin in it. Cook at 170°C (325°F) mark 3 for about 1¾ hours. Remove pâté from roasting tin, spoon off excess fat, leave to cool slightly then cover with greaseproof paper and weight down overnight. Turn out, wrap and refrigerate. Allow to come to for 30 minutes at room temperature, then garnish with remaining watercress sprigs.

To freeze Pack and freeze. To use, thaw at cool room temperature overnight.

SEAFOOD ASPIC
— Serves 6 —

225 g (8 oz) whole cooked
* prawns in the shell*
300 ml (½ pint) dry white
* wine*
225 g (8 oz) cod fillet
bayleaf, peppercorns, slices
* of onion for flavouring*
salt and milled pepper
225 g (8 oz) tomato,
* skinned*
15 ml (1 level tbsp)
* powdered gelatine*
15 ml (1 tbsp) chopped
* parsley*
watercress sprigs
mayonnaise to accompany

Shell the prawns, reserving the shells. Reduce the wine by boiling to 150 ml (¼ pint). Place the cod, prawn shells, flavouring ingredients in a saucepan with the reduced wine and 300 ml (½ pint) water. Bring to the boil, simmer gently, covered for 15 minutes. Strain, reserve the liquor—about 400 ml (¾ pint).

Skin and flake the cod. Quarter and deseed the tomatoes; cut into eighths. Put 45 ml (3 tbsp) water into a saucepan. Sprinkle over the gelatine and leave to soak for 3 minutes. Add the reserved fish liquor to the gelatine mixture. Heat very gently to dissolve. Stir in the parsley. Season well.

Line the base of six 150 ml (¼ pint) soufflé-type dishes with some of the peeled prawns and a few tomato pieces. Cover with a little gelatine mixture. Refrigerate to set.

Place the cod over the jelly, then the remaining prawns and tomatoes. Spoon over the remaining gelatine mixture. Refrigerate to set. To serve, run a blunt knife around aspics and turn on to serving plate. Garnish with watercress.

Not suitable for freezing.

AUBERGINE SAMOSAS
Serves 4

1 small aubergine, about 225 g (8 oz)	milled pepper
salt	125 g (4 oz) shortcrust
15 ml (1 tbsp) oil	pastry made with 125 g
1 clove garlic, skinned and crushed	(4 oz) flour; pinch salt; 25 g (1 oz) butter or
1.25 ml ($\frac{1}{4}$ level tsp) ground allspice	block margarine; 25 g (1 oz) lard; 25–30 ml (1–2 tbsp) chilled water
15 ml (1 level tbsp) tomato paste	oil for deep frying

Finely chop the aubergine. Place in a sieve or colander and sprinkle well with salt. Leave for 1 hour. Rinse *well*. Pat dry with kitchen paper. Sauté the aubergine in the oil with the garlic and allspice for 5–7 minutes or until softened. Stir in the tomato paste. Season with milled pepper only and cool.

Sift the flour and salt. Cut the fat into cubes and add to the flour. Rub in lightly, until it resembles breadcrumbs. Sprinkle the water over and mix in with a round-bladed knife. Form the mixture into a ball, knead lightly for a few seconds and leave it in the fridge for 20–30 minutes.

On a well-floured surface thinly roll out the pastry. Stamp out eight 10-cm (4-inch) rounds.

Spoon a little filling on each round, damp the pastry edges and fold over to form semi-circular shapes. Press the edges well together. Cover loosely and chill for 30 minutes.

Heat the oil to about 180°C (350°F) and fry the samosas until golden, about 4–5 minutes. Drain on kitchen paper. Serve immediately.

Not suitable for freezing.

PÂTÉ DE CAMPAGNE WITH BLACK OLIVES
Serves 8

275 g (10 oz) streaky bacon	175 g (6 oz) onion, skinned
75 g (3 oz) black olives	7.5 ml (1$\frac{1}{2}$ level tsp) salt
450 g (1 lb) belly pork	milled pepper
275 g (10 oz) pie veal	5 ml (1 level tsp) rubbed sage
175 g (6 oz) lamb's liver	30 ml (2 tbsp) olive oil
1 clove garlic, skinned and crushed	15 ml (1 tbsp) lemon juice
	30 ml (2 tbsp) brandy

A day ahead, cut the rind off the bacon and stretch the rashers with the back of a knife. Halve, stone and roughly chop the olives. Pass the belly pork, veal, liver and onion twice through the finest blades of the mincer. Add remaining ingredients, except bacon, and mix well. Layer the bacon and minced ingredients in a 1.1-litre (2-pint) terrine, topping with bacon rashers.

Cover with foil and lid and place in a roasting tin, half filled with boiling water. Cook at 170°C (325°F) mark 3 for about 2 hours. Pour off juices and reserve, weight down pâté and refrigerate overnight.

Skim fat off jellied juices, warm juices to liquefy then spoon over the pâté. Refrigerate to set. Leave at room temperature for 30 minutes before serving.

To freeze Pack and freeze without the juices—use these in soups or gravies. To use, thaw at cool room temperature overnight.

TARAMASALATA
Serves 8

75 g (3 oz) fresh white breadcrumbs	300 ml ($\frac{1}{2}$ pint) vegetable oil
120 ml (8 tbsp) lemon juice	30 ml (2 tbsp) hot water
175 g (6 oz) smoked cod's roe, skinned	35 ml (7 tsp) tomato ketchup
1 clove garlic, skinned	milled black pepper

Soak the breadcrumbs in 60 ml (4 tbsp) lemon juice for about 10 minutes.

Using an electric mixer, beat the cod's roe until smooth. Add the breadcrumbs and crushed garlic and then work in the oil, drop by drop. Beat constantly until all the oil is absorbed using a mixer all the time.

Stir in the remaining lemon juice, hot water and tomato ketchup. Spoon the mixture into a serving dish, cover and chill for 2 hours. Grind over some black pepper before serving with black olives, lemon wedges and pitta bread or fresh fingers of toast.

Not suitable for freezing.

AVOCADO WITH PARMA HAM
Serves 6

50 g (2 oz) Parma ham	salt and milled pepper
90 ml (6 tbsp) vegetable oil	3 spring onions, trimmed
45 ml (3 tbsp) lemon juice	3 ripe avocados
5 ml (1 level tsp) Dijon mustard	French bread to accompany

Cut the ham into fine shreds, using lightly-oiled kitchen scissors. Whisk the oil, lemon juice, mustard and seasoning together—go lightly on the salt. Stir in the spring onions, finely snipped, and the ham. Halve the avocados and twist to remove the stones. If necessary, cut a thin slice off the base of each half so that they will sit flat on the serving plate.

Spoon the ham mixture into the avocados, covering the whole surface to prevent discoloration. Cover with cling film and refrigerate for 2 hours. Serve with hot French bread.

Not suitable for freezing.

The layers of bacon and the olives dotting this Pâté de campagne give it an interesting texture, as well as flavour

CHAPTER TWO

FISH AND SHELLFISH

MUSHROOM & SOLE PROFITEROLES
Serves 6

For the choux pastry
50 g (2 oz) butter; 150 ml
(¼ pint) water; 65 g
(2½ oz) plain flour;
pinch salt; 2 eggs
350 g (12 oz) white button
mushrooms, wiped
225 g (8 oz) fillet of sole,
skinned

150 ml (¼ pint) milk
50 g (2 oz) butter
25 g (1 oz) flour
1.25 ml (¼ level tsp)
ground coriander
60 ml (4 tbsp) dry white
wine
salt and milled pepper

Sift the flour and salt on to a sheet of greaseproof paper. Melt the fat slowly in the water. Bring to a rolling boil and tip in flour and salt. Immediately take off the heat, beat well until the paste forms a ball and leaves the sides of the pan clean. Turn into a bowl, cool slightly and beat in the eggs a little at a time, keeping the mixture stiff. Spoon or pipe the choux pastry into six balls on to a wetted baking sheet. Bake at 200°C (400°F) mark 6 for about 25 minutes or until well risen, golden and crisp. Make a slit in the side of each profiterole. Return to the oven for a further 5 minutes. Cool on a wire rack.

Thinly slice the mushrooms, reserving 125 g (4 oz) for garnish. Slice the fish into thin strips. Poach the mushrooms and fish in the milk for 10–12 minutes. Strain, reserving milk.

Melt 25 g (1 oz) butter in a small pan, stir in the flour and coriander. Cook for 1–2 minutes before adding reserved milk. Bring to the boil, add the wine, simmer for 2 minutes. Fold in the fish and mushrooms. Season and cool.

To serve, fill the cold profiteroles with the cold sauce. Cover loosely and reheat at 190°C (375°F) mark 5 for about 15 minutes. Garnish with the remaining mushrooms sautéed in the remaining butter.

To freeze Freeze the filled profiteroles. To use, reheat from frozen as above for about 1 hour. Cover as necessary during reheating. Garnish as above.

HADDOCK ROULADE
Serves 4

225 g (8 oz) smoked
haddock
300 ml (½ pint) milk
6 peppercorns
3 eggs, separated
50 g (2 oz) butter
50 g (2 oz) plain flour
10 ml (2 tsp) lemon juice
salt and milled pepper
chopped parsley

For the Mushroom Sauce
milk
25 g (1 oz) butter
125 g (4 oz) mushrooms,
thinly sliced
30 ml (2 level tbsp) flour
30 ml (2 tbsp) chopped
parsley
5 ml (1 tsp) lemon juice
salt and milled pepper

Grease and line a 35.5 × 25.5-cm (14 × 10-inch) Swiss roll tin. Place milk, peppercorns and fish in a pan. Simmer, covered for about 7 minutes until fish is tender. Strain and reserve the milk. Flake fish, discarding skin and bones. Place flesh in a bowl and mix in the egg yolks. Melt the fat in a saucepan; add the flour and cook for 1 minute. Off the heat, gradually stir in 150 ml (¼ pint) reserved milk (keep the rest). Boil for 1–2 minutes stirring all the time, until thick. Off the heat, beat in the fish and lemon juice. Season.

Whisk the egg whites until stiff. Fold into the mixture. Pour into the tin and spread to cover the base. Bake at 200°C (400°F) mark 6 for about 12 minutes.

Meanwhile make the mushroom sauce. Make the reserved fish cooking juices up to 300 ml (½ pint) with milk. Melt the fat in a pan and sauté the mushrooms for 2–3 minutes. Add the flour and cook for a further 1–2 minutes. Off the heat, add milk, boil for 2–3 minutes. Stir in the parsley, lemon juice and seasoning. Keep warm.

Place a damp sheet of greaseproof paper on to a working surface. Quickly flip the roulade on to the damp paper.

Make a shallow cut across the bottom edge of the roulade. Spread half the sauce over the bottom two-thirds. Using the paper roll up from the cut end. Lift on to a flat serving dish. Garnish with parsley and serve remaining sauce separately.

Suitable for freezing.

Rich and melting, Haddock roulade is an excellent luncheon entree

Fish in White Wine
Serves 8

1.1 kg (2½ lb) cod fillet, haddock or other white fish
50 g (2 oz) butter
450 g (1 lb) courgettes, thinly sliced
350 g (12 oz) onion, skinned and sliced
30 ml (2 level tbsp) flour
15 ml (1 level tbsp) ground paprika
300 ml (½ pint) dry white wine
396-g (14-oz) can tomatoes
5 ml (1 level tsp) dried basil
1 clove garlic, skinned
salt and milled pepper
190-g (6¾-oz) can pimiento, drained
fried French bread croûtes

Skin the fish and cut into 5-cm (2-inch) pieces. Melt the butter in a large frying pan, add the courgettes, onion, flour and paprika and fry gently for 3–4 minutes, stirring. Stir in the wine, contents of can of tomatoes, basil, crushed garlic and seasoning. Bring to the boil.

In a large ovenproof dish layer up the fish, sliced pimiento and sauce mixture, seasoning well. Cover the dish tightly and cook at 170°C (325°F) mark 3 for 50–60 minutes, adjust seasoning. Garnish with croûtes of French bread.

Not suitable for freezing.

Trout with Grapes
Serves 2

two rainbow trout, about 200 g (7 oz) each
75 g (3 oz) small white grapes
25 g (1 oz) shelled hazelnuts
5 ml (1 level tsp) dried thyme
25 g (1 oz) butter
50 g (2 oz) fresh white breadcrumbs
caster sugar, optional
salt and milled pepper
75 ml (5 tbsp) medium white wine
bayleaf

Clean the trout but leave on the heads. Slit along the belly of the fish to open out completely. Place slit side down and press firmly along backbone of fish to open out a little. Halve the grapes and remove the pips. Roughly chop the hazelnuts. Melt the butter and fry the hazelnuts until beginning to brown. Off the heat stir in the grapes, thyme and breadcrumbs. Add sugar to taste if grapes are tart; season.

Pack the stuffing mixture into the cavity of the trout. Lie them flat in a shallow 1.1-litre (2-pint) ovenproof dish. Pour over the white wine; add the bayleaf. Cover with buttered foil and bake at 190°C (375°F) mark 5 for 25 minutes. Uncover the dish and cook for a further 10 minutes. Serve hot.

Not suitable for freezing.

Smoked Mackerel Gougère
Serves 4

350 g (12 oz) fresh smoked mackerel fillets, flaked
125 g (4 oz) onion, skinned and sliced
150 g (5 oz) butter
175 g (6 oz) plain flour
150 ml (¼ pint) milk
45 ml (3 tbsp) cider
30 ml (2 level tbsp) natural yogurt
salt and milled pepper
4 eggs, beaten
75 g (3 oz) Cheddar cheese, grated
15 ml (1 level tbsp) dried breadcrumbs

To make the sauce, fry the onion in 25 g (1 oz) butter until soft and golden. Add 25 g (1 oz) flour with the milk, stirring briskly, simmer for 3 minutes. Off the heat stir in the cider, yogurt, fish and seasoning; go carefully with the salt. Cover and refrigerate.

For the choux paste, melt the remaining butter in 300 ml (½ pint) water. Bring to the boil, take off the heat and beat in the remaining flour until just smooth. Beat in the eggs, a little at a time, then the cheese.

Spoon the choux paste around the sides of a 1.1-litre (2-pint) shallow ovenproof dish, cover and refrigerate. When required spoon the sauce into the centre of the choux paste, sprinkle with breadcrumbs and bake at 200°C (400°F) mark 6 for 40–45 minutes.

To freeze Pack and freeze dish before baking. Cook from frozen at 200°C (400°F) mark 6 for 1–1¼ hours.

Baked Mackerel with Gooseberry Sauce
Serves 4

4 mackerel cleaned—about 900 g (2 lb) total weight
butter
350 g (12 oz) fresh or frozen gooseberries
45 ml (3 tbsp) water
15 ml (1 level tbsp) flour
200 ml (7 fl oz) chicken stock
fresh chives
salt and milled pepper
sugar

Cut the head and tail from each fish. Make three slashes across one side of each fish to a depth of about 5 mm (¼ in). Rub over with a little butter. Place slashed side uppermost in a deep baking dish. Bake, uncovered, at 190°C (375°F) mark 5 for 25–30 minutes.

Meanwhile stew the gooseberries in the water in a covered pan for 10–15 minutes or until very soft. Purée in an electric blender or rub through a nylon sieve.

Melt 15 g (½ oz) butter in a sauté pan, add the flour. Cook for 1–2 minutes before gradually stirring in the stock. Add 15 ml (1 tbsp) snipped chives, gooseberry purée, seasoning and sweeten to taste. Stir until the mixture is well blended. Bring to the boil, simmer for 2–3 minutes. Serve hot with the mackerel garnished with more snipped chives.

Not suitable for freezing.

Courgettes and garlic bring the flavour of the Mediterranean to Fish in white wine

ROLLED HERRINGS
Serves 4

2 whole herrings, about 450 g (1 lb) total weight	oatflakes to garnish
225 g (8 oz) ripe pears	75 g (3 oz) rolled oats
50 g (2 oz) onion, skinned and chopped	1 small lemon or lime
	50 g (2 oz) butter
	salt and milled pepper

Clean the herrings, remove the heads but leave on the tails. Press along the backbones and remove. Cut each fish in half lengthwise.

Peel and roughly chop the pears, reserving four slices for garnish. Dip slices in oatflakes to coat.

Sauté the onions, rolled oats, finely grated lemon or lime rind and chopped pear in 25 g (1 oz) butter for 3–4 minutes, season. Place a little stuffing on each fillet. Roll up from the head end. Secure with wooden cocktail sticks. Place the herring rolls in a shallow, greased, ovenproof dish. Sprinkle with oatflakes, dot with the remaining butter and garnish each herring with a slice of pear. Bake at 190°C (375°F) mark 5 for 30 minutes.

Not suitable for freezing.

BAKED CRUMBED HADDOCK
Serves 4

30 ml (2 level tbsp) capers	salt and milled pepper
1 egg, hard-boiled	seasoned flour
75 g (3 oz) full fat soft cheese	beaten egg
5 ml (1 tsp) lemon juice	75 g (3 oz) dried white breadcrumbs
two 275 g (12 oz) fresh haddock fillets	50 g (2 oz) butter, melted

Finely chop the capers and hard-boiled egg. Gradually beat into the soft cheese with the lemon juice; season.

Skin the haddock fillets. Spread each one with the cheese mixture and fold in half. Press together well. Dip the stuffed fillets in the flour then brush with beaten egg. Coat well with the dried breadcrumbs. Place the fish side by side in a shallow ovenproof dish. Pour over the melted butter.

Bake at 190°C (375°F) mark 5 for about 40 minutes. Baste occasionally with the melted butter.

Not suitable for freezing.

SOURED CREAM SALMON PIE
Serves 8

450 g (1 lb) frozen Canadian salmon	3 eggs, hard boiled
60 ml (4 tbsp) white wine	30 ml (2 tbsp) chopped parsley
salt and milled pepper	50 g (2 oz) lard
165 g (6½ oz) butter	450 g (1 lb) self-raising flour
40 g (1½ oz) plain flour	30 ml (2 level tbsp) grated Parmesan cheese
200 g (7 oz) Gruyère or Cheddar cheese	beaten egg to glaze
142-ml (5-fl oz) carton soured cream	

Cover the salmon sparingly with cold water, add wine, season and simmer for about 20 minutes. Reserve the fish stock, flake the fish discarding the bones and skin.

Make a sauce from 40 g (1½ oz) butter, the plain flour, 300 ml (½ pint) reserved fish stock and seasoning, bubble for 2 minutes. Off the heat stir in the grated cheese, roughly chopped eggs, soured cream and parsley. Cool.

Prepare the shortcrust pastry from the remaining butter and lard, self-raising flour and Parmesan, binding with a little water. Roll out one-third to a 35.5 × 10-cm (14 × 4-inch) oblong, place on a baking sheet. Top with the sauce mixture, salmon and more sauce. Cover with the remaining pastry, sealing the edges well. Garnish with pastry trimmings. Glaze with beaten egg and bake at 190°C (375°F) mark 5 for about 40 minutes. Serve warm.

Not suitable for freezing.

STAR-GAZEY PIE
Serves 6

12 small fresh sardines, pilchards or herrings, cleaned and boned — about 900 g (2 lb) total weight (heads on)	salt and milled pepper
	3 eggs, beaten
	15 ml (1 tbsp) tarragon vinegar
50 g (2 oz) fresh brown breadcrumbs	60 ml (4 level tbsp) chopped parsley
125 g (4 oz) streaky bacon, rinded and finely chopped	275 g (10 oz) shortcrust pastry, made with 275 g (10 oz) plain flour etc
	beaten egg to glaze

Remove the tails from the fish but leave the heads on. Season the inside of the fish.

Sprinkle breadcrumbs in an even layer over a 28-cm (11-inch) edged ovenproof plate. Arrange the fish in a circle over the crumbs with tail ends to the centre and heads pointing outwards just over the edge of the plate. Cover the fish with the bacon. Beat the eggs with the vinegar and parsley and pour over the fish. Cover the pie with the pastry, indenting it a little between the fish. Trim the pastry to leave the heads sticking out of the pie. Glaze with a little beaten egg.

Bake at 190°C (375°F) mark 5 for 30 minutes, or until the fish is cooked and the pastry golden.

Not suitable for freezing.

Rolled herring in oatmeal have more than a little of the taste of Scotland

SEAFOOD RING
Serves 4

400 g (14 oz) fillets of sole
43-g (1½-oz) can dressed
  crab meat
3 eggs
90 ml (6 tbsp) single cream
568 ml (1 pint) milk
salt and milled pepper

50 g (2 oz) long grain rice,
  cooked
65 g (2½ oz) butter
30 ml (2 level tbsp) flour
2.5 ml (½ tsp) lemon juice
30 ml (2 tbsp) chopped
  parsley

Cut the sole into broad strips and use them to line a 1.1-litre (2-pint) well-greased ring mould.

Liquidise together the crab, eggs, cream and 300 ml (½ pint) milk. Season. Stir in the cooked rice. Carefully pour the crab mixture into the lined ring mould. Cover with buttered foil. Place in a baking dish half filled with water. Bake at 170°C (325°F) mark 3 for 1 hour, or until just set.

Melt 25 g (1 oz) butter in a saucepan. Stir in the flour. Cook, stirring for 2 minutes before adding the remaining milk and lemon juice. Bring to the boil and simmer for 2 minutes. Beat in the parsley and remaining butter; season.

Turn the cooked seafood ring on to a serving dish. Pour off any excess liquid. Coat evenly with warm parsley sauce.

Not suitable for freezing.

BASS WITH FENNEL
Serves 4

2 cleaned bass, each
  weighing about 350 g
  (12 oz)
150 ml (¼ pint) dry white
  wine

oil
salt and milled pepper
10 ml (2 tsp) lemon juice
a few sprigs of fennel
lemon slices to garnish

Rinse the fish, remove scales and fins. Make 3–4 diagonal slits 5 mm (¼ inch) deep on each side of the fish.

Combine the wine, 15 ml (1 tbsp) oil, seasoning and lemon juice in a dish large enough to take the fish. Slip fennel into the slits in the fish, place in the marinade, cover and refrigerate for several hours. Turn and baste from time to time.

To cook, drain the fish, brush with more oil and either barbecue with fennel in a fish cage, or grill on high heat until fish flakes when tested with a knife. The skin should show signs of bubbling. Serve on a bed of lemon slices with a little hot marinade poured over.

Not suitable for freezing.

HADDOCK & MUSHROOM PUFFS
Serves 4

397-g (14-oz) packet puff
  pastry, defrost if frozen
450 g (1 lb) haddock fillet,
  skinned
213-g (7½-oz) can
  creamed mushrooms
5 ml (1 tsp) lemon juice

20 ml (4 tsp) capers,
  chopped
15 ml (1 level tbsp)
  chopped fresh chives or
  5 ml (1 level tsp) dried
salt and milled pepper
1 egg

Roll the pastry into a 40.5-cm (16-inch) square. Using a sharp knife, cut into four squares, trim edges and reserve trimmings. Place the squares on baking sheets. Divide the fish into four and place diagonally across the pastry squares. Combine the creamed mushrooms, lemon juice, capers, chives and seasoning. Mix well, then spoon over the fish.

Brush the edges of each square lightly with water. Bring the four points of each square together and seal the edges to form an envelope. Decorate with pastry trimmings, make a small hole in the centre of each parcel. Refrigerate for several hours.

Glaze the pastry with egg beaten with salt and bake in the oven at 220°C (425°F) mark 7 for about 20 minutes, or until pastry is golden brown and well risen. Serve with baked tomatoes.

To freeze Using fresh fish only, pack and freeze before glazing and baking. To use, bake from frozen at 220°C (425°F) mark 7 for 20 minutes, lay a sheet of foil on top and continue baking for a further 15 minutes.

SEAFOOD STIR FRY
Serves 4

225 g (8 oz) celery,
  washed and trimmed
350 g (12 oz) monkfish
  fillet or coley fillet
350 g (12 oz) Iceberg or
  Cos lettuce
peanut oil
5 ml (1 level tsp) dried
  tarragon

1 clove garlic, skinned and
  crushed
225 g (8 oz) peeled prawns
425-g (15-oz) can whole
  baby sweetcorn, drained
45 ml (3 tbsp) oyster sauce
  or 15 ml (1 tbsp)
  anchovy essence
salt and milled pepper

Slice the celery into thin 5-cm (2-inch) matchsticks. Skin and cut the fish into 2.5-cm (1-inch) chunks. Finely shred lettuce, discarding the core. Heat 15 ml (1 tbsp) oil in a wok or large frying pan until smoky hot. Fry the lettuce for about 30 seconds to lightly cook. Transfer to a serving dish. Keep warm in a low oven.

Heat 30 ml (2 tbsp) oil in the pan until smoky hot. Over a high heat, fry the celery, monkfish, tarragon and garlic for 2–3 minutes, stirring all the time, adding oil if necessary. Reduce the heat, add the prawns, sweetcorn and oyster sauce. Toss well together over the heat for a further 2–3 minutes to coat all the ingredients in the sauce and heat through. The fish will flake apart. Season. Spoon on to the lettuce and serve immediately.

Not suitable for freezing.

Despite their deceptive elegance, Haddock and mushroom puffs will appeal to masculine appetites

SAUTÉ OF FISH & VEGETABLES
Serves 4

700 g (1½ lb) monkfish,
  skinned, or 450 g (1 lb)
  filleted
100 ml (4 fl oz) white wine
1 clove garlic, skinned
salt and milled pepper
225 g (½ lb) carrots, pared
175 g (6 oz) celery

50 g (2 oz) onion, skinned
15 ml (1 tbsp) corn oil
50 g (2 oz) butter
15 ml (1 level tbsp) plain
  flour
2.5 ml (½ level tsp) ground
  paprika

Cut the monkfish into strips about 5 cm (2 inch) long by
1 cm (½ inch) wide, place in a shallow dish. Pour over the
wine, add the crushed garlic with plenty of seasoning, cover
and marinate in the refrigerator for 2 hours. Strain off the
marinade and reserve.

Slice the carrots, celery and onion into match-stick size
pieces. Heat the oil and butter in a sauté pan. Add the
vegetables and sauté over a high heat for 2 minutes, shaking
the pan from time to time. Lift vegetables out of the pan
with a draining spoon.

Toss the drained fish in the flour, paprika and seasoning.
Sauté in the residual fat for 3–4 minutes, turning occasionally.

Return the vegetables to the pan with the marinade,
bring to the boil and simmer, covered for 5 minutes, adjust
seasoning.

Not suitable for freezing

LENTIL TUNA SAVOURY
Serves 4

175 g (6 oz) red lentils
75 g (3 oz) onion
15 g (½ oz) butter or
  margarine
salt and milled pepper

198-g (7-oz) can tuna fish
  in brine
1 large egg
150 ml (¼ pint) milk
25 g (1 oz) salted peanuts

Place the lentils in a saucepan with 600 ml (1 pint) water.
Bring to the boil. *Simmer* for 20–25 minutes until the lentils
are just tender and most of the liquid has evaporated. Stir
occasionally.

Finely chop the onion. Cook in the butter or margarine
until softened. Off the heat stir in the drained tuna. Season.
Beat the lentils, egg and milk into the tuna mixture. Spoon
into a shallow 1.1-litre (2-pint) ovenproof dish.

Finely chop the peanuts. Sprinkle over the dish. Bake at
180°C (350°F) mark 4 for 25–30 minutes.

Not suitable for freezing.

TOSSED SPAGHETTI WITH MACKEREL
Serves 2

175 g (6 oz) spaghetti
salt and milled pepper
peanut oil
275 g (10 oz) smoked
  mackerel fillet, skinned
  and flaked
10 ml (2 tsp) lemon juice

50 g (2 oz) spring onions,
  washed, trimmed and
  roughly chopped
60 ml (4 level tbsp)
  chopped parsley
75 g (3 oz) butter
2 eggs, beaten

Cook the spaghetti in plenty of boiling, salted water until
tender. Drain well. Toss in 30 ml (2 tbsp) oil. Place the
spaghetti and oil in a wok or large frying pan. Toss over a
high heat for 2 minutes, adding a little more oil if necessary.
Add the mackerel, spring onions, parsley, lemon juice and
butter.

Reduce the heat and stir until the butter melts. Off the
heat, stir in the beaten eggs. Toss until the mixture is well
coated and the egg is lightly cooked. Season and serve
immediately.

Not suitable for freezing.

COD WITH CORIANDER IN CREAM
Serves 4

450 g (1 lb) thick cut cod
  fillet
30 ml (2 level tbsp) flour
10 ml (2 level tsp) ground
  coriander
salt and milled pepper

50 g (2 oz) butter
15–30 ml (1–2 tbsp)
  lemon juice
15 ml (1 tbsp) capers
1 egg yolk
90 ml (6 tbsp) single cream

Skin the fish and divide into four portions. Mix the flour,
ground coriander and seasoning together. Coat the fish
pieces with this mixture. Heat the butter in a medium-sized
sauté pan and sauté the fish gently until golden on both
sides, turning only once. Add 15 ml (1 tbsp) lemon juice to
the pan with the capers, cover tightly and continue cooking
for a further 4–5 minutes, or until the fish is tender. Place
the fish on a warm serving dish.

Mix the egg yolk and cream together, stir into the pan
juices and heat gently until the sauce thickens slightly—do
not boil. Adjust seasoning, adding extra lemon juice if
wished and spoon the sauce over the fish.

Not suitable for freezing.

The crunch of coated monkfish contrasts wonderfully with the light sauce of Sauté of fish and vegetables

POACHED SALMON TROUT
Serves 10

1.8 kg (4 lb) salmon trout
  or piece of salmon,
  cleaned
150 ml (¼ pint) dry white
  wine
1 carrot, peeled and sliced
1 onion, skinned and sliced
2 sticks of celery, washed
  and chopped
parsley stalks
bayleaf

5 ml (1 level tsp) salt
8 peppercorns
15 ml (1 tbsp) lemon juice
butter
600 ml (1 pint) liquid
  aspic jelly
7.5-cm (3-inch) piece
  cucumber, thinly sliced
lemon, prawns, whole and
  shelled, and lettuce for
  garnish

Place the fish in a deep roasting tin. Pour over the wine and enough water to three-quarters cover it. Add the carrot,

onion, celery, parsley stalks, bayleaf, salt and peppercorns and lemon juice. Cover the tin with buttered foil. Place in the oven and cook for 15 minutes per 450 g (1 lb) at 170°C (325°F) mark 3. If serving the fish hot, allow an extra 10 minutes at the end of cooking time. Leave to cool, covered.

Carefully lift the fish out of the roasting tin.

Sprinkle gelatine over the surface. Leave to soak for 15 minutes.

Remove the skin from the fish and ease out all the fin bones. Place the fish on a wire rack standing over a rimmed tray or baking sheet. As the aspic begins to set, spoon carefully over the fish. Allow to set. Repeat to build up a good glaze. Dip cucumber, lemon slices and prawns in aspic, use to garnish. Spoon over more aspic. To serve, place on serving plate, garnish with more lemon slices, prawns and lettuce.

Not suitable for freezing.

No other dish quite says summer like cold Poached salmon trout

SEAFOOD PILAFF
Serves 6

This dish looks attractive served on natural scallop shells placed on serving plates. Put soy sauce on the table so people can help themselves—you only need to use a few drops.

225 g (½ lb) tomatoes, skinned
125 g (4 oz) frozen prawns, thawed
125 g (4 oz) white crab meat, fresh or frozen, thawed
142-g (5-oz) jar mussels
50 g (2 oz) butter
75 g (3 oz) onion, skinned and sliced
175 g (6 oz) long grain rice
300 ml (½ pint) light stock
2.5 ml (½ level tsp) ground turmeric
5 ml (1 level tsp) ground paprika
1 green pepper, seeded and diced
1 clove garlic, skinned and crushed
15 ml (1 level tbsp) tomato paste
salt and milled pepper
30 ml (2 tbsp) medium sherry

Quarter and de-seed the tomatoes, reserving the juices; cut each tomato quarter in half lengthwise. Dry the prawns on kitchen paper, flake the crab meat discarding any shell or gristle, drain the mussels.

Melt the butter in a medium-sized flameproof casserole and well brown the onion. Stir in the rice with the turmeric and paprika and cook gently for 1 minute. Stir in the stock with green pepper, garlic, tomato paste and seasoning and bring to the boil.

Cover the dish tightly and cook in the oven at 170°C (325°F) mark 3 for 20 minutes. Remove from the oven and stir in the prepared fish with the tomatoes and their juices and the sherry, mixing well. Cover again and return to the oven for a further 10–15 minutes, or until all liquid has been absorbed and the rice is tender. Adjust seasoning and serve hot.

Not suitable for freezing.

TOP CRUST FISH PIE
Serves 6

Use a pie funnel if you have one to give the pastry a nicely domed appearance. Other white fish can replace the coley. Serve with petits pois, or just a green side salad as a crisp, fresh accompaniment.

700 g (1½ lb) coley fillet
45 ml (3 tbsp) lemon juice
salt and milled pepper
75 g (3 oz) butter or margarine
450 ml (¾ pint) milk
slices of carrot and onion, bayleaf for flavouring
40 g (1½ oz) flour
45 ml (3 tbsp) chopped parsley
225 g (8 oz) frozen prawns, thawed
368-g (13-oz) packet frozen puffed pastry, thawed

Rinse the fish under the cold tap and drain well. Place in a shallow ovenproof dish and pour over the lemon juice; season well and dot with 25 g (1 oz) fat. Cover the dish tightly and bake at 180°C (350°F) mark 4 for about 40 minutes, or until the fish flakes readily apart. Strain off and reserve the cooking liquor; flake the fish discarding skin and bone.

Meanwhile bring the milk to the boil with the flavourings, take off the heat, cover and leave to infuse for 15 minutes.

Melt 50 g (2 oz) fat in a heavy-based pan and off the heat gradually stir in the 40 g (1½ oz) flour until smooth. Strain on the flavoured milk and stir until smooth. Return to the heat and bring to the boil, stirring all the time, bubble for 3 minutes, season well. Off the heat stir in the reserved cooking juices with the parsley, flaked coley and prawns. Turn into a 1.1-litre (2-pint) pie dish and leave to cool.

Roll out the pastry and use to top the pie, sealing edges well. Decorate with pastry trimmings. Stand the pie on a baking sheet, glaze with beaten egg and bake at 220°C (425°F) mark 7 for about 35 minutes or until golden brown and crisp. Keep warm in a cool oven.

Not suitable for freezing.

CHAPTER THREE

MEAT AND OFFAL

BEEF OLIVES
Serves 4

75 g (3 oz) streaky bacon, rinded
1 small onion, skinned and chopped
10 ml (2 tsp) chopped parsley
125 g (4 oz) fresh white breadcrumbs
50 g (2 oz) shredded suet
1.25 ml ($\frac{1}{4}$ level tsp) dried mixed herbs
1 small egg

1 lemon
salt and milled pepper
8 thin slices of beef topside, about 700 g (1$\frac{1}{2}$ lb) total weight
15 ml (1 level tbsp) made English mustard
45 ml (3 level tbsp) seasoned flour
60 ml (4 tbsp) oil
400 ml ($\frac{3}{4}$ pint) beef stock
225 g (8 oz) onion, skinned

Finely chop the bacon and mix with the next six ingredients. Add the grated rind of $\frac{1}{2}$ lemon, 5 ml (1 tsp) juice, seasoning.

Trim the meat and bat out between sheets of cling film. Spread mustard thinly over meat, divide stuffing between the pieces. Roll up, secure with fine string and toss in the flour.

Heat the oil in a shallow flameproof casserole into which the beef olives will just fit. Brown them well, remove from the fat. Stir the remaining seasoned flour into the pan residue and brown lightly. Gradually add the stock and bring to the boil. Season, replace the meat. Slice the onion into rings and scatter over the meat. Cover and cook at 170°C (325°F) mark 3 for about 1$\frac{1}{2}$ hours.

To freeze Cool, pack and freeze. Thaw overnight at cool room temperature. Reheat at 200°C (400°F) mark 6 for 40 minutes.

BRAISED BRISKET WITH RED WINE
Serves 6

15 ml (1 level tbsp) flour
salt and milled pepper
1.1-kg (2$\frac{1}{2}$-lb) piece lean rolled brisket
15 ml (1 tbsp) oil
225 g (8 oz) carrot, pared and roughly chopped
225 g (8 oz) parsnip, peeled and roughly chopped
150 ml ($\frac{1}{4}$ pint) beef stock

175 g (6 oz) onion, skinned and diced
15 ml (1 level tbsp) tomato paste
60 ml (4 tbsp) red wine
2.5 ml ($\frac{1}{2}$ level tsp) dried thyme
bayleaf
10 ml (2 level tsp) cornflour

Season the flour and roll the brisket joint in it until well coated. Heat oil in a 2.3-litre (4-pint) flameproof casserole and brown the joint well. Remove. Stir the vegetables into residual fat and sauté for 2 minutes, add stock, tomato paste, wine, thyme, bayleaf and seasoning. Bring to the boil. Replace meat pushing it well down into the vegetables. Cover tightly and cook in the oven at 170°C (325°F) mark 3 for about 2$\frac{1}{4}$ hours or until the meat is tender when pierced with a fine skewer. Remove the meat and carve into slices. Arrange on a serving dish with the vegetables, cover, keep warm.

Thicken the juices with the cornflour mixed to a paste with a little water. Adjust seasoning and serve separately.

Not suitable for freezing.

Braised brisket in red wine is served with the vegetables with which it was cooked, complemented by crisp potato balls

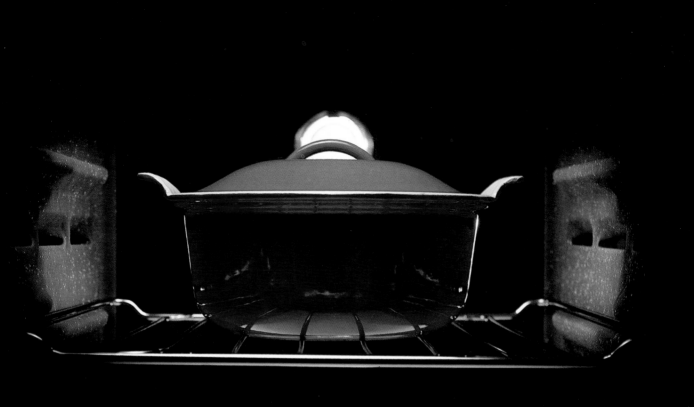

CHILLI BEEF WITH BEANS
Serves 4

275 g (10 oz) rump steak	salt and milled pepper
90 ml (6 tbsp) orange juice	peanut oil
15 ml (1 tbsp) lemon juice	175 g (6 oz) red pepper,
30 ml (2 tbsp) black bean	seeded and diced
sauce or 10 ml (2 level	125 g (4 oz) onion, skinned
tsp) beef extract	and diced
30 ml (2 level tbsp) chilli	225 g (8 oz) black eye
seasoning	beans or peas, boiled
5 ml (1 level tsp) cornflour	

Trim and cut the rump steak into 1-cm (½-inch) cubes. Whisk together the next six ingredients; pour over beef and leave to marinate for 1 hour.

Heat 45 ml (3 tbsp) oil in a wok or large frying pan until smoky hot. Drain beef, reserving marinade; brown a few pieces at a time. Remove with a slotted spoon. Add the pepper and onion to the pan. Fry, stirring all the time, for 2–3 minutes, adding more oil if necessary. Return the beef with the beans or peas and marinade mixture. Cook, stirring, for a further 2–3 minutes, until the sauce thickens and glazes the ingredients. Check seasoning.

Serve immediately with Chinese egg noodles or tagliatelle.

Not suitable for freezing.

ROAST RIB BEEF
Serves 8

2.7 kg (6 lb) rib beef	5 ml (1 level tsp) ground
125 g (4 oz) butter,	mace
softened	5 ml (1 level tsp) ground
1 small clove garlic,	cloves
skinned and crushed	15 ml (1 level tbsp) plain
5 ml (1 level tsp) ground	flour
allspice	400 ml (¾ pint) brown
salt and milled pepper	stock

Wipe meat, place on a rack over a roasting tin. Cream together the butter and all the remaining ingredients, except the flour and stock. Spread this mixture evenly all over the meat. Roast at 200°C (400°F) mark 6 for 15 minutes per 450 g (1 lb) plus 15 minutes over. This gives a rare roast.

Place the meat on a warm serving dish, and keep warm in a low oven.

Pour off all but 30 ml (2 tbsp) of the fat from the roasting tin. Over a low heat stir in the plain flour and blend thoroughly with the fat. Cook gently to a golden brown, stirring frequently. Gradually blend in the stock, bring to the boil and cook for 3–4 minutes. Season to taste, and strain before serving with the roast beef.

Not suitable for freezing.

CHICKEN LIVER BOLOGNESE
Serves 4

225 g (8 oz) onion, skinned	45 ml (3 level tbsp) tomato
125 g (4 oz) carrot, pared	paste
125 g (4 oz) celery	150 ml (¼ pint) beef stock
50 g (2 oz) lard	2.5 ml (½ level tsp) dried
125 g (4 oz) streaky	oregano
bacon, rinded	1 bayleaf
450 g (1 lb) chicken livers,	salt and milled pepper
prepared and chopped	275 g (10 oz) spaghetti
150 ml (¼ pint) red wine	25 g (1 oz) butter, melted

Chop the onion, carrot and celery finely. Melt the lard in a deep frying pan, fry the vegetables till golden. Snip the bacon into the pan, add the liver and fry till coloured. Stir in the tomato paste, red wine and stock. Add the oregano, bayleaf and seasoning, bring to boil, simmer covered for 20 minutes.

Cook the spaghetti in boiling salted water for about 11 minutes. Drain and toss in butter. Season with plenty of milled pepper. Serve with the chicken liver sauce.

To freeze Cool quickly and freeze without the spaghetti. To use, thaw overnight at cool room temperature. Add 30–45 ml (2–3 tbsp) stock, bring to the boil and simmer for 10–15 minutes. Serve with spaghetti as above.

PORK FILLET WITH CIDER & CORIANDER
Serves 4

425 g (1 lb) pork fillet	15 ml (1 level tbsp) ground
(tenderloin)	coriander
225 g (½ lb) celery, wiped	15 ml (1 level tbsp) plain
1 green pepper	flour
125 g (4 oz) onion, skinned	150 ml (¼ pint) dry cider
and chopped	150 ml (¼ pint) stock
30 ml (2 tbsp) oil	salt and milled pepper
50 g (2 oz) butter	

Trim and slice the pork fillet into 5-mm (¼-inch) thick pieces. Place between sheets of cling film and bat out thinly. Refrigerate loosely covered.

Slice the celery into 5-mm (¼-inch) pieces and cut the pepper into rings discarding the cores. Sauté the celery and pepper in the oil and half the butter for 2–3 minutes— choose a wide frying pan. Lift out with a slotted spoon, keep warm. Add the remaining butter and over a high heat, brown pork a few pieces at a time. Take out of the pan, golden fry the onion in the residual fat. Stir in the coriander and flour, cook for 1 minute. Add cider, stock and seasoning, quickly bring to the boil, add the meat and simmer for about 5 minutes. Serve the pork with vegetables. Small new potatoes in thin slices are a suitable accompaniment.

Not suitable for freezing.

Black eye beans, onion and red pepper bring to Chilli beef with beans the piquant taste of South America

SAUSAGE NOODLE BAKE
Serves 8

50 g (2 oz) margarine
225 g (8 oz) onion, skinned
  and thinly sliced
700 g (1½ lb) pork
  sausagemeat or minced
  pork
240 g (8½ oz) smoked pork
  sausage
5 ml (1 level tsp) English
  mustard powder

75 ml (5 level tbsp) flour
900 ml (1½ pints) milk
salt and milled pepper
350 g (12 oz) ribbon
  noodles, boiled
175 g (6 oz) strong
  Cheddar or Double
  Gloucester cheese,
  grated

Melt the margarine in a large saucepan. Sauté the onion until golden. Stir in the sausagemeat and half the smoked sausage, finely chopped. Stir well, breaking up the sausagemeat, for 2–3 minutes. Add the flour and mustard. Cook, stirring, for a further 2 minutes before adding the milk. Bring to the boil, simmer for 2 minutes, season, cool.

In a shallow greased 2.3-litre (4-pint) ovenproof dish layer the noodles and sauce, ending with sauce. Thickly slice the remaining sausage and lay on top. Sprinkle with the cheese. Cool, cover loosely and refrigerate until required.

To serve, uncover and bake at 190°C (375°F) mark 5 for about 1 hour, covering lightly if necessary.

Not suitable for freezing.

SPINACH-STUFFED SHOULDER OF LAMB
Serves 6

225 g (8 oz) onion, skinned
  and finely chopped
15 ml (1 tbsp) oil
227-g (8-oz) packet
  frozen chopped spinach,
  thawed
1 clove garlic, skinned and
  crushed
2.5 ml (½ level tsp) ground
  nutmeg

salt and milled pepper
1.4 kg (3 lb) boned
  shoulder of lamb
slivers of garlic
10 ml (2 level tsp) plain
  flour
300 ml (½ pint) light stock
15 ml (1 level tbsp)
  redcurrant jelly
dash of gravy browning

Soften the onion in the oil in a pan and add the well-drained spinach, garlic, nutmeg and seasoning—add plenty of pepper. Cool.

Fill the spinach mixture into the bone cavity of the lamb and sew up using cotton or fine string. Make small cuts in the fat and insert garlic slivers into them. Place lamb on a rack in a roasting tin. Roast in the oven at 180°C (350°F) mark 4 for about 2 hours 15 minutes. Baste several times during cooking. Place the joint on a shallow serving plate and keep warm.

Drain off all but 15 ml (1 tbsp) fat from the roasting tin, stir flour into pan, cook for 1–2 minutes. Add the stock, redcurrant jelly with seasoning and a dash of gravy browning; boil for 2–3 minutes, stirring. Serve the gravy separately.

Not suitable for freezing.

VEAL GOULASH WITH CARAWAY DUMPLINGS
Serves 8

1.4 kg (3 lb) stewing veal
75 g (3 oz) lard
700 g (1½ lb) onions,
  skinned and thinly sliced
450 g (1 lb) carrots, pared
  and thinly sliced
60 ml (4 level tbsp) ground
  paprika
30 ml (2 level tbsp) plain
  flour
900 ml (1½ pint) chicken
  stock

60 ml (4 tbsp) dry white
  wine
salt and milled pepper
225 g (8 oz) self-raising
  flour
125 g (4 oz) shredded suet
10 ml (2 level tsp)
  caraway seeds
142-g (5-oz) carton
  soured cream
75 ml (5 tbsp) water

Cut up the veal into 4-cm (1½-inch) pieces. Brown well, a little at a time in the hot lard; drain and place in a shallow ovenproof dish—a foil-lined roasting tin will do. Lightly brown the onions and carrot, add the paprika and plain flour and fry for 2 minutes. Stir in the stock, wine and seasoning, bring to boil, pour over veal. Cover tightly, cook at 150°C (300°F) mark 2 for 2 hours.

Prepare sixteen dumplings from the remaining ingredients, seasoning well; place on top of the goulash, sprinkle with extra caraway seeds. Bake covered for about 45 minutes.

Not suitable for freezing.

MINTED LAMB MEATBALLS
Serves 4

225 g (½ lb) crisp cabbage,
  finely chopped
450 g (1 lb) lean minced
  lamb
125 g (4 oz) onion, skinned
  and finely chopped
2.5 ml (½ level tsp) ground
  allspice
salt and pepper
bayleaf

397-g (14-oz) can tomato
  juice
10 ml (2 level tsp) fresh
  chopped mint or 2.5 ml
  (½ level tsp) dried
15 ml (1 tbsp) chopped
  parsley
175 g (6 oz) noodles,
  freshly boiled, to
  accompany

Steam the cabbage for 2–3 minutes, or until softened. Mix together the lamb, cabbage, onion, allspice and seasoning. Beat well. Shape the mixture into 16 small balls. Place the meatballs in a large shallow ovenproof dish. Pour over the tomato juice, mixed with the bayleaf, mint and parsley. Cover tightly and bake at 180°C (350°F) mark 4 for about 1 hour. Skim any fat off the tomato juices then spoon the meatballs and juices on to the noodles for serving.

Not suitable for freezing.

Spinach-stuffed shoulder of lamb would star at any Sunday lunch

LAMB WITH APRICOTS
Serves 4

50 g (2 oz) dried apricots
125 g (4 oz) dried black
  eye beans
salt and milled pepper
550 g (1¼ lb) boned
  casserole lamb
30 ml (2 level tbsp) flour
2.5 ml (½ level tsp) chilli
  seasoning
15 ml (1 level tbsp) ground
  coriander

15 ml (1 tbsp) oil
125 g (4 oz) onion, skinned
  and sliced
125 g (4 oz) mushrooms,
  wiped and sliced
600 ml (1 pint) light stock
45 ml (3 level tbsp) mango
  chutney
141-g (5-oz) carton
  natural yogurt
snipped parsley

Soak the apricots and beans separately overnight. Boil the beans for 10 minutes in salted water; drain.

Cut the lamb into 2.5-cm (1-inch) cubes. Toss it in flour seasoned with chilli, coriander, salt and pepper; brown, a few pieces at a time, in the hot oil in a flameproof casserole. Remove from the fat, using a draining spoon. Add the onion and mushrooms and fry for a few minutes. Stir in the stock, beans, chutney, drained apricots. Replace the lamb. Bring to the boil, cover and cook at 170°C (325°F) mark 3 for about 1 hour, until the meat is quite tender. Stir in the yogurt, adjust seasoning. Garnish with parsley.

To freeze Cool, pack and freeze. To use, thaw overnight at cool room temperature, reheat gently on top of the stove.

QUICK FRIED BEEF
Serves 4

450 g (1 lb) shin of beef
45 ml (3 tbsp) medium
  sherry
30 ml (2 tbsp) lemon juice
15 ml (1 tbsp) soy sauce
10 ml (2 level tsp) ground
  paprika
225 g (8 oz) long grain
  rice

salt and milled pepper
5 ml (1 level tsp) cornflour
peanut oil
225 g (8 oz) onion, skinned
  and thinly sliced
125 g (4 oz) button
  mushrooms, wiped and
  thinly sliced
chopped parsley to garnish

Trim the beef of any fat and sinew, slice wafer thin and shred into matchstick long strips. Place in a mixing bowl. Whisk together the sherry, lemon juice, soy sauce and paprika. Pour over the beef strips, cover and marinate in the refrigerator overnight. Cook the rice in plenty of boiling salted water until just tender. Drain well. Drain the meat and whisk the cornflour into the residual marinade.

Heat 45 ml (3 tbsp) oil in a wok or large frying pan until smoky hot. Add the meat and stir over a high heat for about 2 minutes. Stir in the onion and mushrooms, adding more oil if necessary. Cook for a further 2 minutes before adding the rice and marinade mixture. Reduce the heat and cook, stirring until thoroughly combined and heated through. Season and serve immediately garnished with parsley.

Not suitable for freezing.

SWEET SPICED BACON
Serves 4

450 g (1 lb) bacon chops,
  rinded
432-g (15¼-oz) can
  pineapple slices
5 ml (1 tsp) soy sauce
5 ml (1 level tsp) Chinese
  Five Spice Powder
5 ml (1 level tsp) French
  mustard

5 ml (1 level tsp) cornflour
125 g (4 oz) white cabbage
  or Chinese leaves
125 g (4 oz) prunes,
  soaked overnight
peanut oil
30 ml (2 tbsp) chopped
  parsley
salt and milled pepper

Cut the bacon chops into 1-cm (½-inch) strips. Drain the pineapple slices, reserving the juice; roughly chop the flesh. Whisk the juice together with the soy sauce, spice, cornflour and mustard. Finely shred the cabbage or Chinese leaves. Halve and stone the prunes.

Heat 30 ml (2 tbsp) oil in a wok or large frying pan until smoky hot. Stir in the bacon and cabbage. Fry over a high heat, stirring all the time, for 3–4 minutes, adding a little more oil if necessary. Stir in the soy sauce mixture and pineapple pieces. Bring to the boil, reduce heat and stir in the prunes and parsley. Season and serve immediately.

Not suitable for freezing.

LAMB WITH FENNEL
Serves 4

8 lamb cutlets, about 150 g
  (5 oz) each
125 g (4 oz) cooked ham
450 g (1 lb) Florence
  fennel
10 ml (2 tsp) lemon juice
peanut oil
1 clove garlic, skinned and
  crushed

15 ml (1 level tbsp) tomato
  paste
pinch sugar
90 ml (6 tbsp) red wine
45 ml (3 level tbsp) grated
  Parmesan cheese
12 black olives, stoned
salt and milled pepper

Trim and bone the lamb cutlets, shape into noisettes and secure with wooden cocktail sticks. Thickly slice the ham and cut into diamond shapes. Slice the fennel and toss in the lemon juice. Heat 30 ml (2 tbsp) oil with the garlic in a wok or large frying pan until smoky hot. Add the noisettes and fry for about 4 minutes, until brown on all sides. Stir in the fennel, adding more oil if necessary. Cook over a high heat for a further 4–5 minutes, stirring all the time, until the fennel begins to soften. Add the tomato paste, sugar and red wine. Reduce heat, stir for 2–3 minutes, until well blended. Stir in the Parmesan and olives. Season and serve immediately.

Not suitable for freezing.

The crisp texture and aniseed flavour of the vegetable is a delicious foil for the meat in Lamb with fennel

CROWN ROAST OF LAMB
Serves 6

2 best end necks of lamb, chined, each with 6–7 cutlets
125 g (4 oz) onion, skinned and chopped
125 g (4 oz) celery, wiped and chopped
1 eating apple, peeled and chopped
25 g (1 oz) butter
40 g (1½ oz) dried apricots, soaked overnight
125 g (4 oz) fresh white breadcrumbs
30 ml (2 tbsp) chopped parsley
finely grated rind ½ lemon and 15 ml (1 tbsp) lemon juice
1 small egg
salt and milled pepper
50 g (2 oz) lard
30 ml (2 level tbsp) flour
400 ml (¾ pint) brown stock

Cut away the chine bones and ease out the shoulder blades from both joints. Trim each cutlet bone to a depth of 2.5 cm (1 inch). Bend the joints around fat side inside and sew together to form a crown. Cover the exposed bones with foil.

Sauté the onion, celery and apple in butter until browning. Drain, dry and chop the apricots and stir into the pan with the next five ingredients, season well, cool. Fill the stuffing into the crown of lamb and weigh the joint. Place the joint in a small roasting tin with the lard. Roast at 180°C (350°F) mark 4 for 30 minutes to the 450 g (1 lb) plus 30 minutes. Baste occasionally and cover lightly with foil if necessary.

Make gravy from the pan juices, adding the flour, stock and seasoning. Serve separately.

Not suitable for freezing.

APRICOT AND WALNUT STUFFED SHOULDER OF LAMB
Serves 6

75 g (3 oz) onion, skinned and finely chopped
25 g (1 oz) walnut pieces, roughly chopped
25 g (1 oz) butter or margarine
75 g (3 oz) fresh brown breadcrumbs
25 g (1 oz) chopped dried apricots, soaked overnight
25 g (1 oz) stem ginger, chopped
finely grated rind of ½ lemon
15 ml (1 tbsp) lemon juice
30 ml (2 tbsp) chopped parsley
salt and milled pepper
1.4–1.6 kg (3–3½ lb) boned shoulder of lamb
1 egg, size 6
The glaze
45 ml (3 level tbsp) ginger marmalade

Fry the onions and walnuts in the fat until golden. Turn into a bowl and mix with the remaining stuffing ingredients, seasoning well. When cool, spoon the mixture into the pocket of the boned shoulder and sew up with a needle and fine string. Space the stitches at about 1-cm (½-inch) intervals, making sure that the thread passes through the meat and the fat. Sew up the knuckle hole, too. Weigh the joint and then place on a rack standing over a roasting tin. Score the surface of the fat. Roast at 180°C (350°F) mark 4 allowing 30 minutes per lb, basting occasionally. Thirty minutes before the end of cooking time, spread the marmalade over the surface and return the meat to the oven. Lift the joint on to a warm serving plate and serve with gravy.

Not suitable for freezing.

SPICED VEAL WITH PEPPER
Serves 4

600 g (1¼ lb) pie veal
15 ml (1 tbsp) oil
2.5 ml (½ level tsp) each ground ginger, turmeric, cumin, chilli powder
1.25 ml (¼ level tsp) ground cloves
225 g (8 oz) onion, skinned and sliced
225 g (8 oz) red pepper, seeded and sliced
1 clove garlic, skinned and crushed
225 g (8 oz) tomatoes, skinned and chopped
two 141-g (5-oz) cartons natural yogurt
salt and milled pepper

Trim the veal of fat. Cut into chunky cubes. Heat the oil in a large saucepan. Add the spices, onion, pepper and garlic. Cook for 1 minute before stirring in the tomatoes. Over a low heat, very gradually add the yoghurt. Stir well between each addition. Stir in the veal and seasoning.

Simmer gently, covered, for 30 minutes, uncover and cook for a further 30 minutes or until the veal is tender and the liquid is reduced. Stir occasionally to prevent the meat sticking to the pan. Adjust seasoning.

Not suitable for freezing.

Crown roast of lamb—the king of roasts

A rich centre filling of walnuts and apricots is all that is needed for Apricot and walnut stuffed shoulder of lamb

COLD BEEF IN SOURED CREAM
Serves 4

450 g (1 lb) lean rump
  steak in a thin slice
30 ml (2 tbsp) corn oil
salt and milled pepper
75 g (3 oz) onion, skinned
  and chopped
225 g (8 oz) button
  mushrooms, finely sliced
5 ml (1 level tsp) Dijon
  mustard

10 ml (2 level tsp) chopped
  fresh thyme or 2.5 ml
  (½ level tsp) dried
1 green eating apple
142-ml (5-fl oz) carton
  soured cream
15 ml (1 tbsp) lemon juice
lettuce and French bread
  for serving

Slice the steak into thin strips. Heat the oil in a large frying
pan. When hot, quickly brown the steak in a shallow layer,
turning occasionally. Don't crowd the pan. The meat should
remain pink in the centre. Transfer the beef to a bowl using
a slotted spoon. Season with salt and pepper.

Reheat the residual fat; fry the onion until golden brown.
Add the mushrooms, mustard and thyme. Fry over high
heat for 1 minute. Add to the beef, stir, cover and refrigerate
when cool.

Slice the apple thinly. Combine with the soured cream
and lemon juice, cover and refrigerate for several hours.

To serve, line a shallow dish with crisp lettuce. Combine
contents of bowls. Check seasoning and pile into the centre
of the lettuce. Tuck in slices of freshly toasted bread.

Not suitable for freezing.

APPLE BAKED CHOPS
Serves 4

225 g (8 oz) dessert apples
75 g (3 oz) onion, skinned
50 g (2 oz) raisins
200 ml (7 fl oz)
  unsweetened apple juice
45 ml (3 tbsp) chopped
  parsley

salt and milled pepper
4 pork loin chops, about
  175 g (6 oz) each
3 or 4 green cardamoms,
  lightly crushed
30 ml (2 tbsp) dry white
  wine or cider

Core and finely chop the apple. Finely chop the onion.
Place in a saucepan with the raisins and apple juice. Simmer
gently uncovered for 3–4 minutes until the apple is beginning to soften. Drain off the juices and reserve. Stir the
parsley and seasoning into the apple mixture, cool.

Trim the chops of all fat. Make a horizontal cut through
the flesh, almost to the bone. Open out to form a pocket.
Spoon a little of the stuffing mixture into the pocket of
each chop. Place in a shallow ovenproof dish. Sprinkle
any remaining stuffing around the chops with the crushed
cardamoms. Pour over the reserved juices and wine or
cider. Cover with foil and bake at 190°C (375°F) mark 5 for
about 1 hour.

Drain the juices into a saucepan. Reduce to half quantity.
Brown chops under the grill. Spoon over the juices.

To freeze For chops that have not been frozen previously.
Cool pack and freeze before baking. To use, thaw at cool
room temperature overnight. Cook as above.

CASSEROLED LAMB WITH AUBERGINE
Serves 8

700 g (1½ lb) aubergines
salt and milled pepper
1.8–2 kg (4–4½ lb) leg
  lamb
50 g (2 oz) lard
60 ml (4 level tbsp) plain
  flour
400 ml (¾ pint) chicken
  stock

90 ml (6 tbsp) medium
  sherry
5 ml (1 level tsp) dried
  marjoram or 30 ml
  (2 tbsp) fresh chopped
700 g (1½ lb) tomatoes,
  skinned and sliced
45 ml (3 tbsp) oil
snipped parsley

Cut the aubergines into 5-mm (¼-inch) slices. Sprinkle with
salt and leave for 30 minutes. Rinse under cold water and
dry with absorbent kitchen paper.

Meanwhile, cut the lamb off the bone then slice into thin
strips. Brown well, a few at a time in the hot lard. Drain
from the fat and place in a shallow ovenproof dish. Stir the
flour into the pan juices, add stock, sherry and marjoram.
Season, bring to the boil, pour over the lamb. Top with the
sliced tomatoes and finally the sliced aubergines. Brush
with oil. Cover and bake at 180°C (350°F) mark 4 for
1½ hours. Uncover; brush the aubergines with the cooking
juices and bake at 230°C (450°F) mark 8 for about 20
minutes, or until golden. Sprinkle with parsley.

Not suitable for freezing.

KIDNEY & SAUSAGE FRY
Serves 4

4 small lambs' kidneys
240 g (8½ oz) smoked pork
  sausage
125 g (4 oz) onion, skinned
oil
15 ml (1 level tbsp) ground
  paprika

15 ml (1 level tbsp) tomato
  ketchup
15 ml (1 level tbsp) peanut
  butter
salt and milled pepper
chopped parsley

Skin, halve and core the kidneys. Cut a few criss-cross
slashes halfway through each kidney to form a diamond
pattern on the surface. Skin and thickly slice the sausage.
Slice the onion into thick rings. Heat 45 ml (3 tbsp) oil in a
wok or large frying pan until smoky hot. Add the kidneys,
core-side down. Fry over a high heat for 2–3 minutes to
brown, stirring all the time.

Reduce the heat, stir in the sausage, onion and paprika,
adding more oil if necessary. Fry, stirring, for a further
3 minutes before adding the tomato ketchup and peanut
butter. Cook for a further 2 minutes, until well blended.
Season and serve immediately garnished with plenty of
chopped parsley.

Not suitable for freezing.

Cold beef in soured cream should lower the heat at any summer buffet

PAPER WRAPPED PORK
Serves 4

350 g (12 oz) pork
   tenderloin
10 ml (2 level tsp) grated
   fresh root ginger
1 small clove garlic,
   skinned and crushed
20 ml (4 tsp) lemon juice
75 ml (5 tbsp) ginger wine
salt and milled pepper

43-g (1.5-oz) can dressed
   crab meat
peanut oil
75-g (3-oz) bunch spring
   onions, trimmed
450 g (1 lb) broccoli,
   trimmed
50 ml (¼ pint) light stock
75 g (3 oz) cashew nuts

Very thinly slice the meat. Mix together the ginger, garlic, lemon juice, ginger wine and seasoning. Place the pork, crab and 45 ml (3 tbsp) marinade in a bowl. Cover and marinate for 1 hour.

Cut 12 rectangles of greaseproof paper about 20.5 × 12.5 cm (8 × 5 inches). Brush lightly with oil on both sides. Snip the green onion tops into the pork mixture. Thinly slice the white root ends and reserve. Cut the broccoli into small florets. Divide the pork mixture between the papers. Fold the longest sides over and pleat together, turn the short ends under, tucking one end in the other to secure.

Heat about 45 ml (3 tbsp) oil in a wok or large frying pan, add the parcels and fry over a high heat for 4 minutes, turning occasionally. Transfer to a serving dish. Keep warm. Add 15 ml (1 tbsp) oil to pan. Stir in the broccoli and reserved onion. Fry over a brisk heat for 30 seconds. Reduce the heat, add the remaining marinade, stock and cashew nuts. Cook, stirring, for 4–5 minutes.

Not suitable for freezing.

ROLLED PORK TENDERLOINS
Serves 6

two 350-g (12-oz) fillets
   of pork
125 g (4 oz) celery, chopped
225 g (8 oz) leek, chopped
125 g (4 oz) eating apple,
   peeled, cored and
   roughly chopped

50 g (2 oz) walnut pieces,
   roughly chopped
25 g (1 oz) butter
125 g (4 oz) Edam cheese
salt and milled pepper
60 ml (4 tbsp) oil

Make one slice along each fillet almost through to the base. Open out, lay cut side down on a flat surface. Cover with greaseproof paper and bat out with a rolling pin until completely flat and very thin.

Melt the butter in a large frying pan and sauté the celery, leek, apple and walnuts for 3–4 minutes, until the celery has softened. Take out of the pan and cool. Coarsely grate the cheese. Stir 75 g (3 oz) into the cooled mixture; season.

Lay the pork fillets on a flat surface, overlapping the longest edges by about 2.5 cm (1 inch). Spoon the stuffing mixture evenly along the pork fillets. Fold up the sides to enclose the stuffing. Tie securely at intervals with fine string. Heat the oil in the frying pan and brown the pork well. Transfer pork and oil to a roasting tin, and cook at 200°C (400°F) mark 6 for 40 minutes.

Sprinkle the remaining cheese over the pork. Return to the oven for a further 10 minutes. Serve sliced with gravy made from the pan juices.

Not suitable for freezing.

LIVER & MUSTARD HOT POT
Serves 4

350 g (12 oz) lambs' liver,
   thinly sliced
15 ml (1 level tbsp)
   seasoned flour
30 ml (2 tbsp) oil
125 g (4 oz) streaky
   bacon, chopped
175 g (6 oz) onion, skinned
   and thinly sliced

700 g (1½ lb) floury
   potatoes (such as
   King Edward)
30 ml (2 level tbsp)
   French mustard
salt and milled pepper
300 ml (½ pint) stock
25 g (1 oz) butter

Toss the liver in the seasoned flour. Heat the oil in a large frying pan and brown the liver well on both sides, a few pieces at a time. Remove from pan and set aside. In the same pan, sauté the bacon and onions for 2–3 minutes, until golden brown. Remove from the heat.

Peel and slice the potatoes *very* finely. In a 1.7-litre (3-pint) ovenproof dish layer the potatoes with the liver, bacon and onion mixture, finishing with the potatoes. Whisk the French mustard and seasoning into the stock. Pour into the potato mix. Dot the surface with the butter. Bake uncovered at 180°C (350°F) mark 4 for about 1½ hours.

Not suitable for freezing.

LAMB & COURGETTE KEBABS
Serves 8

half leg lamb, about 900 g
   (2 lb)
450 g (1 lb) courgettes
50 g (2 oz) dried apricots,
   soaked overnight
200 ml (7 fl oz) vegetable
   oil
salt and milled pepper

75 ml (5 tbsp) thyme
   vinegar
15 ml (1 level tbsp) fresh
   chopped thyme, or 5 ml
   (1 level tsp) dried
15 ml (3 level tsp) Dijon
   mustard

Cut the lamb into 2-cm (¾-inch) cubes, discarding the skin and bones. Cut the courgettes into 5-mm (¼-inch) slices. Halve the apricots. Thread the meat, courgettes and apricots on to eight skewers and place in a non-metal dish.

Mix the oil, vinegar, herbs, mustard and seasoning together and spoon over the kebabs. Cover, refrigerate and leave to marinate for several hours, turning once.

Cook the kebabs over a barbecue or under a grill for about 15–20 minutes. Turn and brush with the marinade occasionally. Spoon any remaining marinade over the kebabs to serve.

Not suitable for freezing.

Slices of Rolled pork tenderloin expose their tasty apple, celery and walnut centre

PIQUANT LAMB WITH ROSEMARY
Serves 4

900-g (2-lb) piece leg of
  lamb, about 700 g
  (1½ lb) boned
grated rind of 1 lemon
90 ml (6 tbsp) lemon juice
30 ml (2 level tbsp) fresh
  rosemary or 15 ml
  (1 level tbsp) dried
1 large clove garlic

45 ml (3 tbsp) oil
900 g (2 lb) small new
  potatoes
stock (optional)
10 ml (2 level tsp)
  cornflour
salt and milled pepper
rosemary sprigs to garnish

Cut the lamb into 2.5-cm (1-inch) cubes. Place in a bowl with the lemon rind, lemon juice, rosemary and crushed garlic. Cover and marinate for at least 1 hour. Drain the lamb and reserve the marinade. Heat the oil in a large flameproof casserole. Brown the lamb well, a few pieces at a time. Remove with a slotted spoon.

In the same pan, sauté the potatoes for 1–2 minutes. Return the lamb, marinade and seasoning to pan. Bring to the boil. Cover tightly. Bake at 180°C (350°F) mark 4 for 1–1½ hours or until the lamb and potatoes are tender. Drain the juices from the casserole into a measuring jug. Make up to 150 ml (¼ pint) with water or stock. Whisk in the cornflour. Bring to the boil, stirring. Simmer until thickened and clear. Season. Spoon over lamb; garnish.

Not suitable for freezing.

PAUPIETTES OF BEEF
Serves 4

4 thin slices topside, about
  125 g (4 oz) each
100 g (4 oz) liver sausage
350 g (12 oz) pork
  sausagemeat
15 ml (1 level tbsp) dried
  chives
5 ml (1 level tsp) made
  English mustard

30 ml (2 level tbsp)
  creamed horseradish
salt and milled pepper
50 g (2 oz) butter or
  margarine
450 g (1 lb) onions,
  skinned and thinly sliced
chopped parsley to garnish

Bat out each slice of topside between two sheets of grease-proof paper or cling film until very thin. Finely chop the liver sausage. Mix with sausagemeat, chives, mustard, 5 ml (1 level tsp) horseradish; season. Divide stuffing mixture between the beef slices and roll up from shortest side. Halve and secure with cocktail sticks. Heat 25 g (1 oz) fat in a large frying pan and brown rolls on all sides. Transfer to a shallow ovenproof dish into which they will just fit.

In the same pan melt the remaining fat. Gently fry the onions until soft but not coloured. Off the heat stir in the remaining horseradish. Spoon over the meat. Cover tightly with foil. Cook at 180°C (350°F) mark 4 for about 1¼ hours or until the meat is tender. Skim well. Garnish with chopped parsley to serve.

Not suitable for freezing.

PAPRIKA BEEF
Serves 4

450 g (1 lb) lean shin of
  beef
15 ml (1 level tbsp) flour
1.25 ml (¼ level tsp)
  caraway seeds
1.25 ml (¼ level tsp) dried
  marjoram
7.5 ml (1½ level tsp) mild
  paprika pepper
175 g (6 oz) onion, skinned
  and sliced

salt and milled pepper
225 g (½ lb) carrots, pared
  and sliced
200 ml (7 fl oz) beef stock
15 ml (1 level tbsp) tomato
  paste
1 clove garlic
1 whole clove
125 g (4 oz) button
  mushrooms, wiped and
  sliced

Trim the fat from beef. Cut the meat into chunky cubes and toss in the flour, caraway seeds, marjoram, paprika and seasoning. Layer the meat, onions and carrots in a 2-litre (3½-pint) flameproof casserole.

Whisk together the stock, tomato paste, crushed garlic, and clove. Pour into the casserole. Bring to the boil, bubble, uncovered, for 3–4 minutes. Cover tightly. Bake at 180°C (350°F) mark 4 for about 1½ hours. Stir occasionally. Remove from the oven, stir in the mushrooms. Re-cover and return to the oven for a further 15 minutes or so.

To freeze Cool, pack and freeze after baking, omitting mushrooms. Thaw at cool room temperature overnight. Stir in the mushrooms with a little extra stock. Reheat, covered, at 200°C (400°F) mark 6 for about 30 minutes.

SWEET & SOUR LAMB WITH PASTA
Serves 8

4 large breasts of lamb,
  boned and skinned
30 ml (2 tbsp) vegetable oil
225 g (8 oz) onion, skinned
  and sliced
10 ml (2 level tsp) ground
  ginger
45 ml (3 level tbsp) plain
  flour
300 ml (½ pint) light stock
300 ml (½ pint) dry cider

30 ml (2 tbsp) soy sauce
15 ml (1 tbsp)
  Worcestershire sauce
45 ml (3 tbsp) thin honey
45 ml (3 tbsp) vinegar
340-g (12-oz) can
  pineapple cubes
salt and milled pepper
125 g (4 oz) small pasta
  shells
parsley sprigs

Cut up the lamb into 5-cm (2-inch) fingers discarding excess fat. Cover with cold water, bring to the boil and bubble for 5 minutes, drain and cool.

Well brown the meat a little at a time in the hot oil in a large flameproof casserole, drain from the fat. Add the onion, ground ginger and flour to the residual oil, fry gently for 3 minutes. Stir in the next six ingredients with the strained pineapple juice, seasoning and meat. Bring to boil, cover, cook, 150°C (300°F) mark 2 for 1 hour. Add the pineapple chunks and pasta, re-cover and cook for a further 40 minutes, adjust seasoning. Garnish with snipped parsley.

To freeze Cool, add pineapple cubes, pack and freeze without adding pasta. To use, thaw overnight, bring to the boil, add pasta and complete as above.

Piquant lamb with rosemary—new potatoes invade a classic combination to great effect

Classic Beef Stew
Serves 4–6

700–900 g (1½–2 lb)
  stewing steak, in a piece
4 medium onions, about
  350 g (12 oz) total
  weight, skinned
50 g (2 oz) lard
350 g (12 oz) old carrots,
  peeled and cut into
  chunks

30 ml (2 level tbsp) plain
  flour
600 ml (1 pint) beef stock
15 ml (1 level tbsp) tomato
  paste
salt and milled pepper
1 large garlic clove,
  skinned
2 bayleaves

Trim all skin and excess fat off the meat. Cut the meat into cubes of about 4 cm (1½ inch). Halve the onions lengthwise straight through the root. Trim off the hairy root ends, but don't cut away all the root or the onions will collapse during cooking. Melt the lard in a medium-sized flameproof casserole. Increase the heat and when the fat is just beginning to smoke, add the meat about one-quarter at a time. Fry each batch over a high heat until well browned all over. Remove with draining spoons.

Lower the heat under the casserole and add the prepared onions and carrots. Fry over a moderate heat until the vegetables are lightly browned. Stir gently to brown all sides, taking care not to break up the onions. Remove from the casserole using draining spoons. Off the heat, sprinkle the flour into the residual fat and stir well until evenly blended. The roux should be of a thin consistency as a thick roux will not brown evenly; add a little more lard if necessary. Return to the heat and cook slowly until the roux turns a light russet brown colour. Stir occasionally to prevent the flour sticking. Take the casserole off heat and stir in the stock, tomato paste and seasoning until the mixture is quite smooth. Crush the garlic into the juices. Return to the heat and bring slowly up to the boil, stirring all the time. Add the meat and vegetables with their juices, and the bayleaves.

Cover the casserole tightly and cook in the oven at 170°C (325°F) mark 3 for about 2½ hours or until the meat is tender. Uncover and stir once during cooking; recover and return to the oven. Alternatively, cover and simmer gently on top of the stove for about 2 hours only. Stir occasionally to prevent the stew from sticking. Skim any fat off the surface of the stew and adjust the seasoning.

Suitable for freezing.

Classic beef stew is an anglicised version of a great French dish

BEEF & VENISON IN RED WINE
Serves 8

450 g (1 lb) stewing venison	350 g (12 oz) mushrooms, wiped
900 g (2 lb) shin of beef	60 ml (4 tbsp) oil
175 g (6 oz) onion, skinned	30 ml (2 level tbsp) flour
300 ml (½ pint) dry red wine	450 ml (¾ pint) beef stock
15 ml (1 level tbsp) coriander seeds	salt and milled pepper
2 bayleaves	1 clove garlic, skinned
350 g (12 oz) celery	parsley
	redcurrant jelly to accompany

Cut the venison into chunks and the beef into strips; slice the onion. Add the wine, coriander seeds and bayleaves. Marinate in a cool place for 24 hours, turning occasionally.

Strain off the marinade and reserve, discarding the bay-leaves. Slice the celery into 7.5-cm (3-inch) lengths. Slice the mushrooms.

Heat the oil in a large flameproof casserole, brown the meat and onions in batches. Remove, add the celery and mushrooms, quickly brown. Sprinkle over the flour; add stock, seasoning, marinade and crushed garlic; bring to the boil, replace meat and onion. Cover the casserole, cook in the oven at 150°C (300°F) mark 2 for about 3 hours or until tender. Garnish with snipped parsley. Serve with redcurrant jelly.

To freeze Cool, pack and freeze without garnish. To use, thaw overnight at cool room temperature. Reheat, covered, in the oven at 220°C (425°F) mark 7 for about ½ hour, reduce oven to 150°C (300°F) mark 2 for 20 minutes.

GAMMON POCKETS
Serves 4

four 125 g (4 oz) smoked gammon steaks or gammon rashers	salt and milled pepper
125 g (4 oz) carrot, pared	100 ml (4 fl oz) fresh orange juice
1 small green pepper, about 125 g (4 oz)	15 ml (1 tbsp) each soya sauce, cider vinegar, runny honey
50 g (2 oz) onion, skinned	10 ml (2 level tsp) cornflour
298-g (10½-oz) can bamboo shoots	

Snip the rind off the gammon steaks then lay them on a chopping board. Cover with damp greaseproof paper and bat out *lightly* with a rolling pin.

Coarsely grate the carrot. Halve, de-seed and thinly slice the pepper. Thinly slice the onion and drained bamboo shoots. Mix together the carrot, pepper, onion and bamboo shoots with seasoning. Divide the vegetable mixture between the gammon steaks. Fold up the sides to enclose the mixture and secure with wooden cocktail sticks. Place the filled steaks in a shallow ovenproof dish. Whisk together the orange juice, soya sauce, vinegar and honey. Pour over the gammon. Cover with foil. Bake at 190°C (375°F) mark 5 for 50 minutes.

Drain the cooking juices into a saucepan. Re-cover the gammon and keep warm in a low oven. Mix the cornflour to a smooth paste with a little water. Stir into the juices. Bring to the boil, stirring, simmer until thickened. Season. Pour over the gammon to serve.

Not suitable for freezing.

BRAISED OXTAIL
Serves 6

2 small oxtails cut up — about 1.4 kg (3 lb) total weight	150 ml (¼ pint) red wine
30 ml (2 level tbsp) flour	15 ml (1 level tbsp) tomato paste
salt and milled pepper	pared rind ½ lemon
40 g (1½ oz) lard	2 bayleaves
350 g (12 oz) onions, skinned and sliced	225 g (½ lb) carrots, pared
900 ml (1½ pints) stock	450 g (1 lb) parsnips, peeled
	snipped parsley

Coat the oxtails in the seasoned flour. Brown a few pieces at a time in the hot lard in a large flameproof casserole. Take out of the pan. Add the onions to the casserole and lightly brown. Stir in any remaining flour followed by the next five ingredients, season well. Bring to the boil, replace meat. Cover the pan and simmer for 2 hours, skim well.

Cut the carrots and parsnips into chunks and stir into the casserole. Re-cover the pan and simmer for a further 2 hours, or until the meat is quite tender. Skim all fat off the surface of the casserole, adjust seasoning and garnish with parsley.

To freeze Cool, pack and freeze. To use, thaw overnight at cool room temperature, reheat gently on top of the stove.

LIVER & BACON CHOPS
Serves 4

4 loin of lamb chops, about 75 g (3 oz) each	50 g (2 oz) margarine
75 g (3 oz) onion, skinned and finely chopped	30 ml (2 level tbsp) Dijon mustard
175 g (6 oz) lambs' liver, chopped finely	30 ml (2 tbsp) chopped parsley
25 g (1 oz) fresh breadcrumbs	salt and milled pepper
	4 thin rashers streaky bacon, rinded

Place the trimmed lamb chops on a greased baking sheet. Fold the ends of the chops in to form a circle. Sauté the onion in the margarine for 3–4 minutes until softened. Off the heat stir in the liver and breadcrumbs. Add 15 ml (1 level tbsp) mustard, the parsley and seasoning.

Divide the stuffing mixture between the chops, spooning it into the centre of each one. Spread the remaining mustard on the outside of the chops. Stretch the bacon rashers with the back of a knife. Wrap around each chop to enclose the stuffing. Secure with skewers. Bake at 190°C (375°F) mark 5 for 45–50 minutes. Cover with foil after 25 minutes.

Not suitable for freezing.

VEAL WITH OKRA & APPLE

Serves 4

2 veal escalopes, about
    175 g (6 oz) each
seasoned flour
85-g (3-oz) packet full fat
    soft cheese
1 egg, beaten
50 g (2 oz) dried white
    breadcrumbs
peanut oil

125 g (4 oz) green dessert
    apple
15 ml (1 tbsp) cider
    vinegar
350 g (12 oz) okra,
    washed and trimmed
200-ml (7.04-fl oz) carton
    apple juice
salt and milled pepper

Place the veal escalopes between sheets of cling film. Bat out with a rolling pin until very thin. Coat in flour. Spread one side of one escalope with the cream cheese. Place the other escalope on top and press down well. Slice the veal into 1-cm ($\frac{1}{2}$-inch) wide strips. Coat again in seasoned flour, egg and breadcrumbs. Chill well for about 30 minutes.

Quarter, core and thickly slice the apple. Place in a bowl with the cider vinegar. Toss well to coat. Heat 90 ml (6 tbsp) oil in a wok or large frying pan. Fry the veal slices over a medium heat for 4–5 minutes, until golden brown. Remove with a slotted spoon. Keep warm.

Add the okra to the pan, adding extra oil if necessary. Fry, stirring, over a medium heat for 3–4 minutes. Add the apple juice. Bring to the boil and simmer, covered, for about 10 minutes. Stir in the apple slices and vinegar. Season.

Return the veal strips to the pan. Shake over a high heat for a further 2–3 minutes to heat through. Serve immediately.

Not suitable for freezing.

Okra, a neglected vegetable, makes Veal okra and apple into something special

LANCASHIRE HOT POT

Serves 4

900 g (2 lb) middle neck of
    lamb, divided into eight
    cutlets
175 g (6 oz) lambs'
    kidneys
450 g (1 lb) trimmed leeks
225 g ($\frac{1}{2}$ lb) carrots, pared
900 g (2 lb) potatoes

40 g (1$\frac{1}{2}$ oz) lard or
    dripping
5 ml (1 level tsp) dried
    thyme
salt and milled pepper
600 ml (1 pint) brown
    stock

Trim any excess fat off the lamb; skin, halve and core the kidneys and divide each half into three or four pieces. Slice the leeks into 1-cm ($\frac{1}{2}$-inch) thick pieces, discarding the roots, wash and drain well. Thickly slice the carrots, peel and thinly slice the potatoes. Heat the lard in a frying pan and brown the lamb, a few pieces at a time. Lightly brown the kidneys.

In a 3.4-litre (6-pint) ovenproof casserole layer up the meats, leeks, carrots and three-quarters of the potatoes, sprinkling herbs and seasoning between the layers. Pour in the stock and top with a neat layer of overlapping potato slices. Brush with the residual lard from the frying pan.

Cover the casserole and cook at 170°C (325°F) mark 3 for 2 hours. Uncover, increase the temperature to 220°C (425°F) mark 7 and continue cooking until the potatoes are golden brown and crisp—about 30 minutes.

To freeze Cool, overwrap and freeze. To use, thaw at cool room temperature overnight. Reheat, loosely covered at 220°C (425°F) mark 7 for about 1$\frac{1}{4}$ hours.

KIDNEY & CELERY SAUTÉ

Serves 4

450 g (1 lb) lamb's kidneys
2 sticks celery, trimmed
15 ml (1 tbsp) corn oil
25 g (1 oz) butter
30 ml (2 tbsp) brandy

150 ml ($\frac{1}{4}$ pint) brown
    bone stock
1 clove garlic, skinned
salt and milled pepper

Skin each kidney, halve and snip out the cores. Halve them again. Slice the celery into 2.5-cm (1-inch) diagonal pieces.

Heat the oil and butter in the base of a sauté pan and, when it is hot, add the kidney pieces a few at a time. Cook quickly until brown. Remove the kidneys from the pan and keep them warm.

Add the celery pieces, cover and cook them for 5 minutes, shaking the pan from time to time. Replace the kidneys. Add the brandy to the pan and set alight. Add the stock, crushed garlic and seasoning and bring to the boil. Heat through to serving temperature.

Not suitable for freezing.

Illustrated in colour on page 52

Take the lid off this Lancashire hot pot to reveal layers of succulent lamb, leeks and carrots

Spring Lamb Casserole
Serves 8

1.6 kg (3½ lb) lean boned
  lamb (leg)
350 g (12 oz) each carrot,
  turnip, onion, prepared
45 ml (3 tbsp) oil
45 ml (3 level tbsp) flour
45 ml (3 level tbsp) tomato
  paste
300 ml (½ pint) orange
  juice (unsweetened)

300 ml (½ pint) light stock
bayleaf
salt and milled pepper
225 g (8 oz) button
  mushrooms, wiped
chopped parsley
4 egg quantity of choux
  pastry (see Mushroom
  and Sole Profiteroles,
  page 16)

Cut the lamb into 2.5-cm (1-inch) cubes. Roughly chop the carrot, turnip and onion. Heat the oil in a large flameproof casserole. Add the meat and vegetables. Stir over a high heat for 2–3 minutes. Add the flour and tomato paste. Cook, stirring, for a further 2 minutes before adding the orange juice, stock and bayleaf. Bring to the boil, season. Cover and cook at 180°C (350°F) mark 4 for 1½ hours or until lamb is tender. Stir in the mushrooms. Spoon into a shallow 3.4-litre (6-pint) ovenproof dish. Cool completely. Beat 30 ml (2 tbsp) parsley into the choux pastry. Spoon over the lamb. Bake at 200°C (400°F) mark 6 for about 1 hour, or until choux is risen and golden brown. Cover loosely towards end of cooking time if necessary. Garnish with parsley.

To freeze Open freeze after covering lamb with pastry. Cover. Bake from frozen at 200°C (400°F) mark 6 for about 2 hours.

Casserole of Rolled Stuffed Veal
Serves 8

2 kg (4½ lb) breast of veal
  with bone
75 g (3 oz) breadcrumbs
113 g (4 oz) ham pâté
30 ml (2 tbsp) snipped
  chives
60 ml (4 level tbsp) soured
  cream
25 g (1 oz) chopped walnuts

15 ml (1 level tbsp) whole
  grain mustard
salt and milled pepper
450 g (1 lb) mushrooms,
  wiped and sliced
150 ml (¼ pint) white
  stock, veal bone
30 ml (2 tbsp) white wine
parsley for garnish

Trim all the fat from the breast of veal, removing bones. Mix together the breadcrumbs, pâté, chives, 30 ml (2 tbsp) soured cream, mustard, and walnuts. Spread the stuffing mixture over the inside of the meat. Roll up the meat as tightly as possible and sew together with fine string or thick thread.

Place the mushrooms in the bottom of a flameproof casserole. Pour over stock and wine, bring to the boil. Place the veal on top of the casserole, cover tightly, cook in the oven at 150°C (300°F) mark 2 for about 3 hours.

Remove the meat from casserole to slice for serving. Stir the remaining soured cream into the mushrooms and juices and boil to reduce for about 5 minutes. Pour over the veal. Garnish with snipped parsley.

Not suitable for freezing.

Orange Glazed Gammon
Serves 8–10

1.8 kg (4 lb) corner
  gammon
30 ml (2 level tbsp) Dijon
  mustard
45 ml (3 level tbsp) orange
  marmalade
salt and milled pepper

1.25 ml (¼ level tsp)
  ground allspice
50 g (2 oz) demerara
  sugar
1 orange
cloves

Cover the gammon with cold water, soak for 2–3 hours. Drain. Place the joint, skin side down, in a large pan of cold water. Bring to the boil, skim, reduce heat and simmer, covered, for half the cooking time, allowing 25 minutes per 450 g (1 lb).

Drain. Wrap in foil and place in a roasting tin. Cook in the oven at 180°C (350°F) mark 4 for the rest of the time.

Mix the next six ingredients. Raise the oven temperature to 200°C (400°F) mark 6. Unwrap the joint, strip off the rind, slash the fat and spread with half the glaze. Return to the oven in a foil-lined baking tin. Cook for 20 minutes.

Cut the orange into thin slices, reserve three and halve the rest. Using cloves, attach the orange pieces to the joint. Brush with remaining glaze. Return to oven for 10 minutes. Serve hot with orange slices and pickled walnuts.

Not suitable for freezing.

Cider Pork Sauté
Serves 4

450 g (1 lb) green dessert
  apples, peeled and cored
450 g (1 lb) potatoes,
  peeled and cubed
salt and milled pepper
50 g (2 oz) butter
450 g (1 lb) pork escalope

15 ml (1 tbsp) oil
50 g (2 oz) onion, finely
  chopped
15 ml (1 level tbsp) flour
300 ml (½ pint) dry cider
30 ml (2 level tbsp) capers
beaten egg to glaze

Thickly slice half of the apples. Cook with potatoes in boiling, salted water for 20 minutes. Drain and mash. Beat in half of the butter. Season. Pipe into both ends of a 1.5-litre (2½-pint) ovenproof dish. Cut the pork into fine strips. Thickly slice the remaining apples. Keep covered in cold water. Heat the remaining butter and oil in a large sauté pan. Brown the pork strips. Remove with a slotted spoon. Add the onion, sauté for 2–3 minutes. Return the pork, stir in the flour. Cook, stirring, for 1–2 minutes. Add cider. Stir in the apples, simmer gently for 4–5 minutes. Stir in the capers; season.

Spoon into the centre of the dish. Brush the potato with beaten egg. Bake at 200°C (400°F) mark 6 for 25–30 minutes.

Not suitable for freezing.

Cider pork sauté borders the rich mix of apple and pork with browned and creamy potatoes

CHAPTER FOUR

POULTRY AND GAME

CHICKEN WITH CUMIN & CIDER
Serves 4

1 large red-skinned eating
    apple
15 ml (1 tbsp) corn oil
50 g (2 oz) butter
4 chicken leg portions
225 g ($\frac{1}{2}$ lb) cooking
    apples, peeled
15 ml (1 level tbsp) flour

50 g (2 oz) onion, skinned
    and sliced
5 ml (1 level tsp) ground
    cumin
300 ml ($\frac{1}{2}$ pint) jellied
    chicken stock
150 ml ($\frac{1}{4}$ pint) dry cider
salt and milled pepper

Quarter and core the eating apple, halve each quarter length-wise. Heat the oil and butter in a sauté pan and sauté the apple until crisply golden, remove from fat and reserve.

Sauté the chicken joints in the residual fat until golden, take out of the pan. Add the cooking apple and onion, sauté for 3 minutes, stir in the cumin and flour and cook for a further 1 minute. Stir in the stock and cider, season and bring to the boil, replace the chicken. Cover the pan and simmer gently for 15 minutes, turn the chicken pieces over. Re-cover the pan and cook for a further 15 minutes, or until the chicken is quite tender.

Garnish the dish with the sautéed apple.

Not suitable for freezing.

TURKEY PAUPIETTES WITH CUMIN
Serves 8

8 thin turkey escalopes or
    700 g (1$\frac{1}{2}$ lb) turkey
    fillet
salt and milled pepper
450 g (1 lb) pork
    sausagemeat or sausages
60 ml (4 level tbsp) mango
    chutney
50 g (2 oz) salted peanuts,
    chopped
30 ml (2 tbsp) vegetable oil
450 g (1 lb) parsnips,
    peeled and sliced

25 g (1 oz) butter
450 g (1 lb) medium
    onions, skinned and
    sliced
15 ml (1 level tbsp) ground
    cumin
45 ml (3 level tbsp) plain
    flour
45 ml (3 level tbsp)
    desiccated coconut
400 ml ($\frac{3}{4}$ pint) chicken
    stock

Bat out escalopes or fillet between sheets of damp grease-proof paper into eight *thin* pieces; season well. Mix the sausagemeat (or skinned sausages) with 30 ml (2 level tbsp) chutney, the nuts and seasoning. Divide between the escalopes. Roll up and secure with cocktail sticks.

Brown the paupiettes in the hot fat in a shallow flameproof casserole. Drain from fat. Add the parsnips, onions, cumin, flour and coconut to residual oil, fry for 2–3 minutes. Stir in the stock, remaining chutney and seasoning; bring to the boil, replace the paupiettes in a single layer. Cover the dish and cook at 150°C (300°F) mark 2 for about 1$\frac{1}{2}$ hours, skim before serving.

Not suitable for freezing.

Cumin is an intriguing ingredient in gently spicy Turkey paupiettes with cumin

SAUTÉ OF CHICKEN WITH ORANGE
Serves 4

8 chicken thighs
15 ml (1 tbsp) vegetable oil
25 g (1 oz) butter
15 ml (1 level tbsp) flour
200 ml (7 fl oz) jellied
　chicken stock
2 oranges
2.5 ml (½ level tsp) dried
　tarragon or 15 ml
　(1 tbsp) chopped fresh
　tarragon
salt and milled pepper
400-g (14-oz) can
　artichoke hearts

Trim the chicken thighs, remove any excess fat and the skin if preferred. Heat the oil and butter in a medium-sized sauté pan and sauté the chicken until golden brown all over. Sprinkle the flour into the pan, stir in the stock with the finely grated rind and strained juice of one orange. Add the herbs, season well and bring to the boil. Cover the pan and *simmer* for about 20 minutes, or until the chicken is almost tender—a skewer should easily pierce the flesh.

Strip the remaining orange free of skin and white pith, halve each segment. Slice each artichoke heart in two. Tuck the artichoke and orange in around the chicken, cover and heat through gently for 5 minutes. Skim the sauce, if necessary, before serving.

Not suitable for freezing.

TURKEY & HAM PARCELS
Serves 8

700 g (1½ lb) turkey
　escalopes
8 thin slices ham
100 g (4 oz) Cheddar
　cheese with onion and
　chives
salt and milled pepper
15 ml (1 level tbsp)
　creamed horseradish
20 ml (4 level tsp) flour
1 egg, beaten
90 ml (6 level tbsp) dried
　white breadcrumbs
oil

Cut the escalopes into sixteen even-sized pieces. Bat out *thinly* between sheets of cling film. Halve each ham slice and cut the cheese into sixteen small pieces. Wrap a piece of cheese, a little horseradish and seasoning in each slice of ham. Enclose each one in a slice of turkey meat securing firmly with wooden cocktail sticks. Coat the turkey parcels in flour, beaten egg and crumbs. Chill for at least 2 hours.

Brush the parcels with plenty of oil and barbecue or grill for about 8 minutes a side.

To freeze Use fresh turkey only. Pack and freeze uncooked. To use, thaw overnight at cool room temperature; refrigerate before cooking.

N.B. If turkey escalopes are unavailable use eight chicken breast fillets; halve them then bat out as above.

Two excellent one-pan dishes: Sauté of chicken with orange (left)
and Kidney and celery sauté (page 46)

Roast Goose & Apple Sauce
— Serves 8–10 —

4–5 kg (9–11 lb) oven-ready goose	900 g (2 lb) cooking apples
salt and milled pepper	50 g (2 oz) butter
sage and onion stuffing	60–90 ml (4–6 level tbsp) granulated sugar

Prick the skin of the goose with a fork in several places. Pull inside fat out of bird, reserve. Rub salt over skin. Spoon stuffing into the goose, skewer the neck skin to the back of the bird, then truss or tie up the goose with string. Put on a rack placed over a roasting tin. Cover with the reserved fat and foil. Roast at 200°C (400°F) mark 6 for 15 minutes per 450 g (1 lb) plus 15 minutes, basting frequently. Remove foil for the last 30 minutes to brown.

Meanwhile, prepare the apple sauce. Peel, quarter, core and slice the apples and place in a saucepan with 75 ml (5 tbsp) water. Cover and cook gently until soft, about 10 minutes. Beat the fruit well, then purée in a blender, or pass through a sieve. Beat in the butter and sweeten to taste.

Serve the goose with roast potatoes, Chestnut & Sprout Sauté (see page 67), gravy and warm apple sauce.

To freeze Freeze the apple sauce. To use, thaw, reheat.

Turkey Steaks with Ginger Wine & Apricots
— Serves 4 —

two 225-g (8-oz) packs of turkey steaks	50 g (2 oz) butter
salt and milled black pepper	15 ml (1 tbsp) oil
50 g (2 oz) dried apricots, soaked overnight	90 ml (6 tbsp) ginger wine
	90 ml (6 tbsp) jellied chicken stock

Divide the steaks into four portions and bat out thinly. Season generously with milled black pepper. Drain and slice the apricots.

Brown the turkey well in melted butter with oil. Reduce the heat and cook for 5–7 minutes, until tender. Remove to serving dish and keep warm.

Stir the ginger wine and chicken stock into the pan, scraping up any sediment. Reduce until syrupy. Add the sliced apricots. Adjust seasoning. Heat to serving temperature and pour over the turkey steaks.

Not suitable for freezing.

Roast goose and Orange-glazed gammon (page 48) —two traditional highlights of the holiday season

CHICKEN DAUPHINOISE
Serves 6

900 g (2 lb) old potatoes,
   peeled and thinly sliced
salt and pepper
6 chicken breast fillets,
   skinned—about 125 g
   (4 oz) each
30 ml (2 level tbsp)
   seasoned flour
50 g (2 oz) butter

5 ml (1 level tsp) chopped
   fresh tarragon or 2.5 ml
   ($\frac{1}{2}$ level tsp) dried
200 ml (7 fl oz) double
   cream
1 large clove garlic,
   skinned
tarragon sprigs

Cook the potatoes in boiling, salted water for 2–3 minutes. Drain well. Coat the chicken fillets in the seasoned flour. In a large sauté pan melt the butter with the chopped or dried tarragon. Sauté the chicken fillets for 2–3 minutes until lightly browned on both sides. Remove the chicken with a slotted spoon. Reserve the tarragon butter.

Arrange the chicken and potatoes in overlapping layers in a shallow 2-litre (3$\frac{1}{2}$-pint) ovenproof dish. Season the cream *well* with salt, pepper and crushed garlic. Spoon over the chicken and potatoes. Cook uncovered at 170°C (325°F) mark 3 for about 1 hour 15 minutes.

Brush reserved butter over the chicken and potatoes. Lightly brown under a hot grill. Garnish with tarragon.

Not suitable for freezing.

BONED STUFFED POUSSINS
Serves 4

300-g (10.6-oz) packet
   leaf spinach, thawed
1 medium onion, chopped
125 g (4 oz) mixed nuts
75 g (3 oz) butter
125 g (4 oz) fresh white
   breadcrumbs
1 lemon
1 egg
salt and milled pepper

two 700 g (1$\frac{1}{2}$ lb) boned
   poussins, legs and wings
   attached
450 ml ($\frac{3}{4}$ pint) chicken
   stock
150 ml ($\frac{1}{4}$ pint) dry
   vermouth
10 ml (2 level tsp) cornflour
gravy browning
a few sprigs of watercress

Squeeze and finely chop spinach. Fry the onion and nuts in 50 g (2 oz) butter for 2–3 minutes. Add spinach and stir over a high heat for a few minutes. Mix in the breadcrumbs, finely grated rind of $\frac{1}{2}$ lemon, 30 ml (2 tbsp) lemon juice, the egg and seasoning. Leave to cool. Stuff the birds and sew up, using fine string. Run a skewer through the leg and wing joints and tie the knuckle ends together. Place in a roasting tin and spread remaining butter over breasts. Pour over 150 ml ($\frac{1}{4}$ pint) stock and the vermouth. Roast at 200°C (400°F) mark 6 for about 1 hour, basting frequently, until tender. Remove string and skewers and cut each bird in half. Place on a serving platter, cover and keep warm. Mix the cornflour to a smooth paste with a little water. Add to the roasting tin with the remaining stock. Cook for 1–2 minutes, stirring. Adjust seasoning, add a dash of gravy browning; serve separately. Garnish with watercress sprigs.

Not suitable for freezing.

Boned and stuffed poussins—one small bird will be quite sufficient for each guest

JUGGED HARE
Serves 6

1 hare, jointed—about
   1.6 kg (3$\frac{1}{2}$ lb) with its
   blood
75 ml (5 level tbsp)
   seasoned flour
125 g (4 oz) rindless
   streaky bacon
5 ml (1 tsp) vinegar
50 g (2 oz) butter
900 ml (1$\frac{1}{2}$ pint) stock

150 ml ($\frac{1}{4}$ pint) port
5 ml (1 level tsp) dried
   marjoram
45 ml (3 level tbsp)
   redcurrant jelly
2 medium onions, skinned
12 cloves
salt and milled pepper
snipped parsley

Wipe the hare and divide into smaller pieces if necessary. Toss in the seasoned flour. Snip the bacon into small pieces. Mix blood with vinegar, cover, refrigerate.

Brown the bacon in its own fat in a large flameproof casserole, take out of the pan. Add the butter to the pan and lightly brown the hare portions. Add the stock, port, herbs and redcurrant jelly with the onions studded with the cloves. Replace the bacon, season well. Bring to the boil, cover and cook at 170°C (325°F) mark 3 for 3 hours, or until tender.

Take the hare out of its juices, place in a deep serving dish, cover and keep warm. Discard the onions.

Mix the blood with some cooking juices until smooth. Add to the pan and heat through without boiling, adjust seasoning, pour over the hare and garnish with parsley.

To freeze Cool, pack and freeze. To use, thaw overnight at cool room temperature. Reheat, covered at 200°C (400°F) mark 6 for about 40 minutes.

Fit for the son of the Sun King, Chicken dauphinoise turns a classic potato recipe into a main dish

PHEASANT WITH CRANBERRIES
Serves 4

175 g (6 oz) cranberries
30 ml (2 level tbsp) caster
  sugar
75 g (3 oz) each onion,
  celery, streaky bacon
75 g (3 oz) butter or
  margarine
salt and milled pepper

125 g (4 oz) fresh brown
  breadcrumbs
1 large oven-ready
  pheasant
15 ml (1 tbsp) oil
15 ml (1 level tbsp) flour
150 ml (¼ pint) red wine
150 ml (¼ pint) stock

Place the cranberries, caster sugar and 10 ml (2 tsp) water in a small pan over a low heat. Heat gently, covered, until the cranberries burst. Uncover, raise the heat for 2–3 minutes until the excess moisture has evaporated, cool.

Skin the onion, wash and trim the celery. Finely chop with the bacon. Sauté in 25 g (1 oz) fat for 3–4 minutes, stir in the breadcrumbs and cranberries. Season then cool.

With poultry shears or strong scissors cut along the backbone and breastbone of the pheasant to split the bird in two. Pack the stuffing into the halves. Place the oil and remaining butter in a small roasting tin. Add the pheasant halves skin side down and roast at 230°C (450°F) mark 8 for 10 minutes, then at 200°C (400°F) mark 6 for a further 25–30 minutes.

To serve, split each piece of pheasant in half; keep warm. Make a gravy from pan juices and remaining ingredients. Spoon a little over pheasant and serve the rest separately.

Not suitable for freezing.

ROAST PHEASANT
Serves 4

1 brace oven-ready
  pheasants
50 g (2 oz) streaky bacon,
  rinded
50 g (2 oz) butter, softened
30 ml (2 level tbsp) plain
  flour

300 ml (½ pint) stock
salt and milled pepper
For the garnish
100 g (4 oz) fresh white
  breadcrumbs
25 g (1 oz) butter
watercress

Truss the birds and cover the breasts with bacon; place in a roasting tin. Spread the butter over the legs and wings. Roast at 230°C (450°F) mark 6 for 15–20 minutes, basting frequently. Remove from oven, discard bacon and sprinkle the breasts with flour. Baste with butter; cook for a further 15 minutes.

Fry the breadcrumbs in the butter until golden. Put the pheasants on a heated serving dish and remove the trussing strings. Spoon the fried crumbs round the birds, garnish with watercress and keep hot. Skim the fat from the cooking juices. Add the stock and stir to loosen any sediment. Boil for 2–3 minutes and season to taste. Serve the gravy with the pheasants.

Not suitable for freezing.

Illustrated in colour on page 2

PEACH GLAZED CHICKEN LEGS
Serves 4

50 g (2 oz) brown rice
15 ml (1 level tbsp) ground
  turmeric
salt and milled pepper
125 g (4 oz) spring onions,
  trimmed
50 g (2 oz) butter or
  margarine
2.5 ml (½ level tsp) ground
  ginger

25 g (1 oz) Brazil nuts
411-g (14½-oz) can peach
  halves
4 chicken legs, about 1 kg
  (2.2 lb) total weight
15 ml (1 level tbsp) golden
  syrup
5 ml (1 level tsp) cornflour
15 ml (1 tbsp) malt
  vinegar

Cook the brown rice with the turmeric in boiling salted water for about 45 minutes. Drain well. Finely chop the spring onions and nuts and sauté with the ginger in 25 g (1 oz) fat for 2–3 minutes. Off the heat, stir in the rice and one chopped peach half—reserve peach juices. Season. Cool.

Cut and ease the bones out of the chicken legs, keeping the skin and flesh as intact as possible. Spoon a little stuffing into each chicken leg. Carefully fold over to enclose stuffing. Sew up neatly.

Liquidise the remaining peaches with half the juice, the golden syrup, cornflour and vinegar. Reduce by boiling to half its original quantity, stirring all the time.

Melt the remaining fat in a shallow 1.1-litre (2-pint) flameproof casserole. Brown the chicken parcels. Pour over the peach sauce. Cook at 200°C (400°F) mark 6 for about 40 minutes. Skim.

Not suitable for freezing.

DUCK WITH MANGO
Serves 4

175 g (6 oz) celery,
  washed and trimmed
1 ripe, but still firm mango
4 duck portions, about
  275 g (10 oz) each
2.5 ml (½ level tsp) ground
  allspice

peanut oil
50 g (2 oz) walnut pieces
45 ml (3 level tbsp) plum
  jam
20 ml (4 tsp) wine vinegar
salt and milled pepper

Thickly slice the celery. Skin and thickly slice mango if necessary. Remove any excess fat from the duck portions. Divide each portion into three. Cover with cold water, bring to the boil then simmer gently for 15–20 minutes. Drain well. Pat dry on absorbent paper. Trim the bones.

Heat 60 ml (4 tbsp) oil in a wok or large frying pan until smoky hot. Add the duck portions and allspice. Brown well on all sides. Add the celery and walnuts, adding more oil if necessary. Fry, stirring all the time, for 2–3 minutes, until browned. Stir in the plum jam, and wine vinegar. Stir over the heat for a further 2–3 minutes, until the ingredients are well glazed. Stir in the mango. Season and serve immediately.

Not suitable for freezing.

Peach-glazed chicken legs hide a scrumptious stuffing studded with brazil nuts

RABBIT & FORCEMEAT PIE
— Serves 4 —

225 g (8 oz) each, small
  onion, button
  mushrooms
4 rabbit portions, 550 g
  (1¼ lb) total weight
30 ml (2 level tbsp) flour
1 clove garlic, skinned and
  crushed
25 g (1 oz) lard
100 ml (4 fl oz) port
300 ml (½ pint) stock

12 juniper berries, crushed
350 g (12 oz) sausagemeat
45 ml (3 tbsp) chopped
  parsley
30 ml (2 level tbsp) made
  English mustard
salt and milled pepper
shortcrust pastry made
  with 225 g (8 oz) plain
  flour etc

Skin and quarter the onions. Trim the mushrooms. Toss
the rabbit portions in the flour. Sauté the onions, mushrooms
and garlic in the lard until beginning to brown. Remove
with a slotted spoon to a 1.7-litre (3-pint) pie dish. In the
same pan brown the rabbit portions. Stir the port, stock
and juniper berries into the pan. Bring to the boil, scraping
any sediment from the bottom. Add to dish.

Mix together the sausagemeat, parsley, mustard and
seasoning. Shape into 8 balls. Add to pie dish. Cover with
shortcrust pastry. Bake at 190°C (375°F) mark 5 for 30
minutes. Cover loosely with foil. Reduce temperature to
180°C (350°F) mark 4 for a further 1 hour.

Not suitable for freezing.

CHICKEN WITH VERMOUTH & OLIVES
— Serves 4 —

8 chicken thighs, skinned
  —about 900 g (2 lb)
40 g (1½ oz) seasoned
  plain flour
50 g (2 oz) butter
300 ml (½ pint) chicken
  stock
150 ml (¼ pint) dry
  vermouth or white wine

1 small clove garlic,
  skinned and crushed
142-ml (5-fl oz) carton
  soured cream
50 g (2 oz) black olives,
  stoned and sliced
salt and milled pepper
flaky pastry scraps and
  parsley sprigs to garnish

Toss the chicken thighs in seasoned flour. In a deep frying
pan melt the butter, brown the chicken well all over. Remove
from fat, put aside. Stir in the remaining seasoned flour,
cook for 2–3 minutes. Gradually stir in the stock, vermouth
and crushed garlic. Boil for 2–3 minutes, stirring. Replace
the chicken, cover and simmer gently for about 1 hour.
Remove the chicken pieces to serving dish and keep warm.

Stir the soured cream into the pan juices. Heat gently for
3–4 minutes, without boiling. Just before serving add the
olives. Adjust the seasoning and spoon over the chicken.

For garnish, cut pastry scraps into crescents, bake at
220°C (425°F) mark 7 for about 12 minutes.

Not suitable for freezing.

CASSEROLED PIGEON IN PORT WINE
— Serves 8 —

8 pigeons
flavouring vegetables,
  peppercorns and
  bayleaves
50 g (2 oz) butter or
  margarine
450 g (1 lb) onions,
  skinned and diced
350 g (12 oz) celery, diced

450 g (1 lb) swede, peeled
  and diced
45 ml (3 level tbsp) plain
  flour
60 ml (4 tbsp) port
salt and milled pepper
parsley sprigs or celery
  leaves for garnish

Remove the breasts from the pigeons, skin and slice into
fork-sized pieces. Place carcasses, flavouring vegetables,
bayleaves and peppercorns with 1.1 litre (2 pint) water in a
large saucepan. Simmer for about 1 hour or until reduced
to 600 ml (1 pint).

Heat the butter in a large pan and quickly brown the
pigeon pieces, a few at a time. Remove from the pan and
add the diced vegetables. Cover the pan, reduce the heat
and cook for about 5 minutes, or until beginning to soften.
Stirring well, toss in the flour and cook for 2 minutes. Add
port with 400 ml (¾ pint) stock and bring to the boil. Season
well. Stir in the pigeon pieces.

Place in a large ovenproof dish. Cover and cook in the
oven at 150°C (300°F) mark 2 for about 3 hours. Garnish.

Not suitable for freezing.

*Any guest at a country cottage — or town house — would be tempted
by Rabbit and forcemeat pie*

*Chicken with vermouth and olives uses herby fortified wine to lend
distinction*

TURKEY KEBABS WITH CHILLI PEANUT SAUCE
Serves 3

450 g (1 lb) white diced
   turkey casserole meat or
   whole breast fillet
185-g (7½-oz) can button
   mushrooms, drained
150 ml (¼ pint) vegetable
   oil
30 ml (2 tbsp) lemon juice
5 ml (1 level tsp) each
   ground cumin, sugar,
   salt

300 ml (½ pint) milk
45 ml (3 level tbsp)
   desiccated coconut
60 ml (4 level tbsp) peanut
   butter
pinch of chilli powder or
   20 ml (4 level tsp) chilli
   seasoning
salt and milled pepper
beansprouts and spring
   onions

Thread six skewers alternately with turkey meat and whole mushrooms. Combine the next five ingredients and marinate the kebabs for at least 2 hours, turning occasionally.

Bring the milk to boil. Add the coconut, infuse for 10 minutes. In a heavy-based pan heat the peanut butter with chilli powder. Cook gently for 1 minute. Gradually stir in the coconut milk, bring to boil then simmer for 2–3 minutes. Season.

Cook the kebabs under a low grill for 10–15 minutes, turning two or three times and basting with the marinade. Spoon a little sauce over the kebabs, and serve the rest separately. Garnish the kebabs with beansprouts and spring onions tassels.

Not suitable for freezing.

CHICKEN & STILTON ROULADES
Serves 4

125 g (4 oz) Stilton
   cheese, crumbled
75 g (3 oz) unsalted
   butter, softened
4 chicken breasts, skinned
   and boned
8 rashers smoked back
   bacon
15 ml (1 tbsp) vegetable oil

25 g (1 oz) butter
1 glass red wine made up
   to 300 ml (½ pint) with
   chicken stock
5 ml (1 level tsp)
   arrowroot
salt and milled pepper
watercress for garnish

Cream the Stilton and unsalted butter to a smooth paste.

Bat out the chicken breasts between two sheets of damp greaseproof paper. Spread Stilton butter evenly on one side of each breast. Roll up the chicken breasts, wrap in rinded bacon rashers and secure with cocktail sticks.

In a heavy based pan, heat oil and butter and brown the chicken rolls well. Pour in the red wine and stock, season, bring to the boil, cover and simmer very gently for 35–40 minutes turning occasionally. Remove the meat to a serving dish, keep warm.

Thicken the pan juices with a smooth paste of arrowroot and water. Season. Spoon the sauce over meat and garnish with watercress sprigs.

Not suitable for freezing.

CIDER BAKED RABBIT WITH CABBAGE
Serves 8

60 ml (4 tbsp) vegetable oil
225 g (½ lb) streaky bacon
   rashers, rinded and
   chopped in small pieces
225 g (8 oz) onion, skinned
   and sliced
350 g (12 oz) cooking
   apple, peeled and sliced
1.4 kg (3 lb) white cabbage
salt and milled pepper

8 rabbit joints, about
   1.4 kg (3 lb) total
   weight
60 ml (4 level tbsp) plain
   flour
15 ml (3 level tsp) French
   mustard
300 ml (½ pint) dry cider
450 ml (¾ pint) light stock
snipped parsley

Heat the oil in a large frying pan and lightly brown the bacon, onion and apple. Lift out of the pan with draining spoons, mix with the cabbage and plenty of seasoning and place in a *large* ovenproof casserole.

Brown the rabbit joints well in the reheated residual oil and place on top of the cabbage. Stir the flour and mustard into the pan. Gradually add the cider and stock, stirring. Season and bring to the boil. Pour over the rabbit; cover tightly and cook in the oven at 170°C (325°F) mark 3 for 1½–1¾ hours, or until the rabbit is tender, adjust seasoning. Garnish with plenty of parsley.

Not suitable for freezing.

CURRIED TURKEY WITH AVOCADO
Serves 4

350 g (12 oz) turkey fillet
1 bunch spring onions,
   about 75 g (3 oz) in
   weight
1 ripe but still firm
   avocado
15 ml (1 tbsp) lemon juice
30 ml (2 level tbsp) flour
1 egg, beaten

15 ml (1 level tbsp) each,
   ground cumin, ground
   ginger
peanut oil
1 clove garlic, skinned and
   crushed
225-g (8-oz) can bamboo
   shoots, drained
salt and milled pepper

Slice the turkey fillet into pencil thin 5-cm (2-inch) long strips. Wash, trim and roughly chop the spring onions. Peel, halve and stone the avocado. Thickly slice and coat in lemon juice. Toss the turkey in the flour, cumin and ginger. Stir in the beaten egg until the strips are well coated.

Heat 45 ml (3 tbsp) oil, with the garlic in a wok or large frying pan until smoky hot. Stir fry the turkey strips, over a high heat, until all are golden brown, adding a little oil if necessary.

Reduce the heat, stir in the thinly sliced bamboo shoots and spring onions. Cook, stirring, for 1–2 minutes. Off the heat, gently fold in the avocado and lemon juice. Season and serve immediately.

Not suitable for freezing.

Turkey kebabs with chilli peanut sauce boast the spicy nuttiness characteristic of Malaysian cooking

ROAST DUCKLING
Serves 4

1.8–2 kg (4–4½ lb) oven-
  ready duckling
3 medium oranges
salt and milled pepper
150 ml (¼ pint) medium
  dry white wine
1 large lemon
15 ml (1 level tbsp) caster
  sugar

15 ml (1 tbsp) white wine
  vinegar
30 ml (2 tbsp) brandy
150 ml (¼ pint) giblet stock
15 ml (1 level tbsp)
  cornflour
trimmed watercress sprigs
  to garnish

Pull out any excess fat from the inside of the duckling. Using a potato peeler thinly pare the rind off one orange and place inside the duckling cavity with salt and pepper. Weigh the bird then put it on a wire rack placed over a roasting tin. Prick the skin all over with a fork, sprinkle generously with salt.

Roast the duckling at 180°C (350°F) mark 4 for 20 minutes to the 450 g (1 lb) plus an extra 20 minutes. Baste the bird occasionally. After 1 hour tip all the fat out of the roasting tin and then pour the wine over the bird. Baste well then return to the oven to complete the cooking; baste occasionally.

Meanwhile, finely grate the rind of one orange and place in a small bowl. Add the strained juice of two oranges, about 135 ml (9 tbsp) with 45 ml (3 tbsp) strained lemon juice. Cut all peel and pith away from the remaining orange. Cut out the segments, discarding membrane. Reserve segments.

Place sugar and vinegar in saucepan and warm gently until the sugar dissolves. Boil slowly until the mixture turns to a golden caramel then remove from the heat. At once pour in the fruit juice mixture and add the brandy. Return to the heat and simmer for about 5 minutes, or until the final ingredients are evenly blended. Stir occasionally; set aside.

When cooked place the duckling on a large chopping board. Using strong kitchen or game scissors split the bird in half along the breast bone. Cut out and discard the backbone. Using a sharp knife, make a diagonal cut to divide each side into a leg and wing joint. Cut off the wing pinions and knobbly leg ends. Place the duckling on a serving plate; keep warm, loosely covered.

Pour all remaining fat out of the roasting tin, reserving the duckling juices. Add the fruit juices and stock to the pan and bubble up scraping the sediment off the bottom of the pan. Mix the cornflour to a smooth paste with a little water. Add to the pan juices and bring to the boil, stirring. Cook for 2 minutes, season, add the orange segments. Spoon over the duckling. Garnish with watercress sprigs.

Not suitable for freezing.

Our Duckling with orange segments is a subtler dish than the more usual version à l'orange

SESAME LEMON CHICKEN
Serves 4

8 small chicken drumsticks, about 75 g (3 oz) each
30 ml (2 level tbsp) cornflour
1 egg, beaten
225 g (8 oz) leek, washed and trimmed
1 lemon
60 ml (4 tbsp) dry sherry

15 ml (1 tbsp) each soy sauce, cider vinegar, demerara sugar
sesame oil
peanut oil
45 ml (3 level tbsp) sesame seeds
salt and milled pepper

Cover the drumsticks with cold water, bring to the boil. Simmer for about 30 minutes. Drain and pat dry with absorbent paper. Mix together the cornflour and eggs; use to coat the chicken drumsticks thoroughly.

Cut the leeks into 1-cm (½-inch) slices. Whisk together the grated lemon rind, soy sauce, cider vinegar, sugar and sherry. Peel and thinly slice the lemon.

Heat 15 ml (1 tbsp) sesame oil and 30 ml (2 tbsp) peanut oil in a wok or large frying pan until smoky hot. Brown the drumsticks a few at a time. Remove with a slotted spoon. Over a medium heat, fry the leeks and sesame seeds for 1–2 minutes, adding more oil if necessary. Return the drumsticks and sauce mixture to the pan. Raise heat, bring to the boil and simmer for 3–4 minutes, stirring occasionally. Season.

Transfer to a warmed serving dish. Lightly sauté the lemon slices in the wok or frying pan. Garnish the drumsticks with the lemon and serve immediately.

Not suitable for freezing.

CHICKEN WITH WATERCRESS & APRICOTS
Serves 4

1 large bunch watercress
400 ml (15 fl oz) oil
150 ml (5 fl oz) white wine vinegar
45 ml (3 tbsp) chopped parsley
salt and milled pepper

1 small onion, skinned and finely chopped
1.4 kg (3 lb) oven-ready chicken
225 g (½ lb) fresh ripe apricots
watercress sprigs to garnish

A day ahead, wash and drain the watercress, pat dry with absorbent kitchen paper, then finely chop. Mix 350 ml (12 fl oz) oil with the vinegar, parsley, watercress, onion and seasoning. Heat the remaining oil in a medium-sized flame-proof casserole. Brown the chicken all over in the hot oil.

Pour half the dressing over the chicken and bring to the boil. Cover the casserole and cook in the oven at 170°C (325°F) mark 3 for about 1½ hours; baste occasionally. To test the chicken, pierce a leg with a fine skewer; when done, the juices will run clear. Cool in the cooking liquor.

Drain the chicken then joint into small pieces. Arrange on a serving platter. Cover and refrigerate. Halve and stone apricots, stir into remaining dressing; cover tightly, refrigerate.

To serve, take the chicken from refrigerator. Gently stir the apricots in the dressing and spoon over the chicken. Garnish with watercress sprigs.

Not suitable for freezing.

ORANGE & CHICKEN LIVER SKEWERS
Serves 4

200 ml (7 fl oz) orange juice
2 small oranges
5 ml (1 level tsp) fresh chopped tarragon or 2.5 ml (½ level tsp) dried
1 green pepper

450 g (1 lb) whole firm chicken livers
2 slices bread, crumbed
butter or margarine
100 g (4 oz) onion
275 g (10 oz) beansprouts
small bunch chives
salt and milled pepper

Simmer the orange juice, grated rind of 1 orange and tarragon for 2–3 minutes. Reduce by half. Segment oranges.

Cut the livers in half; toss lightly in breadcrumbs. Place in a lightly-greased grill pan and grill for 2 minutes each side. De-seed and roughly chop the pepper and onion. Thread on to four skewers alternately with the livers, and place in grill pan, spoon over a little orange juice. Grill, basting, for 2–3 minutes on each side.

Meanwhile, steam the beansprouts for 2–3 minutes. Warm the orange with the remaining juice. Add snipped chives and seasoning to beansprouts and arrange on a serving dish. Top with the skewers and spoon over orange and juices.

Not suitable for freezing.

Chicken with watercress and apricots transforms cold chicken into a sophisticated centrepiece

CHAPTER FIVE

VEGETABLES AND SALADS

CAULIFLOWER & COURGETTE BAKE
— Serves 4 —

700 g (1½ lb) trimmed
  cauliflower
salt and milled pepper
225 g (8 oz) courgettes,
  thinly sliced
45 ml (3 level tbsp) flour

50 g (2 oz) butter or
  margarine
150 ml (¼ pint) milk
3 eggs, separated
15 ml (1 level tbsp) grated
  Parmesan cheese

Cut the cauliflower into small florets. Cook in boiling, salted water for 10–12 minutes until tender. Drain well. Cook the courgettes in half the fat until beginning to soften.

Melt the remaining fat in a saucepan. Stir in the flour. Cook, stirring, for 1–2 minutes before adding the milk. Bring to the boil, stirring all the time. Simmer until thickened. Liquidise or sieve together the cauliflower, warm sauce and egg yolks. Season well.

Stiffly whisk the egg whites and fold in the cauliflower mixture. Place half in a 1.6-litre (2¾-pint) deep soufflé dish. Spoon over the sautéed courgettes, reserving a few for garnish. Finish with the remaining cauliflower mixture and reserved courgettes. Sprinkle over the Parmesan cheese. Bake at 190°C (375°F) mark 5 for 35–40 minutes, or until golden and just firm to the touch. Serve immediately.

Not suitable for freezing.

SPINACH POTATO WEDGES
— Serves 4 —

450 g (1 lb) potatoes,
  peeled
50 g (2 oz) onion, skinned
  and chopped
450 g (1 lb) fresh spinach,
  cooked
50 g (2 oz) Ricotta or
  cottage cheese
65 g (2½ oz) Parmesan
  cheese

30 ml (2 tbsp) oil
50 g (2 oz) salami
1 egg, 1 egg yolk
pinch nutmeg
salt and milled pepper
3.75 ml (¾ level tsp)
  baking powder
125 g (4 oz) plain flour
parsley sprigs

Boil 350 g (12 oz) potatoes until tender, drain well. Meanwhile coarsely grate the remaining potato. Fry with the onion in the oil for 2 minutes. Add the *well drained* finely chopped spinach, fry for 2 minutes. Off the heat add the Ricotta, 50 g (2 oz) Parmesan, the shredded salami, the egg yolk, nutmeg and seasoning. Cool.

Peel and sieve the cooked potatoes. Beat in the egg, baking powder and flour. Knead on a well-floured surface. Roll out the pastry to a 23-cm (9-inch) square. Place on a greased baking sheet. Pile the spinach mixture in the centre of the dough. Bring the corners of dough to the centre, pressing lightly together. Mark lines on the pastry. Sprinkle over the remaining Parmesan. Bake at 200°C (400°F) mark 6 for about 40 minutes. Serve hot, cut into wedges and garnished with parsley.

Not suitable for freezing.

Spinach potato wedges are surprisingly light but very satisfying

PRAWN BAKED POTATOES
Serves 6

3 large even-sized potatoes, about 350 g (12 oz) each	150 ml (5 fl oz) milk
salt and milled pepper	125 g (4 oz) Brie, rinded grated rind and juice of
30 ml (2 tbsp) oil	1 lemon
50 g (2 oz) butter	175 g (6 oz) cooked, shelled prawns
15 ml (1 level tbsp) flour	2 egg whites

Wash the potatoes well, then dry. Rub the skins with salt and oil. Place in a shallow baking dish and cook at 200°C (400°F) mark 6 for about 1½ hours, or until cooked through.

Meanwhile melt 25 g (1 oz) butter in a saucepan. Stir in the flour. Cook, stirring for 1–2 minutes before stirring in the milk. Bring to the boil, simmer for 2 minutes. Off the heat, beat in the roughly chopped Brie. Beat until completely melted. Stir in the grated lemon rind and 10 ml (2 tsp) juice. Cover with damp greaseproof paper.

Cut the potatoes in half, horizontally. Carefully scoop out the flesh, leaving the skins intact. Rub the skins with the remaining butter. Mash the potato flesh, stir into the sauce, beating until smooth. Stir in the prawns; season. Lightly whisk the egg whites. Fold into the prawn mixture. Spoon back into the scooped-out shells. Bake for a further 25–30 minutes to brown. Serve with a mixed salad.

Not suitable for freezing.

HAM & POTATO GNOCCHI
Serves 4

450 g (1 lb) even-sized floury potatoes, scrubbed	25 g (1 oz) butter or margarine
150 g (5 oz) plain flour	400 ml (¾ pint) milk
1 egg	75 g (3 oz) Cheddar cheese
50 g (2 oz) cooked ham	25 g (1 oz) grated Parmesan cheese
salt and pepper	

Boil the potatoes in their skins until tender, about 20 minutes. Finely chop the ham. Drain, skin, then mash the potatoes. Add 125 g (4 oz) flour, egg and ham. Season and beat well to mix. Using damp hands, shape the potato mixture into 24 small balls.

Bring a large pan of water to the boil. Drop in several of the balls and boil for at least 8 minutes. They will become fluffy when cooked. Lift out of the water with a slotted spoon; place in a shallow flameproof dish. Cover and keep warm. Repeat until all the potato balls are cooked.

Make a sauce with the fat, remaining flour and milk. Off the heat grate the Cheddar cheese into the sauce. Add the Parmesan and season well. Pour the sauce over the gnocchi and place under a hot grill to brown. Serve with a crisp lemon-dressed green salad.

Not suitable for freezing.

VEGETABLE CANNELLONI
Serves 4

salt and milled pepper	226-g (8-oz) can tomatoes
15 ml (1 tbsp) oil	150 ml (¼ pint) red wine
8 sheets wide lasagne verdi, about 150 g (5 oz) total weight	175 g (6 oz) Mozzarella cheeze, grated
450 g (1 lb) cabbage	142-ml (5-fl oz) carton single cream
75 g (3 oz) butter	568 ml (1 pint) milk
45 ml (3 level tbsp) flour	1 egg

Bring to the boil a large saucepan of salted water. Add the oil. Cook the lasagne for 10–12 minutes until just tender. Drain well. Separate the sheets and keep under cold water.

Trim, quarter and core the cabbage. Shred finely. Sauté the cabbage in 50 g (2 oz) butter for 5–7 minutes. Add 15 ml (1 level tbsp) flour, the tomatoes and wine. Cover, simmer for 10 minutes until the cabbage retains some bite and much of the liquid has been absorbed. Season and cool.

Pat the lasagne dry with absorbent paper. Spread the cabbage mixture and half the Mozzarella on the sheets and roll up. Pack together in a shallow greased ovenproof dish. Make a white sauce from the remaining butter, flour, cream and milk. Off the heat stir in the remaining Mozzarella and egg. Pour evenly over the cannelloni. Bake uncovered at 180°C (350°F) mark 4 for 45 minutes.

Not suitable for freezing.

CABBAGE & HAZELNUT CROQUETTES
Makes 16

450 g (1 lb) potatoes, peeled	50 g (2 oz) flour
900 g (2 lb) cabbage, trimmed and roughly chopped	50 g (2 oz) chopped, toasted hazelnuts
45 ml (3 tbsp) milk	salt and milled pepper
50 g (2 oz) margarine	2 eggs
	dried white breadcrumbs
	fat for deep frying

Boil the potatoes in salted water and mash without adding any liquid. Cook the cabbage in boiling salted water until just tender. Drain well. Purée in an electric blender, adding the milk if required—you should have 450 ml (¾ pint) of purée.

Make a sauce with the margarine, flour and cabbage purée, cook for 2 minutes, stirring. Add the hazelnuts. Stir the mashed potatoes into the sauce, season and mix well. Transfer to a bowl, cool, cover and chill well for at least 1½ hours or until firm.

With dampened hands shape into 16 croquettes, place on greased baking sheet and chill again. Coat croquettes in beaten egg and breadcrumbs. Deep fry at 180°C (350°F) for about 4 minutes, or shallow fry turning occasionally.

To freeze Open freeze the croquettes uncooked. Pack when firm. To use, thaw for 2 hours only, then fry as above.

WATERCRESS & OATMEAL CROQUETTES
Makes 12

700 g (1½ lb) medium-
  sized floury potatoes
15 g (½ oz) butter
1 bunch watercress
2 eggs
salt and milled pepper

15 ml (1 level tbsp) flour
50 g (2 oz) fresh white
  breadcrumbs
50 g (2 oz) medium
  oatmeal
oil for frying

Scrub the potatoes, boil in their skins until tender, about 20 minutes. Drain well. Peel, then sieve the potatoes into a bowl or mash *well*. Beat in the butter.

Wash, drain and finely chop the watercress. Add to the bowl with one egg and seasoning; mix well.

Mould the potato mixture into 12 'cork'-shaped pieces. Coat each croquette lightly in flour. Break the remaining egg on to a plate; beat lightly. Combine the breadcrumbs and oatmeal on another plate. Brush the croquettes with egg, then coat in the breadcrumb mixture, pressing it on firmly. Chill for at least 30 minutes. Deep fry the croquettes for about 4 minutes or until golden brown. Drain on kitchen paper before serving.

To freeze Open freeze before deep frying. Pack into freezer bags when firm. To use, unwrap, thaw at cool room temperature for 4–5 hours. Cook as above.

CHESTNUT & SPROUT SAUTÉ
Serves 8

900 g (2 lb) chestnuts or
  879-g (1 lb 15-oz) can
  whole chestnuts
600 ml (1 pint) chicken
  stock
770 g (1½ lb) Brussels
  sprouts, prepared

salt and milled pepper
225 g (8 oz) celery,
  washed and trimmed
450 g (1 lb) medium
  onions, skinned
125 g (4 oz) butter
grated rind of 1 lemon

If using fresh chestnuts, snip the brown outer skins, or nick with a sharp knife. Place in boiling water for 3–5 minutes. Lift out, a few at a time, and peel off both the brown and inner skins. Cover with the stock and simmer for 40–45 minutes or until tender. Drain well.

Meanwhile cook the sprouts in boiling salted water for 3–4 minutes only; drain well. Cut the celery into 2.5-cm (1-inch) pieces; quarter the onions and separate out the layers.

Melt the butter in a large sauté or frying pan. Sauté the celery and onions with the lemon rind until softening, about 2–3 minutes. Add the cooked chestnuts. Brussels sprouts and seasoning. Sauté for a further 1–2 minutes to heat through before serving.

Not suitable for freezing.

TURNIPS IN CURRY CREAM SAUCE
Serves 4

700 g (1½ lb) small turnips
50 g (2 oz) butter or
  margarine
125 g (4 oz) onion, skinned
  and finely chopped
125 g (4 oz) cooking
  apple, peeled
5 ml (1 level tsp) mild
  curry powder

50 g (2 oz) sultanas
5 ml (1 level tsp) plain
  flour
150 ml (¼ pint) dry cider
142-ml (5-fl oz) carton
  single cream
10 ml (2 tsp) lemon juice
salt and milled pepper

Peel the turnips, boil in salted water for 10–15 minutes until just tender. Meanwhile melt the butter, add the onion, cover and cook gently until soft and tinged with colour. Uncover and stir in the finely chopped apple, sultanas, curry powder and flour. Cook stirring 3–4 minutes.

Pour the cider into pan, bring to the boil, bubble gently for 2 minutes, stirring. Off the heat stir in the cream, lemon juice and seasoning. Keep warm without boiling.

Drain the turnips. Place in a heated dish and pour the sauce over.

Not suitable for freezing.

VEGETABLE LASAGNE
Serves 4

175 g (6 oz) lasagne verdi
225 g (½ lb) onion, skinned
350 g (12 oz) tomatoes,
  skinned
350 g (12 oz) courgettes
15 ml (1 tbsp) oil
2.5 ml (½ level tsp) dried
  basil
15 ml (1 level tbsp) tomato
  paste
25 g (1 oz) walnut pieces,
  chopped

salt and milled pepper
454-g (16-oz) carton
  natural yogurt
2 eggs
1.25 ml (¼ level tsp)
  ground cumin
75 g (3 oz) Cheddar
  cheese, grated
oil
fried croûtons to
  accompany

Cook the lasagne in boiling salted water for 15 minutes. Finely slice the vegetables. Reserve a few courgettes, fry the vegetables in oil until tomatoes begin to break down. Stir in the basil, tomato paste and season well.

Grease a 2-litre (3½-pint) deep-sided roasting tin and layer lasagne, vegetables, nuts, ending with lasagne. Season the yogurt, beat in the eggs, stir in the cumin and cheese, and pour over the lasagne. Garnish with the reserved courgettes. Brush with oil. Bake in the oven at 200°C (400°F) mark 6 for about 40 minutes until set. Place croûtons between the courgettes to serve.

Not suitable for freezing.

CURRIED EGGS & BROCCOLI
Serves 4

700 g (1½ lb) broccoli
6 eggs, hard-boiled
30 ml (2 level tbsp) mango
  chutney
50 g (2 oz) butter or
  margarine
225 g (8 oz) onion, skinned
  and finely chopped
20 ml (4 level tsp) mild
  curry paste

5 ml (1 level tsp) ground
  turmeric (optional)
30 ml (2 level tbsp) plain
  flour
300 ml (½ pint) milk
two 142-ml (5-fl oz)
  cartons soured cream
salt and milled pepper
fried flaked almonds

Trim about 175 g (6 oz) off the broccoli stalks. Wash the stalks and heads, drain. Cook the stalks in boiling salted water until tender; drain and chop finely. Halve the eggs, sieve the yolks and mix with the chopped broccoli, chopped chutney and seasoning. Spoon back into the egg halves, mounding up well.

Melt the fat in a medium-sized saucepan and sauté the onion with the curry paste and turmeric until soft, about 5 minutes. Stir in the flour and milk, bring to the boil and simmer for 2 minutes, stirring. Add the soured cream, season.

Cook the broccoli in simmering water for about 8 minutes until just tender, drain well. Arrange the eggs and broccoli in a serving dish and spoon the sauce over the eggs. Garnish with flaked almonds.

Not suitable for freezing.

MIXED GLAZED VEGETABLES
Serves 4

175 g (6 oz) carrot, pared
175 g (6 oz) leek, washed
  and trimmed
175 g (6 oz) celery,
  washed and trimmed
175 g (6 oz) cauliflower
  florets
225 g (8 oz) broccoli,
  washed and trimmed or
  225 g (8 oz) frozen
  green beans

small piece of fresh root
  ginger, peeled
425-g (15-oz) can whole
  baby sweetcorn, drained
sesame oil
peanut oil
50 g (2 oz) demerara
  sugar
45 ml (3 tbsp) lemon juice
salt and milled pepper

Thinly slice the carrots, leeks and celery diagonally. Split the cauliflower into small florets and cut the broccoli into small heads. Finely shred 5 ml (1 tsp) root ginger. Halve the baby sweetcorn if large.

Heat 15 ml (1 tbsp) each of the oils in a wok or large frying pan until smoky hot. Add all the vegetables and half the ginger. Cook over a high heat, stirring, for 2–3 minutes, adding more oil if necessary. Stir in the sugar and lemon juice. Reduce the heat, cook, stirring, for a further 3–4 minutes, until all the vegetables are just tender, yet still crunchy. Season. Garnish with the remaining ginger and serve immediately.

Not suitable for freezing.

POTATO & COURGETTE SAVOURY
Serves 6

900 g (2 lb) potatoes,
  peeled
salt and milled pepper
75 g (3 oz) butter or
  margarine
450 g (1 lb) courgettes,
  thinly sliced
3 eggs

225 g (8 oz) onion, thinly
  sliced
400 ml (¾ pint) milk
15 ml (1 level tbsp) Dijon
  mustard
5 ml (1 level tsp) dried
  basil

Cut the potatoes into 3-mm (⅛-inch) thick slices. Blanch in boiling, salted water for 5–7 minutes, or until just tender. Drain well.

In a large frying pan, melt half the fat. Add the courgettes and onions and sauté for 10–12 minutes, or until softened. Remove from the pan using slotted spoons. In the same pan, melt the remaining fat. Sauté the potato slices until pale golden. Beat together the eggs, milk, mustard, basil and seasoning. Layer the vegetables and milk mixture in a shallow 1.7-litre (3-pint) ovenproof dish, ending with a neat potato layer. Place the dish in a roasting tin, half filled with water. Bake at 170°C (325°F) mark 3 for about 1¼ hours until set and well browned.

Not suitable for freezing.

Curried eggs with broccoli is an ideal dish for lunch or late supper

Tiny corn on the cob are a novel touch in Mixed glazed vegetables

CRISP LETTUCE WITH ORANGE
Serves 8

1 large crisp lettuce
½ bunch watercress
2 large oranges
2 slices white bread, crusts
  removed
salad oil

salt and milled pepper
60 ml (4 tbsp) white wine
  vinegar
2.5 ml (½ level tsp) caster
  sugar

Remove any coarse or torn outside leaves from the lettuce. Cut it into eight wedges, trimming away the hard core. Wash and pat dry with kitchen paper. Wash and trim the watercress and dry.

With a small serrated knife, working over a bowl to catch the juices, cut away all the skin and pith from the oranges. Thinly slice the flesh. Arrange the lettuce, watercress and orange in a serving bowl, cover and refrigerate.

Cut the bread into 1-cm (½-inch) squares. Fry in a little oil until crisp and golden. Drain well and sprinkle with salt.

Whisk 60 ml (4 tbsp) oil, the vinegar, sugar and seasoning into the orange juice. Pour over the salad and add the croûtons just before serving.

Not suitable for freezing.

CRISP POTATO BALLS
Serves 6

900 g (2 lb) old potatoes
2 eggs
100 g (4 oz) fresh white
  breadcrumbs

salt and milled pepper
90 ml (6 tbsp) chopped
  parsley
100 g (4 oz) margarine

Boil the peeled potatoes, drain and return to the heat to dry. Mash well.

Separate the eggs. Beat the yolks into the hot mash, seasoning well. Cool. Shape into 20 balls.

Mix the breadcrumbs and parsley. Coat the potato balls in whisked egg white and then in the crumbs. Do this twice.

Melt the margarine in a roasting tin. Place the potato balls in the tin, and shake gently to coat with fat.

Bake for 1½ hours at 170°C (325°F) mark 3.

Suitable for freezing before cooking.

Illustrated in colour on page 29

CORN & CHEESE ROULADE
Serves 4

50 g (2 oz) butter
1 clove garlic, skinned and
  crushed
30 ml (2 level tbsp) flour
200 ml (7 fl oz) milk
4 large eggs, separated
salt and milled pepper
Parmesan cheese

198-g (7-oz) can
  sweetcorn kernels
1 cap canned pimiento,
  roughly chopped
15 ml (1 tbsp) chopped
  parsley
125 g (4 oz) Lancashire
  cheese, grated

Butter a 330 × 225 × 15-mm (13 × 9 × ⅝-inch) Swiss roll tin and line with buttered greaseproof paper.

Melt 25 g (1 oz) butter, stir in the garlic and flour. Cook for 1 minute before stirring in the milk. Bring to boil, simmer for 2 minutes. Cool slightly before breaking in the egg yolks, season. Fold in the stiffly whisked egg whites. Turn evenly into the prepared tin. Cook at 180°C (350°F) mark 4 for about 15 minutes until pale golden and light and spongy to the touch.

Turn out on to greaseproof sprinkled with Parmesan, cool for 1 minute, peel off the greaseproof paper. Scatter on the corn, pimiento and parsley with all but 30 ml (2 tbsp) cheese; roll up from the longest edge. Slip on to a greased ovenproof dish discarding the paper, sprinkle with the remaining Lancashire cheese and a little Parmesan. Dot with remaining butter.

Return to the oven for about 7 minutes. Serve immediately.

Not suitable for freezing.

SPINACH & LENTIL ROULADE
Serves 4

175 g (6 oz) red lentils
50 g (2 oz) onion, skinned
  and finely chopped
30 ml (2 level tbsp) tomato
  ketchup
15 ml (1 level tbsp)
  creamed horseradish
125 g (4 oz) butter

salt and milled pepper
450 g (1 lb) spinach,
  trimmed
50 g (2 oz) plain flour
300 ml (½ pint) milk
2 eggs, separated
dried breadcrumbs

Grease and line a 285 × 185 × 15-mm (11⅜ × 7⅜ × ¾-inch) Swiss roll tin. Cook the lentils with the onion in plenty of boiling salted water. Drain well, return to heat to drive off excess moisture. Purée together with the tomato ketchup, horseradish and 50 g (2 oz) butter. Season.

Wash the spinach. Cook, covered, with salt and no extra liquid for 3–4 minutes. Drain well, finely chop. Preheat the oven to 200°C (400°F) mark 6.

Make a white sauce with the remaining butter, flour and milk. Stir in the spinach and egg yolks. Season. Stiffly whisk the egg whites. Gently fold into the spinach mixture. Spoon into prepared tin. Level surface. Bake for 20 minutes, or until well risen and golden.

Turn out on to greaseproof paper sprinkled with dried breadcrumbs. Peel off the outer greaseproof. Spread the lentil purée over surface. Roll up one long edge. Return to the oven for 5 minutes.

Not suitable for freezing.

STIR FRIED BEETROOT & CABBAGE
— Serves 4 —

350 g (12 oz) red cabbage
225 g (8 oz) cooked
  beetroot, skinned
125 g (4 oz) onion, skinned
  and thinly sliced

peanut oil
30 ml (2 level tbsp)
  creamed horseradish
salt and milled pepper

Finely shred the red cabbage, discarding the core. Coarsely grate or finely chop the beetroot.

Heat 30 ml (2 tbsp) oil in a wok or large frying pan until smoky hot. Stir in the cabbage and onion. Cook over a high heat for 3–4 minutes, stirring all the time, until the cabbage has softened a little but still retains its crispness. Add a little more oil if necessary. Stir in the beetroot, horseradish and seasoning. Cook, stirring, for a further few minutes to heat through. Serve immediately.

Not suitable for freezing.

CREAMED PARSNIPS
— Serves 8 —

1.8 kg (4 lb) parsnips,
  peeled and roughly
  chopped
salt and milled pepper
100 g (4 oz) butter
15 ml (1 level tbsp) flour

2.5 ml (½ level tsp)
  English mustard powder
200 ml (7 fl oz) milk
142-ml (5-fl oz) carton
  soured cream

Boil the parsnips in salted water for about 30 minutes, or until tender. Drain well. Mash with potato masher or push through a large wire sieve.

Melt 50 g (2 oz) butter in a large saucepan. Stir in the flour and mustard powder. Cook stirring for 1–2 minutes before adding the milk and soured cream. Bring to the boil, stirring, simmer for 2 minutes. It will look slightly curdled.

Slowly pour the sauce on to the sieved parsnips, beating well. Return the mixture to the saucepan. Stir over a low heat while beating in the remaining butter. Season.

To freeze Cool, pack and freeze without the extra butter. To use, thaw overnight at cool room temperature. Reheat in saucepan stirring all the time, while beating in the butter.

BRUSSELS SPROUT & BACON SOUFFLÉ
— Serves 4 as a light lunch with salad —

700 g (1½ lb) Brussels
  sprouts, trimmed weight
125 g (4 oz) smoked bacon
  rashers, rinded
50 g (2 oz) butter

pinch grated nutmeg
50 g (2 oz) plain flour
300 ml (½ pint) milk
3 eggs, separated
salt and milled pepper

Butter a 1.3-litre (2¼-pint) soufflé dish. Preheat the oven to 200°C (400°F) mark 6. Cook the brussels sprouts in boiling salted water until tender. Drain well.

Snip the bacon into a small saucepan and sauté in its own fat for about 2 minutes. Stir in the butter, flour and nutmeg, continue stirring while adding milk. Bring to the boil, beat once the sauce starts thickening. Simmer 2 minutes.

Chop half the sprouts. In a blender or food processor purée the rest of the sprouts with the egg yolks and a little sauce. Fold into the sauce with the chopped sprouts. Season well.

Stiffly whisk the egg whites. Gently fold into the brussels sprout mixture. Turn into the soufflé dish. Bake in the oven for 30–35 minutes. Serve immediately.

Not suitable for freezing.

SWEETCORN POTATO PUFFS
— Serves 4 —

350 g (12 oz) medium-
  sized potatoes
salt and milled pepper
75 g (3 oz) butter
65 g (2½ oz) plain flour,
  sieved
2 eggs, beaten

198-g (7-oz) can of
  sweetcorn kernels,
  drained
oil for deep frying
chopped parsley
finely grated rind of
  1 lemon

Wash the potatoes well. Cook in boiling, salted water for 20 minutes, or until tender. Drain well. Peel, then mash or sieve until smooth. Beat in 25 g (1 oz) butter.

In a small saucepan, slowly melt the remaining butter in 150 ml (¼ pint) water. Bring to the boil. Remove from the heat and immediately add all the flour. Beat until just smooth. Cool slightly. Gradually beat the eggs into the cooled mixture. Stir in the sweetcorn, mashed potato and seasoning. Heat the oil to 190°C (375°F) and carefully add a few large spoonfuls of mixture to the hot oil. Fry for at least 5–6 minutes, or until deep golden and crisp. Drain well on absorbent paper. Keep warm, uncovered, in a low oven until all the mixture is cooked. Serve hot, garnished with chopped parsley and grated lemon rind.

Not suitable for freezing.

SWEET POTATOES WITH ORANGE
Serves 4

900 g (2 lb) medium-sized
  sweet potatoes
salt
2 large oranges
15 ml (1 level tbsp) black
  peppercorns

30 ml (2 tbsp) oil
25 g (1 oz) butter
2.5 ml ($\frac{1}{2}$ level tsp) ground
  cinnamon
30 ml (2 level tbsp)
  chopped parsley

Scrub the potatoes. Cook in boiling, salted water until almost tender, about 20 minutes. Meanwhile peel and seg-ment one orange, squeeze the juice from the other. Crush the peppercorns using a pestle and mortar or the end of a rolling pin in a strong bowl. Drain the potatoes and peel off their skins while still hot. Cut the potatoes into large chunks.

At once heat the oil in a large-sized frying pan. Add the butter and when it is frothing, tip in all the potatoes. Fry over a moderate heat, turning occasionally, until the potatoes are golden brown and beginning to flake. Off the heat stir in the cinnamon, peppercorns, parsley, orange juice and seg-ments and salt. Mix well and spoon into a serving dish. Keep warm, uncovered, in a low oven.

Not suitable for freezing.

The tang of citrus and cinnamon enliven Sweet potatoes with orange

New Potatoes & Spiced Hollandaise
Serves 4

900 g (2 lb) new potatoes
salt and milled pepper
ground turmeric
2 egg yolks
175 g (6 oz) unsalted
    butter, softened

1 clove garlic, skinned
30 ml (2 level tbsp)
    natural yogurt
toasted flaked almonds to
    garnish

Wash the potatoes; do not peel. Cook in boiling, salted water with 30 ml (2 level tbsp) ground turmeric added. Boil for 10–15 minutes, according to size; drain well.

Meanwhile place the egg yolks and crushed garlic in a small bowl, fitted over a pan of simmering water. Stir all the time until the eggs thicken *slightly*. Gradually add the butter, whisking or stirring well between each addition until all the butter is incorporated. Do not overheat or the sauce may curdle.

Lastly stir the yogurt into the sauce with 1.25 ml ($\frac{1}{4}$ level tsp) turmeric and seasoning. Stir over a gentle heat for a further minute. Spoon the warm sauce over the potatoes for serving and sprinkle with toasted almonds.

Not suitable for freezing.

Baked Onions Hollandaise
Serves 4

75 g (3 oz) dried mung
    beans
4 large onions, each about
    225 g (8 oz), skinned
2 medium cloves garlic,
    skinned and crushed
butter

75 g (3 oz) Lancashire
    cheese, grated
salt and milled pepper
2.5 ml ($\frac{1}{2}$ level tsp) dry
    mustard
hollandaise sauce for
    serving

Soak the beans overnight, then boil for about 30 minutes. Drain and place in a large mixing bowl; mash lightly to roughly break down. Boil the onions in salted water for about 30 minutes, until tender (the point of a knife should go in easily). Drain. When cool enough to handle, cut each onion in half from root to stem end and scoop out some of the centre.

Chop up the onion centres and mix with the beans. Add the garlic, cheese, 25 g (1 oz) softened butter, seasoning and dry mustard; season well. Arrange onions cut side uppermost in a baking dish. Fill the centres with bean stuffing, dot with butter. Cover and bake at 200°C (400°F) mark 6 for about 40 minutes. Serve with hollandaise sauce.

Not suitable for freezing.

Spiced Wheat Peppers
Serves 4

175 g (6 oz) bulgar wheat
2 green peppers, about
    150 g (5 oz) each
2 yellow peppers, about
    150 g (5 oz) each
25 g (1 oz) butter or
    margarine
175 g (6 oz) tomatoes,
    skinned and roughly
    chopped

225 g (8 oz) onion, skinned
    and chopped
15 ml (1 level tbsp) chilli
    seasoning
salt and milled pepper
two 141-g (5-oz) cartons
    natural yogurt
75 g (3 oz) cucumber,
    finely chopped

Cover the bulgar wheat with cold water. Soak for 1 hour. Cut a thin slice from the stalk end of each pepper. Reserve. Remove the seeds. Cut each pepper in half horizontally and place alternate colours side by side in a shallow buttered ovenproof dish.

Melt the butter in a saucepan, sauté the onion with the chilli seasoning for 3–4 minutes. Add the tomatoes and well-drained bulgar wheat. Cook, stirring for 1–2 minutes; season. Fill peppers with the chilli mixture. Replace tops. Cover tightly with buttered foil. Bake at 190°C (375°F) mark 5 for about 40 minutes. Gently heat together the natural yogurt, and cucumber, whisking. Season. Serve separately.

Not suitable for freezing.

Mung bean and cheese-stuffed Baked onions Hollandaise

CHICK PEA & VEGETABLE CASSEROLE
— Serves 4 —

350 g (12 oz) dried chick
  peas, soaked overnight
100 g (4 oz) brown rice
salt and pepper
600 ml (1 pint) stock
100 g (4 oz) carrot, pared
  and thinly sliced
1 bayleaf

100 g (4 oz) onion, skinned
  and thinly sliced
1 clove garlic
397-g (14-oz) can
  tomatoes
450 g (1 lb) broccoli, cut
  into small florets
lemon juice

Ahead of time cook the soaked chick peas in boiling water until tender—about 1½ hours. Drain. Wash rice, cook in boiling salted water for about 35 minutes until tender. Drain.

Place the stock, carrot, onion, bayleaf, crushed garlic and seasoning in a large saucepan. Bring to the boil; simmer for 5–10 minutes. Add the tomatoes and broccoli to the stock. Simmer covered for about 10 minutes, or until the broccoli is just tender. Gently stir in the cooked rice and chick peas and heat through gently. Adjust seasoning and add a dash of lemon juice.

Not suitable for freezing.

CAULIFLOWER GOUGÈRE
— Serves 4 —

700 g (1½ lb) cauliflower
25 g (1 oz) butter
25 g (1 oz) flour
300 ml (½ pint) milk
30 ml (2 tbsp) chopped
  parsley
salt and milled pepper

50 g (2 oz) lean ham,
  chopped (optional)
2 egg quantity choux
  pastry made with plain
  wholemeal flour (see
  page 16)

Cut the cauliflower into small florets. Cook in boiling salted water for about 10 minutes, or until just tender. Drain well.

Melt the butter, stir in the flour. Cook, stirring for 1–2 minutes before adding the milk. Bring to the boil, add the parsley and ham. Simmer for 2–3 minutes. Season. Fold the cauliflower into the sauce. Spoon into four scallop shells or shallow ovenproof dishes.

Spoon or pipe the choux mixture round the edge of the scallop shells or ovenproof dishes. Bake at 200°C (400°F) mark 6 for 35–40 minutes, or until well risen and brown. Serve immediately.

Not suitable for freezing.

JELLIED TOMATO RING
— Serves 4 —

30 ml (2 level tbsp) sweet
  mint jelly
25 g (1 oz) powdered
  gelatine
salt and milled pepper
125 g (4 oz) tomatoes

330-ml (11½-fl oz) can
  V8 Tomato and
  Vegetable juice
watercress or mint to
  garnish

Place the mint jelly in a saucepan with 150 ml (¼ pint) water. Sprinkle over 10 ml (2 level tsp) gelatine. Leave to soak for 5–10 minutes. In a saucepan make the V8 juice up to 600 ml (1 pint) with water. Season. Sprinkle over the remaining gelatine. Leave to soak for 5–10 minutes. Slowly dissolve both gelatine mixtures over a low heat. Pour half of the mint mixture into a 1-litre (1¾-pint) ring mould. Refrigerate to set.

Peel, quarter and de-seed the tomatoes. Arrange over the set mint jelly. Carefully pour round the remaining mint jelly. Refrigerate to set.

Finally pour the tomato mixture into the mould. Refrigerate for a further 4–5 hours to set. Quickly dip mould into hot water to loosen the jelly ring, then turn it out on to a flat plate. Garnish.

Not suitable for freezing.

STIR FRIED GREENS
— Serves 4 —

450 g (1 lb) spring greens
50 g (2 oz) streaky bacon,
  rinded
peanut oil
125 g (4 oz) frozen peas

50 g (2 oz) alfalfa sprouts
salt and milled pepper
141-g (5-oz) carton
  natural yogurt

Trim and wash the spring greens. Shred very finely. Thinly slice the bacon. Heat 30 ml (2 tbsp) oil in a wok or large frying pan until smoky hot. Stir in the greens, bacon and peas. Cook over a high heat for 3–4 minutes until the peas are tender. Stir all the time, adding a little more oil if necessary. Stir in the alfalfa sprouts. Cook for 1 minute to heat through. Season well and serve immediately drizzled with the yogurt.

Not suitable for freezing.

LEEK & CORN SLAW
Serves 8

700 g (1½ lb) leeks
350 g (12 oz) white
  cabbage
335-g (11.8-oz) can
  sweetcorn kernels,
  drained

30 ml (2 level tbsp) tomato
  ketchup
30 ml (2 level tbsp)
  mayonnaise
salt and milled pepper

Trim then thinly slice the leeks and wash them well. Thinly slice the cabbage. Blanch together in boiling salted water for 2 minutes. Drain immediately. Rinse with cold water. Drain well.

Toss together the cabbage, leeks and sweetcorn. Add the tomato ketchup and mayonnaise and seasoning, stirring well to mix.

Spoon into a serving bowl, cover and refrigerate for several hours before serving. Take out of the refrigerator 30 minutes before eating, stir well.

Not suitable for freezing.

CHILLI POTATO SALAD
Serves 6

900 g (2 lb) even-sized
  waxy potatoes, scrubbed
medium green pepper,
  seeded and roughly
  chopped
medium red pepper, seeded
  and roughly chopped
200 ml (7 fl oz) vegetable
  oil

75 ml (5 tbsp) garlic
  vinegar
15 ml (1 level tbsp) chilli
  seasoning
salt and pepper
100 g (4 oz) onion, skinned
  and chopped
30 ml (2 level tbsp) sesame
  seeds

Boil the potatoes in their skins until tender, about 20 minutes. Drain well. Meanwhile blanch the peppers in boiling water for 1–2 minutes and drain well.

In a large mixing bowl whisk together the oil, vinegar and seasonings. Peel the potatoes and cut them into large chunks. While still hot stir into the dressing with the onion and pepper. Cool, cover and chill for about 2 hours.

Toast the sesame seeds and stir through the salad to serve. Adjust seasoning.

Not suitable for freezing.

ENDIVE, ORANGE & WALNUT
Serves 8

During the winter frilly endive is a crisp alternative to lettuce and doesn't wilt so quickly. Don't use the outside 'fronds', choose the whitish paler green ones.

2 endive
6 oranges
25 g (1 oz) walnut pieces
15 ml (1 level tbsp) caster
  sugar

142-ml (5-fl oz) carton
  soured cream
salt and milled pepper
60 ml (4 tbsp) corn oil
30 ml (2 tbsp) lemon juice

Pull the endive apart, wash, dry thoroughly. Tear into pieces. Place in a salad bowl. Grate the rind of one orange into a bowl and squeeze in the juice. Remove the skin and all pith from the remaining oranges and segment free of membrane. Add to the endive. Chop and add the walnuts. Cover and keep refrigerated.

Just before serving combine the sugar, soured cream, reserved orange juice and rind. Beat in the oil gradually and stir in the lemon juice. Spoon the completed dressing over the endive and then toss the mixture lightly with two forks.

Not suitable for freezing.

CELERIAC WITH TOMATO DRESSING
Serves 8

The mild flavour of celeriac and its interesting texture go particularly well with this mustardy mayonnaise.

2 large celeriac, about
  1.8 kg (4 lb)
lemon juice
300 ml (½ pint)
  mayonnaise
2.5 ml (½ level tsp) French
  mustard
2.5 ml (½ level tsp)
  paprika pepper

salt and milled pepper
90 ml (6 level tbsp) tomato
  chutney
1.25 ml (¼ tsp)
  Worcestershire sauce
few drops of tabasco sauce
30 ml (2 tbsp) water
snipped parsley for garnish

Peel the celeriac. Cut into narrow slices and then into matchsticks. Blanch at once in boiling salted water with a good squeeze of lemon juice for 2–3 minutes. Drain and cool. In a large bowl, combine the other ingredients. Season carefully as celeriac absorbs a lot of flavour. Add the blanched celeriac and toss the salad well. Cover and refrigerate for several hours. Turn the mixture again in the dressing before serving. Garnish with snipped parsley.

Not suitable for freezing.

CHAPTER SIX

PUDDINGS AND DESSERTS

ICED STRAWBERRY SOUFFLÉ
Serves 8

450 g (1 lb) strawberries
60 ml (4 tbsp) Amaretto
  di Saronno (almond
  liqueur
30 ml (2 tbsp) lemon juice
15 ml (1 level tbsp) icing
  sugar

50 g (2 oz) small ratafias
400 ml (15 fl oz) double
  cream
15 ml (1 level tbsp)
  powdered gelatine
4 eggs, separated
175 g (6 oz) caster sugar

Marinate the strawberries in the Amaretto, lemon juice and icing sugar for 30 minutes. Liquidise half the strawberries; sieve to remove the seeds.

Tie a double band of greaseproof paper around the edge of a 1.1-litre (2-pint) straight-sided soufflé dish to form a 5-cm (2-inch) collar. Place a straight-sided 450-g (1-lb) jam jar in the centre of the dish.

Finely crush half the ratafias. Lightly whip 300 ml ($\frac{1}{2}$ pint) cream until it just holds its shape.

In a small saucepan sprinkle the gelatine over 45 ml (3 tbsp) water. Leave to soak for 2–3 minutes until it becomes sponge-like in texture. Dissolve *slowly* over a gentle heat. Meanwhile whisk together the egg yolks and caster sugar with an electric whisk until very light and creamy. Fold in the strawberry purée, whipped cream and dissolved gelatine.

Whisk the egg whites until stiff but not dry, and fold into the strawberry mixture. Pour the mixture into the prepared dish, keeping the jam jar in the centre. Chill for 1–2 hours to set. Freeze until firm—at least 3 hours.

To serve: 2 hours before eating, fill the jam jar with hot water. Gently twist and remove it from the centre of the dish. Fill the centre with the remaining strawberries. Ease off the paper collar and coat the sides with crushed ratafias. Decorate with remaining cream whipped and the whole ratafias. Transfer to the refrigerator for about 2 hours before serving.

To freeze As above.

CRÈME CARAMEL
Serves 4

This recipe involves boiling sugar—take care not to spill any on your hands as it can burn badly. Clean the caramel pan by boiling fresh water in it.

125 g (4 oz) granulated
  sugar (plus 15 ml
  (1 level tbsp))
2 whole eggs
2 egg yolks

568 ml (1 pint) milk
1.25 ml ($\frac{1}{4}$ tsp) vanilla
  essence
pouring cream to
  accompany

Warm a 15-cm (6-inch) ovenproof soufflé dish. Heat 125 g (4 oz) sugar gently in a saucepan with 150 ml ($\frac{1}{4}$ pint) water, without boiling, until all the sugar has dissolved. Bring to boil and boil rapidly until the syrup reduces, thickens and starts to brown, shaking the pan to ensure even browning. When the caramel is golden brown, remove from the heat and leave a few seconds to darken. Immediately take the warmed dish out of the oven and stand on a heatproof surface. Pour the caramel into the warmed dish and leave to cool. Warm the milk in a saucepan. Place the eggs and yolks in a mixing bowl and add the remaining sugar. Whisk, then pour on the warm milk. Add the vanilla essence, then strain the custard on to the cool caramel. Cover the dish with greased greaseproof paper to prevent skin forming. Stand the crème caramel in a roasting tin containing enough water to come halfway up the sides of the dish. Bake at 170°C (325°F) mark 3 for about an hour, until firm but not solid. Remove from the tin and allow to cool. Cover tightly with cling film and refrigerate for several hours, preferably overnight. The longer chilling time makes it easier to remove the Crème Caramel from the dish.

Half an hour before serving loosen from the dish with fingertips. Turn out carefully on to a serving dish, and leave for a few minutes until the caramel trickles out. Stand the cooking dish in hot water to soften remaining caramel and pour over crème caramel.

Not suitable for freezing.

Crème caramel is a simple yet sophisticated dessert

CHERRY SYLLABUB
Serves 6

225 g (8 oz) dark ripe
  cherries, stoned
brandy
2 egg whites
75 g (3 oz) caster sugar
30 ml (2 tbsp) lemon juice

150 ml ($\frac{1}{4}$ pint) sweet
  white wine
284-ml (10-fl oz) carton
  double cream
whole cherries for
  decoration

Finely chop the cherries and place in the base of six tall glasses. Spoon 5 ml (1 tsp) brandy over the cherries in each glass.

Place the egg whites in a medium-sized bowl and whisk until stiff. Gently fold in the sugar, lemon juice and white wine. In a separate bowl lightly whip the cream and fold into the wine mixture.

Spoon the syllabub mixture into the glasses and refrigerate for several hours, preferably overnight. Decorate each with a whole cherry.

Not suitable for freezing.

PEAR & ALMOND FRITTERS
Serves 4

150 ml ($\frac{1}{4}$ pint) orange
  juice
15 ml (1 tbsp) corn oil
1 egg, separated
125 g (4 oz) plain flour
salt
4 large ripe dessert pears

60 ml (4 level tbsp) ground
  almonds
15 ml (1 level tbsp) caster
  sugar
25 g (1 oz) butter
caster sugar for dusting

Put the orange juice, oil and egg yolk into an electric blender; add the flour and a pinch of salt. Switch on for 1 minute, then leave for $\frac{1}{2}$ hour in the fridge. Whisk the egg white in a bowl until stiff, but not dry, and lightly fold into the batter.

Peel and core the pears. Halve lengthwise. Mix together the almonds, sugar and butter. Press a little of this mixture into the centre of each pear half. Dip each pear half in the batter. Deep fry at 180°C (350°F) for 3–4 minutes until golden brown. Dust lightly with caster sugar. Serve quickly.

Not suitable for freezing.

PINEAPPLE CHEESECAKE
Serves 10

175 g (6 oz) plain
  chocolate wholewheat
  biscuits
75 g (3 oz) butter
227-g (8-oz) carton
  cottage cheese
100 g (4 oz) full fat cream
  cheese
thinly pared rind and juice
  of 1 large lemon

142-ml (5-fl oz) carton
  soured cream
3 eggs, separated
50 g (2 oz) caster sugar
15 ml (3 level tsp)
  powdered gelatine
two 432-g (14$\frac{1}{4}$-oz) cans
  sliced pineapple
60 ml (4 level tbsp) sieved
  apricot jam

Roughly crush the biscuits and add the melted butter. Base line a 23-cm (9-inch) spring release cake tin and press the crumb mixture on top, refrigerate to set.

Place the cottage and cream cheeses, lemon rind and 45 ml (3 tbsp) juice, the soured cream in a blender goblet and switch on until smooth. Whisk the egg yolks and sugar until thick. Soak the gelatine in 45 ml (3 tbsp) water and dissolve in the usual way, whisk into the egg yolks with the cheese mixture. Drain and roughly chop three-quarters of the pineapple, reserving juices. Fold into the setting cheese mixture with stiffly whisked egg whites; pour into crust, refrigerate.

Carefully remove the sides of the cake tin then, using a fish slice, lift and slide the cheesecake off the base on to a serving plate. Decorate with reserved pineapple. Boil down the juices with jam to a thick glaze, cool, spoon over the pineapple.

To freeze Open freeze, overwrap when firm. To use, un-wrap, thaw at cool room temperature for 7–8 hours.

FRESH CHERRY & LEMON CHEESECAKE
Serves 10

75 g (3 oz) butter
125 g (5 oz) caster sugar
150 g (5 oz) plain flour
1 egg yolk
225 g ($\frac{1}{2}$ lb) full fat cream
  cheese
226-g ($\frac{1}{2}$-lb) carton
  cottage cheese, sieved
2 eggs, separated
finely grated rind and juice
  of 2 lemons

142-ml (5-fl oz) carton
  soured cream
284-ml (10-fl oz) carton
  double cream
15 ml (1 level tbsp)
  powdered gelatine
225 g ($\frac{1}{2}$ lb) fresh red
  cherries, halved and
  stoned or 213-g (7$\frac{1}{2}$-oz)
  can cherries, drained
angelica to decorate

Cream the butter with 75 g (3 oz) sugar. Mix to a firm dough with the flour and 1 egg yolk. Roll out half to fit the base of a 20.5-cm (8-inch) spring release cake tin, and the other half to fit a 20.5-cm (8-inch) flan ring placed on a baking sheet. Bake both at 180°C (350°F) mark 4 for about 15 minutes. Cut the flan ring round into ten wedges and cool on a wire rack. Leave the other round in the tin.

With an electric mixer beat together the cheeses, 2 egg yolks, the lemon rind, 75 ml (5 tbsp) lemon juice, remaining sugar and soured cream. Stir in half the double cream. Soak the gelatine in 45 ml (3 tbsp) water and dissolve, stir into the cheese mixture. Refrigerate until beginning to set.

Fold the cherries and whisked egg whites into the cheese mixture, turn into tin, refrigerate. Cover when firm. Remove from mould. Place pastry wedges on top. Decorate with angelica.

Not suitable for freezing.

STRAWBERRY CUSTARD FLAN
Serves 6–8

125 g (4 oz) butter	40 g (1½ oz) cornflour
175 g (6 oz) plain flour	400 ml (¾ pint) milk
125 g (4 oz) caster sugar	few drops vanilla essence
3 eggs	350 g (12 oz) strawberries

Rub the butter into the flour and 25 g (1 oz) sugar. Bind to a soft dough with one egg. Knead lightly on a floured surface. Wrap and chill for 30 minutes. Line a 23-cm (9-inch) flan dish with the pastry. Bake blind at 200°C (400°F) mark 6 for 20 minutes, or until pale golden and cooked through. Cool in the dish.

Mix the cornflour to a smooth paste with a little milk and the egg yolks. Bring the remaining milk to the boil with the sugar and vanilla essence. Off the heat pour in the cornflour mixture, return to the boil, stirring, and boil for 2 minutes until thickened. Cover with damp greaseproof paper and cool. (Whisk if necessary to remove lumps.)

Thinly slice the strawberries into the base of the flan, reserving a few for garnish. Whisk the egg whites until stiff and fold into the cold custard mixture. Evenly smooth the custard mixture over the strawberries. Chill to set. Eat within 2 hours of completion garnished with reserved strawberry slices. Serve with cream.

To freeze Pack and freeze the cooked pastry case. To use, thaw the pastry case for about 1 hour, complete as above.

APRICOT MERINGUE TRANCHE
Serves 8

4 egg whites	700 g (1½ lb) fresh ripe
225 g (8 oz) caster sugar	apricots, halved and
75 g (3 oz) ground	stoned
almonds	30 ml (2 tbsp) almond
25 g (1 oz) flaked almonds	liqueur
50 g (2 oz) granulated	142-ml (5-fl oz) carton
sugar	double cream

Draw two oblongs 30.5 × 10 cm (12 × 4 inch) on sheets of non-stick paper. Place upside down on baking sheets.

Whisk the egg whites until stiff but not dry. Whisk in 60 ml (4 level tbsp) caster sugar until the meringue stands in stiff peaks. Fold in remaining caster sugar and ground almonds. Spoon the meringue into a piping bag fitted with a 1-cm (½-inch) plain nozzle. Pipe in lines across the width of the 'frame' marked on the non-stick paper. Sprinkle flaked almonds over one layer. Dry in the oven at 100°C (200°F) mark low for about 2 hours. Peel paper off. Cool on a wire rack.

Dissolve the granulated sugar in 200 ml (7 fl oz) water. Poach the apricots in syrup until just tender. Reserve ten apricot halves. Drain the remainder, purée in an electric blender with the almond liqueur until just smooth. Leave until cold.

Whip the cream until it holds its shape and spread over the plain meringue layer. Spoon on the apricot purée and top with the second meringue layer. Refrigerate for 2 hours. Decorate with reserved apricot halves.

Not suitable for freezing.

FROZEN BRANDY CREAMS
Serves 4

4 egg yolks	142-ml (5-fl oz) carton
150 g (5 oz) caster sugar	double cream
90 ml (6 tbsp) brandy	coffee dragées to decorate

Place the egg yolks, caster sugar and brandy in a medium-sized, deep mixing bowl. Using a wooden spoon, stir well until thoroughly mixed. Place the bowl over a pan of simmering water; the bowl base should not touch the water. Stir the mixture all the time until it thickens slightly and will just coat the back of the spoon. Do not overheat or the eggs may curdle. Take off the heat, cool.

Lightly whip the cream and stir half into the cold brandy mixture. Pour into four small soufflé or ramekin dishes. Freeze until firm, at least 5 hours. Decorate each with a whirl of the remaining whipped cream, top with a coffee dragée. Serve at once.

To freeze Treat as ice cream.

APPLE BREAD & BUTTER PUDDING
Serves 4–6

250 g (9 oz) medium-	125 g (4 oz) soft light
sliced white bread	brown sugar
40 g (1½ oz) butter	2.5 ml (½ level tsp) ground
350 g (12 oz) cooking	nutmeg
apples	3 eggs
125 g (4 oz) stoned dates	568 ml (1 pint) milk

Cut the crusts off the bread and spread with half the butter. Peel, quarter, core and thinly slice the apples. Roughly chop the dates.

Well grease a 1.4-litre (2½-pint) shallow ovenproof dish with the remaining butter. Layer the bread, butter side uppermost, with the apples, dates, sugar and spice, reserving a little sugar. Top with a layer of bread. Stand the dish on a baking sheet.

Whisk the eggs and mix with the warmed milk. Strain over the bread mixture, pressing the bread well down into the milk. Sprinkle with reserved sugar. Bake in the oven at 180°C (350°F) mark 4 for about 1 hour, or until the pudding is just set and the top golden brown. Serve warm.

Not suitable for freezing.

GOLDEN SYRUP ROLL

Serves 6

275 g (10 oz) self-raising
  flour
150 g (5 oz) shredded suet
75 g (3 oz) demerara
  sugar
1 egg
50 g (2 oz) fresh white
  breadcrumbs

about 150 ml (5 fl oz) milk
225 g (8 oz) golden syrup
50 g (2 oz) walnuts,
  chopped
golden syrup and clotted
  cream or custard sauce
  for serving

Mix the flour, suet and 50 g (2 oz) sugar well together. Bind to a firm dough with the egg and milk beaten together. Roll out the dough to an oblong about 38 × 30.5 cm (15 × 12 inches). Scatter over the crumbs to within 2.5 cm (1 inch) of the edges. Spoon the golden syrup and half the nuts on top. Fold the edges of dough up over the filling, dampen them and roll up from the narrow edge, sealing well. Place seam-side down in a well-greased 28 × 10-cm (11 × 4-inch) loaf dish. Mix the remaining nuts and sugar together and scatter over the dough.

Stand the loaf dish on a baking sheet and bake at 180°C (350°F) mark 4 for about 1¼ hours covering lightly when well browned. Spoon over golden syrup before serving with clotted cream or custard.

Not suitable for freezing.

A traditional nursery pudding—Golden syrup roll still brings delight to grown-ups

JELLIED MELON SALAD
Serves 8

225 g (8 oz) black grapes
1 large honeydew melon—
  about 2.2 kg (5 lb)
50 g (2 oz) caster sugar
45 ml (3 tbsp) lemon juice

60 ml (4 tbsp) white wine
  (optional)
15 ml (1 level tbsp)
  powdered gelatine

Halve and pip the grapes. Halve the melon lengthways, remove the seeds. With a melon baller scoop out all the flesh into a bowl. Scrape out any remaining flesh from the melon shells, roughly chop and add to the bowl with the grapes. Trim a thin slice from the rounded side of each shell so that they will sit flat on a plate. Stir the sugar, lemon juice and 150 ml ($\frac{1}{4}$ pint) water into the melon balls. Cover and refrigerate for about 1 hour.

Strain the juices from the melon into a measuring jug and make up to 300 ml ($\frac{1}{2}$ pint) with water and wine if used. Sprinkle over the gelatine. Leave to soak for 5 minutes. Stand the measuring jug in a pan of simmering water until the gelatine dissolves. Cool slightly before stirring into the fruit. Spoon the mixture back into the prepared shells. Chill for at least 2 hours to set before serving. This can be made the day before.

Not suitable for freezing.

BROWN BREAD ICE CREAM
Serves 8

225 g (8 oz) fresh brown
  breadcrumbs
50 g (2 oz) icing sugar
1-litre (1$\frac{3}{4}$-pint) carton
  vanilla ice cream
few drops vanilla essence
1 egg, beaten

25 ml (5 tsp) lemon juice
75 g (3 oz) dried apricots,
  soaked overnight
225 g (8 oz) rhubarb,
  washed and cut up
50 g (2 oz) caster sugar

Place the breadcrumbs and icing sugar on a large baking sheet. Toast under the grill until golden, turning occasionally; cool.

In a large mixing bowl, beat together the ice cream, vanilla essence, egg and 15 ml (1 tbsp) lemon juice. Fold in the cooled breadcrumbs. Spoon back into carton. Refreeze till firm, about 2 hours.

Meanwhile prepare the sauce. Place the apricots with 150 ml ($\frac{1}{4}$ pint) soaking liquor, the rhubarb, caster sugar and remaining lemon juice in a saucepan. Simmer, covered for 10–15 minutes. Cool slightly before liquidising contents of pan. Adjust sweetening to taste; chill to serve.

Transfer the ice cream to refrigerator about 1$\frac{1}{4}$ hours before serving with the sauce.

To freeze Pack and freeze the ice cream and sauce separately. To use, thaw the sauce at cool room temperature overnight.

SWISS APPLE FLAN
Serves 6

50 g (2 oz) block
  margarine
25 g (1 oz) lard
175 g (6 oz) self-raising
  flour
4 good-sized dessert apples,
  about 600 g (1$\frac{1}{4}$ lb)
  total weight

5 ml (1 level tsp) ground
  cinnamon
150 ml (10 tbsp) milk
25 g (1 oz) caster sugar
1 whole egg
1 egg yolk
30 ml (2 level tbsp)
  demerara sugar

Rub the margarine and lard into the flour and cinnamon. Bind to a dough with a little cold water. Chill for 10 minutes. Line a 25-cm (9$\frac{1}{2}$-inch) loose-based fluted flan tin with the pastry. Chill again for about 15 minutes.

Peel and core the apples. Cut each in half vertically. With cut side down slice thinly crosswise, keeping the apple halves in shape. Arrange the sliced apple halves on the flan base, fanning out the slices a little. Bake in the oven uncovered at 200°C (400°F) mark 6 for 20 minutes.

Whisk together the milk, caster sugar, egg and yolk. Pour evenly over the apples. Lower oven to 190°C (375°F) mark 5, return flan for about 25 minutes until custard is just set. Sprinkle the surface with the demerara sugar. Grill until lightly caramelised. Serve warm.

Not suitable for freezing.

OLD ENGLISH TRIFLE
Serves 6

568 ml (1 pint) milk
$\frac{1}{2}$ vanilla pod
2 whole eggs, 2 egg yolks
30 ml (2 level tbsp) caster
  sugar
box of 8 trifle sponges
100 g (4 oz) macaroons,
  lightly crushed

100 g (4 oz) apricot jam
100 ml (4 fl oz) medium
  sherry
284-ml (10-fl oz) carton
  whipping cream
50 g (2 oz) glacé cherries
40 g (1$\frac{1}{2}$ oz) flaked
  almonds, toasted

Scald the milk with the vanilla pod. Cover the pan and leave to infuse for 20 minutes. Beat together the eggs, egg yolks and sugar; add the milk, strained. Cook over a gentle heat, without boiling, stirring all the time until the custard thickens slightly. Pour out into a bowl, lightly sprinkle the surface with sugar, cool.

Spread the trifle sponges with jam, cut up and place in a 2-litre (3$\frac{1}{2}$-pint) shallow serving dish with the macaroons. Spoon over the sherry, then pour over the cold custard. Top with lightly-whipped cream. Cover tightly with cling film and refrigerate for at least 12 hours.

Wash, dry and thinly slice the cherries; mix with the almonds. Use to decorate the trifle just before serving.

Not suitable for freezing.

LEMON PASSIONFRUIT GÂTEAU
Serves 8–10

50 g (2 oz) butter	icing sugar
4 eggs	142-ml (5-fl oz) carton
125 g (4 oz) caster sugar	whipping cream
finely grated rind and juice	142-ml (5-fl oz) carton
of 1 lemon	soured cream
125 g (4 oz) plain flour	3 passionfruit
225 g (8 oz) strawberries	

Grease and base line a 20.5-cm (8-inch) deep round cake tin. Dust out with sugar and flour. Cream the butter until *very* soft and of thick pouring consistency.

Whisk together the eggs, caster sugar and lemon rind with an electric whisk until very pale and thick. The mixture should be thick enough to leave a trail on itself. Sift over the flour and drizzle the butter over the surface. Fold in thoroughly, taking care not to knock out the air. Transfer the mixture to the prepared tin. Bake at 190°C (375°F) mark 5 for 35–40 minutes, test with a fine skewer. Turn out on to a wire rack to cool.

Meanwhile thinly slice the strawberries, marinate in lemon juice and 25 g (1 oz) icing sugar. When cold split the cake in half. Drizzle both halves with the marinade from the strawberries.

Lightly whip the cream, fold in the soured cream and passionfruit seeds. Sandwich the cakes together with the strawberries and cream mixture. Dust with icing sugar to serve.

To freeze Pack and freeze gâteau without the fruit or cream. To use, thaw wrapped and complete as above.

LEMON MERINGUE PIE
Serves 6

150 g (5 oz) butter or	45 ml (3 level tbsp)
block margarine	cornflour
175 g (6 oz) plain flour	100 g (4 oz) caster sugar
2 medium lemons	for the meringue
75–100 g (3–4 oz) caster	pouring cream to
sugar for the filling	accompany
2 eggs, separated	

Rub 125 g (4 oz) fat into the flour until the mixture resembles fine breadcrumbs. Bind to a soft dough with 45 ml (3 tbsp) water and knead lightly until just smooth. Roll out the pastry and use to line a 20.5-cm (8-inch) fluted flan ring placed on a baking sheet (a loose-bottomed tin is not deep enough). Bake blind until golden brown and dried out.

Finely grate the lemon rind straight into a small saucepan. Add 90 ml (6 tbsp) strained lemon juice made up to 300 ml (½ pint) with water and 75 g (3 oz) caster sugar. Warm gently until the sugar dissolves. Mix the cornflour to a smooth paste with 45 ml (3 tbsp) water; off the heat stir quickly into the lemon mixture and blend until smooth. Return to the heat and bring slowly to the boil, stirring all the time, simmer for 3–4 minutes. Cool a little then beat in the egg yolks with the remaining butter. Taste for sweetness and add up to an extra 25 g (1 oz) sugar, but remember that the meringue's sweetness will balance the tartness of the lemon filling. Pour into the cooked pastry case.

Stiffly whisk the egg whites, then whisk in 10 ml (2 level tsp) of the sugar, keeping the egg whites stiff. Fold in the remaining sugar, then spoon the meringue over the lemon mixture, spread it out to the edges and make peaks on the surface. Bake at 150°C (300°F) mark 2 for about 30 minutes.

Not suitable for freezing.

RICE & PEACH BRÛLÉES
Serves 4

400 ml (¾ pint) milk	425-g (15-oz) can sliced
75 g (3 oz) flaked rice	cling peaches, drained
5 ml (1 level tsp)	90 ml (6 level tbsp)
granulated sugar	demerara sugar

Put the milk in a saucepan, add the rice and granulated sugar. Bring to the boil then simmer for about 10 minutes, or until the rice is cooked, stirring occasionally. Cut the peaches into small pieces and add to the rice mixture. Spoon into four 150-ml (¼-pint) greased ramekin dishes, filling almost to the brim.

Sprinkle on the demerara sugar, to completely cover the surface. Place under a hot grill until the sugar caramelises. Serve hot.

Not suitable for freezing.

RASPBERRY HIGHLAND CREAM
Serves 4

50 g (2 oz) medium	60 ml (4 tbsp) thin honey
oatmeal	45 ml (3 tbsp) whisky
284-ml (10-fl oz) carton	350 g (12 oz) fresh
double cream	raspberries

Place the oatmeal in a grill pan (without the rack) and toast until golden brown, turning occasionally with a spoon. Cool. Whip the cream until it just holds its shape then stir in the honey, whisky and cool oatmeal.

Pick over the raspberries, reserving a few for decoration. Layer up the raspberries and cream mixture in four tall glasses, cover with cling film and refrigerate. Allow to come to room temperature for 30 minutes before serving. Decorate with reserved raspberries.

Not suitable for freezing.

Lemon meringue pie is an import from America which has become a British favourite

SPICED TAPIOCA
Serves 4

568 ml (1 pint) milk
50 g (2 oz) tapioca
50 g (2 oz) granulated
    sugar

50 g (2 oz) seedless raisins
1.25 ml ($\frac{1}{4}$ level tsp)
    ground mixed spice
golden syrup

Place the milk in a medium-sized heavy-based saucepan, add the tapioca, sugar, raisins and spice. Stir well. Bring the milk up to the boil. Reduce heat and simmer for about 25 minutes, or until the tapioca is cooked and most of the milk absorbed. Stir occasionally to prevent the tapioca from sticking to the base of the pan. Serve at once with a little warmed golden syrup poured over.

Not suitable for freezing.

OLD-FASHIONED RICE PUDDING
Serves 4

75 g (3 oz) pudding (short
    grain) rice
900 ml (1$\frac{1}{2}$ pints) milk
bayleaf

75 g (3 oz) caster sugar
nutmeg
knob of butter

Place the first four ingredients in a greased 1.4-litre (2$\frac{1}{2}$-pint) shallow ovenproof pie dish. Add a little grated nutmeg and stir gently to mix. Dot the surface of the pudding with the butter. Stand the dish on a baking sheet and bake at 170°C (325°F) mark 3 for about 2$\frac{1}{2}$ hours, or until most of the milk has been absorbed and a brown skin has formed on top of the pudding. Serve warm with freshly stewed fruit.

Not suitable for freezing.

GOOSEBERRY BISCUIT FLAN
Serves 4

75 g (3 oz) ginger biscuits
75 g (3 oz) digestive
    biscuits
75 g (3 oz) butter or block
    margarine
1 large orange
350 g (12 oz) fresh or
    frozen gooseberries,
    thawed

10 ml (2 level tsp)
    powdered gelatine
75–100 g (3–4 oz)
    granulated sugar
170-g (6-oz) can creamed
    rice
142-ml (5-fl oz) carton
    double cream

Crush all the biscuits finely in an electric blender or coffee grinder or put the biscuits in a plastic bag and crush them with a rolling pin. Add to the melted butter then use to line a 18-cm (7-inch) fluted ceramic flan dish. Chill to set.

Pare off a few strips of orange rind with a potato peeler and cut into needle shreds. Blanch, drain and reserve. Soak the gelatine in 30 ml (2 tbsp) water.

Stew the gooseberries until thick and pulpy with the remaining orange rind, finely grated, and 45 ml (3 tbsp) orange juice. Push the gooseberries through a nylon sieve, or purée in an electric blender then sieve to remove the pips. While still warm stir in the sugar to taste with the soaked gelatine; mix until both have dissolved; chill to setting point.

Spoon the creamed rice into the crumb crust. Level off and spread the gooseberry mixture over. Refrigerate to set. Decorate with whipped cream and orange shreds.

Not suitable for freezing.

LEMON CRUMB PUDDING
Serves 4

50 g (2 oz) plain flour
5 ml (1 level tsp) baking
    powder
125 g (4 oz) soft light
    brown sugar
225 g (8 oz) fresh
    breadcrumbs, half
    brown, half white
50 g (2 oz) cut mixed peel
finely grated rind and juice
    of 2 large lemons

125 g (4 oz) shredded suet
2 eggs, beaten
about 150 ml ($\frac{1}{4}$ pint) milk
lemon walnut sauce:
    2 lemons; 75 g (3 oz)
    soft light brown sugar;
    300 ml ($\frac{1}{2}$ pint) water;
    20 ml (4 level tsp)
    arrowroot; 25 g (1 oz)
    butter; 50 g (2 oz)
    walnut pieces

Grease a 1.1-litre (2-pint) pudding basin.

Sift the flour and baking powder into a large mixing bowl and stir in the sugar, breadcrumbs, suet and peel. Add the lemon rinds into the bowl and stir in the strained juice with the eggs and milk. Beat to a soft dropping consistency, adding more milk if necessary. Spoon into the prepared basin and cover with greased greaseproof paper and foil.

Steam for about 2$\frac{1}{2}$–3 hours, turn out on to a warmed plate and serve with lemon walnut sauce.

To make the lemon walnut sauce, finely grate the rind from the lemons into a medium-sized saucepan, then squeeze out the juice—about 90 ml (6 tbsp). Add to the pan with sugar and water, heat gently until the sugar dissolves. Blend the arrowroot to a smooth paste with a little water. Add to the pan and bring to the boil, stirring constantly, bubble mixture gently for 1 minute. Take the pan off the heat, stir in the butter and roughly chopped walnut pieces.

Not suitable for freezing.

The golden crust on Old-fashioned rice pudding is the secret to its success

SPOTTED DICK
— Serves 4 —

175 g (6 oz) fresh white
  bread
75 g (3 oz) self-raising
  flour
pinch of salt

75 g (3 oz) shredded suet
50 g (2 oz) caster sugar
175 g (6 oz) currants
1 lemon
75–90 ml (5–6 tbsp) milk

Take a preserving pan or a deep saucepan at least 20.5-cm (8-inch) wide and two-thirds fill with water. Cover and bring to the boil. Use a baking sheet or foil to make a lid for the preserving pan. Place the breadcrumbs, flour, salt, suet, sugar and currants in a mixing bowl. Grate the rind of half a lemon finely and add to the dry ingredients. Stir well until thoroughly mixed. Pour the milk over the dry ingredients, cutting it through with a palette knife, until well mixed. Using one hand only, bring the ingredients together to form a soft, slightly sticky dough. Turn out on to a floured surface. Dust it lightly with flour to prevent your hands sticking to it, then knead gently until just smooth. Over-handling the dough can toughen the pudding. Shape the dough into a neat roll about 15 cm (6 inch) in length.

Make a 5-cm (2-inch) pleat across a fine textured, colour-fast tea towel or pudding cloth. Encase the roll in the cloth, pleating the open edges tightly together. Tie the ends securely with string to form a cracker shape. Make a string handle across the top. Lower the suet roll into the pan of boiling water, curling it if necessary to fit the pan. Cover the pan, lower the heat to a gentle boil and cook for 2 hours. Top up with boiling water at intervals to ensure that the roll is covered with water. Lift the spotted dick out of the water using the string handle provided. Place on a wire rack standing over a plate and allow excess moisture to drain off. Snip the string and gently roll the pudding out of the cloth or foil on to a serving plate. Mop up any moisture on the plate with kitchen paper. Slice the spotted dick for serving.

Not suitable for freezing.

     Spotted dick is a beloved recipe whose popularity survives from Victorian times

SPICED FRUIT GALETTE
Serves 8

370-g (13-oz) packet puff
 pastry
beaten egg to glaze
450 g (1 lb) tart eating
 apples
5 ml (1 level tsp) mixed
 spice

284-ml (10-fl oz) carton
 double cream
350 g (12 oz) strawberries
30 ml (2 level tbsp) icing
 sugar
icing sugar to decorate

On a lightly-floured surface thinly roll out the pastry and cut out three 20.5-cm (8-inch) rounds and eight 5-cm (2-inch) fluted rounds, folding and re-rolling the pastry as necessary. Place the larger rounds on damp baking sheets; glaze. Prick two large rounds with a fork; lightly mark the third into eight wedges and place one of the smaller fluted rounds on each wedge. Chill for 20–25 minutes. Bake the pastries at 220°C (425°F) mark 7 for about 20 minutes, or until well risen and golden. Cool on a wire rack.

Peel and thinly slice the apples. Cook gently with the mixed spice and 30 ml (2 tbsp) water until very soft. Mash or liquidise to a pulp. Cool. Lightly whip the cream until it just holds its shape. Roughly chop the strawberries, reserving a few for decoration. Fold the strawberries, apple purée and icing sugar into the cream.

Layer the pastry rounds with the fruit cream and top with the wedged round. Decorate with icing sugar and strawberries.

Not suitable for freezing.

BASIC VANILLA ICE CREAM
Serves 8–10

568 ml (1 pint) milk
1 vanilla pod
175 g (6 oz) granulated
 sugar

6 egg yolks
568 ml (1 pint) whipping
 cream

Bring the milk and vanilla pod almost to the boil. Take off the heat and leave for at least 15 minutes. Beat egg yolks and sugar together, stir in the milk and strain back into the pan. Cook the custard gently over a low heat, stirring until it coats the back of a wooden spoon. Do *not* boil.

Pour into a chilled, shallow container and leave to cool. Freeze until slushy—about 2 hours. Turn into a large, chilled basin and mash with a flat whisk or fork. Fold in the lightly-whipped cream. Freeze again until slushy then mash again. Return to freezer to become firm.

To freeze Overwrap according to type of container.
N.B. Do not whip cream if using a mechanical churn or cream maker. Agitate chilled custard and unwhipped cream together.

VARIATIONS
Chocolate Break up 175 g (6 oz) plain chocolate, heat with the milk, whisking until smooth.
Coffee Stir 60 ml (4 tbsp) coffee essence into made custard.
Praline Stir 60 ml (4 tbsp) crushed praline into the completed, nearly frozen ice cream, before it is left to harden.

LEMON SORBET
Serves 8

A cool, refreshing sorbet is just right to follow a rich main course. Serve in chilled glasses accompanied by small thin crisp biscuits.

4 large thin-skinned lemons
2 egg whites

225 g (8 oz) granulated
 sugar

Pare the rinds, yellow part only, off the lemons using a potato peeler. Squeeze the juice, there should be 180 ml (12 tbsp). Dissolve the sugar in 600 ml (1 pint) water then boil for 2 minutes. Take off the heat. Add the lemon rinds, cover the pan and leave to infuse for 10 minutes.

When cool, add the lemon juice to the syrup then strain into a shallow container. Freeze until mushy, about 2 hours.

Whisk the egg whites until stiff and fold through the mixture. Return to the freezer until firm. Transfer to the refrigerator for 45 minutes–1 hour before serving.

To freeze Treat as ice cream.

TIPSY FRUIT COMPOTE
Serves 8

275 g (10 oz) dried
 prunes, soaked overnight
275 g (10 oz) dried
 apricots, soaked
 overnight
50 g (2 oz) sultanas,
 soaked overnight
75 g (3 oz) dried apple
 rings, soaked overnight
cinnamon stick

60 ml (4 tbsp) whisky
600 ml (1 pint)
 unsweetened orange
 juice
15 ml (1 level tbsp) soft
 brown sugar
thinly pared rind of
 1 lemon, cut in
 needleshreds
3 bananas

Drain the soaked fruit and place in an ovenproof dish with the cinnamon stick. Combine the whisky, orange juice, sugar and lemon rind. Pour over the fruit.

Cover with foil and bake at 180°C (350°F) mark 4 for about 30 minutes. Leave to cool, add sliced bananas before serving.

Not suitable for freezing.

BAKED ALASKA

Serves 6

For the sponge
lard for greasing
10 ml (2 level tsp) caster
* sugar*
5 ml (1 level tsp) plain
* flour*
2 eggs, size 2
50 g (2 oz) caster sugar
1 orange
50 g (2 oz) plain flour

For the filling
225 g (½ lb) fresh or frozen
* raspberries*
30 ml (2 tbsp) orange-
* flavoured liqueur*
483-ml block Golden
* Vanilla Ice Cream*
4 egg whites, at room
* temperature*
175 g (6 oz) caster sugar

Place a little lard in a small saucepan and heat gently until it just melts. Brush all over the inside of a 20.5-cm (8-inch) non-stick flat tin. When the lard has set sprinkle over 10 ml (2 level tsp) caster sugar and tilt the tin to give an even coating of sugar. Add 5 ml (1 level tsp) plain flour and coat similarly, knocking out any excess. Place the two whole eggs and 50 g (2 oz) caster sugar in a deep bowl and whisk vigorously with an electric hand mixer until *very* thick. Finely grate the orange rind over the mixture then sift flour over the surface. Fold gently through with a metal spoon, turn into a tin and level the surface by tilting.

Place on a baking sheet in the oven at 180°C (350°F) mark 4 for 20–25 minutes until golden brown. Turn out carefully on to a wire rack to cool.

Place fresh or frozen raspberries on a shallow dish and sprinkle over the liqueur. Cover and leave to marinate for 2 hours, turning occasionally. Place the cold sponge flan on a large ovenproof serving dish and spoon the raspberries together with all their juices into the centre of the flan.

Place the egg whites in a dry bowl and beat until the mixture stands in stiff peaks. Add 20 ml (4 level tsp) of remaining sugar and whisk, then spoon over the remaining sugar and fold through gently until no traces of it remain.

Fit a good sized piping bag with a large star vegetable nozzle and spoon the meringue mixture into it. Place the block of ice cream on top of the raspberries. Pipe the meringue on top, starting from the sponge base then around and over the ice cream until it is completely covered. Immediately place the completed Alaska in the preheated oven at 230°C (450°F) mark 8 for 3–4 minutes. At this stage the meringue should be nicely tinged with brown. Watch the meringue carefully as it burns easily. Do not overcook or the ice cream will become too soft. Serve at once.

Not suitable for freezing.

This Baked Alaska improves on the original by incorporating fresh raspberries

ALMOND EVE'S PUDDING
Serves 4

700 g (1½ lb) cooking
  apples
5 ml (1 level tsp) ground
  cinnamon
175 g (6 oz) demerara
  sugar
125 g (4 oz) butter,
  softened
125 g (4 oz) self-raising
  flour

2 eggs, beaten
25 g (1 oz) ground
  almonds
2.5 ml (½ tsp) almond
  essence
30 ml (2 tbsp) milk
25 g (1 oz) flaked almonds
icing sugar
cinnamon cream

Peel, quarter, core and thickly slice the cooking apples into a 1.4-litre (2½-pint) ovenproof dish. Combine the cinnamon with 50 g (2 oz) of the sugar, scatter over the apple. Cover tightly with cling film while preparing the topping.

Beat the butter, add the remaining demerara sugar and cream together. Then gradually beat in the eggs. Lastly, by hand, *lightly* beat in the flour, ground almonds, essence and milk and spread over the apples. Place the flaked almonds on top in six squares to form a checkerboard effect. Bake at 180°C (350°F) mark 4 for 50–60 minutes.

Dredge icing sugar between the flaked nut squares.

Serve with cinnamon cream.

Not suitable for freezing.

Nuts transform Almond Eve's pudding into a sublime, but still light, dessert

CINNAMON-APPLE PANCAKES
Serves 4–6 (about 12 pancakes)

about 300 ml (½ pint) milk
or milk and water mixed
1 egg
125 g (4 oz) plain flour
1.25 ml (¼ level tsp) salt
125 g (4 oz) fresh white
breadcrumbs
75 g (3 oz) butter

grated zest and juice of
1 lemon
700 g (1½ lb) cooking
apples
50 g (2 oz) caster sugar
5 ml (1 level tsp) ground
cinnamon

Put milk and egg into an electric blender, add the flour and salt and switch on for 1 minute.

Heat an 18-cm (7-inch) frying pan and brush the surface with lard or corn oil. Raise the handle side slightly and pour in a tablespoonful of batter so that a very thin skin flows over the pan. Brown over a moderate heat then, turning over, cook the second side. Repeat, greasing the pan.

Fry the crumbs in 50 g (2 oz) butter until golden, stirring. Place the rest of the butter, grated zest and juice of lemon, peeled and sliced apple, sugar and cinnamon in a saucepan. Cover and cook to a purée. Add the crumbs, divide between the pancakes and roll up. Place in an ovenproof dish. Cap with foil and heat at 170°C (325°F) mark 3 for about 20 minutes. Dust with sifted icing sugar.

To freeze Freeze the rolled-up pancakes before heating in the oven. To use, thaw, then reheat.

VANILLA & BUTTERSCOTCH MOULD
Serves 6

75 g (3 oz) cornflour
1.1 litres (2 pints) milk
150 g (5 oz) granulated
sugar
vanilla essence

65 g (2½ oz) soft light
brown sugar
25 g (1 oz) butter
12 walnut halves

Blend the cornflour to a paste with 150 ml (¼ pint) milk. Place in saucepan with the remaining milk. Bring to the boil and boil gently, stirring, for 4–5 minutes until thickened.

Pour 400 ml (¾ pint) of the mixture into a measuring jug. Beat in 50 g (2 oz) granulated sugar and a few drops of vanilla essence. Pour into a 1.3-litre (2¼-pint) wetted brioche type mould. Beat the brown sugar and butter into the remaining mixture. Spoon evenly on to the vanilla custard. Cool, cover and refrigerate to set for about 4 hours.

Place the remaining sugar and walnuts in a small saucepan. Slowly melt the sugar over a low heat without stirring. When caramelised, stir to coat the walnuts. Lift each coated walnut out separately on to an oiled baking sheet. Cool. To turn out, ease the mixture gently away from the sides of the mould. Invert on to a serving dish. Before serving decorate with the caramelised walnuts.

Not suitable for freezing.

BISCUIT TORTONI
Serves 6–8

3 eggs
275 g (10 oz) caster sugar
400 ml (¾ pint) milk
300 ml (10 fl oz) whipping
cream
75 ml (3 fl oz) medium dry
sherry
125 g (4 oz) ground
almonds

15 ml (1 level tbsp) rice
flour
few drops almond essence
icing sugar

Chilled Plum Sauce
450 g (1 lb) ripe red plums
50 g (2 oz) granulated sugar
7.5 ml (1½ level tsp) cornflour

Place 2 egg yolks and 1 whole egg into a mixing bowl. Add 50 g (2 oz) of the sugar and whisk lightly. Warm the milk, then pour it on to the eggs, whisk again before returning the mixture to the saucepan. Stir over a low heat until the custard thickens *slightly*. Do *not* boil or it will curdle. Pour the custard back into the bowl to cool.

In a large bowl lightly whip the ice cream until it just holds its shape. Using a metal spoon gently stir in the sherry. Pour in the cold custard and stir gently. Pour the custard mixture into a shallow freezer-proof container. Cover and place in the freezer until mushy, about 3 hours.

Meanwhile, preheat the oven to 180°C (350°F) mark 4. Place the 2 egg whites into a bowl. Lightly whisk to just break up the whites. Add the remaining sugar, ground almonds, rice flour and almond essence. With a wooden spoon beat all the ingredients together until smooth. Line 2 baking sheets with non-stick paper. Spoon the mixture into a piping bag fitted with a plain 1 cm (½ inch) nozzle. Pipe 2.5 cm (1 inch) buttons of mixture, well apart, on to the paper. Bake for about 17 minutes. When cooked the ratafias should be golden brown, firm to the touch and have a cracked appearance. Leave to cool for about 1 minute before transferring to a wire rack to cool.

Place the ratafias in a strong polythene bag and crush to fine crumbs with a rolling pin. Place three-quarters of them into a bowl and add the mushy ice cream. Whisk to break up ice crystals. Pour into a non-stick loaf tin with top measurement $25 \times 125 \times 65$ mm ($8\frac{7}{8} \times 4\frac{7}{8} \times 2\frac{3}{8}$ inch), cover with foil. Refreeze until firm.

Dip the base and side of the loaf tin into hot water for a few seconds to loosen the tortoni. Invert on to a serving plate, shaking the mould. Using a palette knife, press the remaining ratafia crumbs over the top and sides of the tortoni. Place the tortoni in the freezer until ready to serve.

Cut out three 15-cm (6-inch) long 2.5-cm (1-inch) wide strips of greaseproof paper. Place these diagonally at regular intervals along the top of the tortoni. Dust generously with icing sugar. Remove the paper strips and serve immediately, cut into slices, with chilled plum sauce.

Halve and stone the plums. Dissolve the sugar in 400 ml (¾ pint) water. Add the plums, simmer for 2–3 minutes. Cool, then purée until smooth. Mix the cornflour to a smooth paste with a little water. Stir into the plum mixture and boil for 1–2 minutes, stirring. Pour into a bowl and cool. Chill well.

Suitable for freezing.

Biscuit tortoni is a luscious import from the kitchens of Italy

CHAPTER SEVEN

CAKES AND BISCUITS

HAZELNUT TRUFFLES

50 g (2 oz) hazelnuts	icing sugar
125 g (4 oz) plain chocolate	30 ml (2 tbsp) brandy
50 g (2 oz) butter	50 g (2 oz) chocolate vermicelli
125 g (4 oz) trifle sponges	

Toast the hazelnuts under the grill until well browned, almost charred. Immediately wrap the nuts in a tea towel or kitchen paper and rub them vigorously to loosen and remove the skins. Leave the nuts to cool, then chop finely. Break up the chocolate and place it in a medium-sized bowl with the cut-up butter. Place the bowl over a pan of simmering water and heat gently until the chocolate and butter melt. Stir gently occasionally, but do not overheat or the chocolate will crust on to the edges of the bowl. Remove from the heat and leave to cool for about 10 minutes.

Meanwhile rub the trifle sponges through a coarse sieve or turn them into fine crumbs using a food processor. Stir the crumbs and 50 g (2 oz) sieved icing sugar into the chocolate mixture. Beat well until beginning to thicken then stir in the hazelnuts and brandy. Cover the mixture and refrigerate until it is firm enough to handle. Lightly dust your fingers with icing sugar and then roll the mixture into small balls—there should be about 24 balls. After shaping, roll the balls in chocolate vermicelli until evenly coated. Spread out the truffles on to baking sheets lined with non-stick paper. Refrigerate until quite firm then cover tightly with cling film.

Take the truffles out of the refrigerator about 30 minutes before serving and leave at cool room temperature.

To freeze Truffles freeze well. Thaw in the refrigerator for about 12 hours.

WALNUT LAYER CAKE

4 eggs, separated	For the butter frosting
125 g (4 oz) caster sugar	40 g (1½ oz) butter
75 g (3 oz) walnuts, finely chopped	75 g (3 oz) icing sugar
25 g (1 oz) fresh brown breadcrumbs	For the American frosting
25 g (1 oz) plain flour	225 g (8 oz) caster or granulated sugar
10 ml (2 tsp) coffee essence	60 ml (4 tbsp) water
walnut halves for decoration	pinch of cream of tartar
	1 size 2 egg white

Grease and base line two 18-cm (7-inch) sandwich tins. Dredge with extra caster sugar and flour. Whisk together the egg yolks and caster sugar until very pale. Fold in the walnuts, breadcrumbs and flour.

Whisk the egg whites until stiff, but not dry. Stir one large spoonful into egg yolk mixture to loosen. Fold in the remainder. Divide between the tins. Level the surface. Bake at 180°C (350°F) mark 4 for about 30 minutes. Turn out on to a wire rack to cool.

Prepare the butter icing. Cream the butter until of a spreading consistency. Gradually beat in the icing sugar, milk and coffee essence. Use to sandwich the two cakes together.

To make the American frosting: place the sugar, water and cream of tartar in a pan, heat to dissolve the sugar without boiling. Meanwhile, whisk the egg white until stiff. Bring the syrup to the boil, without stirring, and boil to reach 118°C (240°F). Remove from the heat, then pour on to the egg white in a thin stream, whisking all the time. Continue to whisk until the mixture is very thick, shows signs of going dull round the edge and is almost cold. Don't under whisk or the icing will run off the cake. Use at once. Coat the cake completely, working quickly to ensure a glossy frosting. Decorate at once with the walnut halves.

Not suitable for freezing.

This Walnut layer cake has antecedents in the Slavic traditions of Poland and the Austro-Hungarian Empire

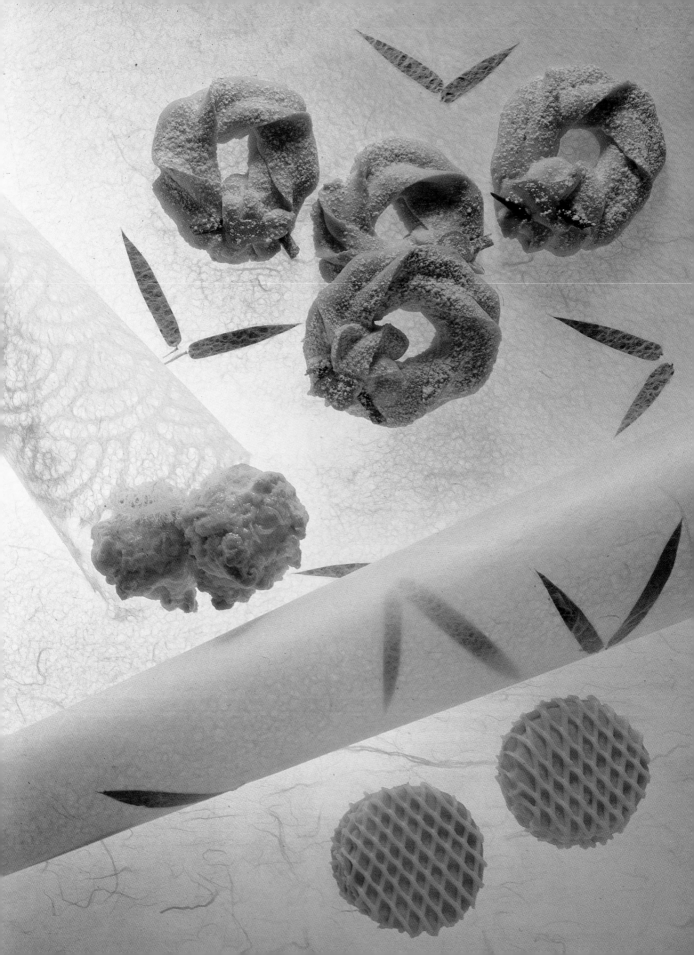

CHERRY GARLANDS
Makes 24

225 g (8 oz) soft tub
  margarine
50 g (2 oz) icing sugar
200 g (7 oz) plain flour
150 g (5 oz) cornflour
vanilla essence

50 g (2 oz) glacé cherries,
  very finely chopped
whole cherries and angelica
  to decorate
icing sugar

Cream the margarine and icing sugar together until pale and fluffy. Beat in the flours, a few drops of vanilla essence and the chopped cherries. (If using an electric handmixer, beat for 3–4 minutes. By hand, beat until the mixture is very soft.) Spoon half the mixture into a piping bag fitted with a 1-cm (½-inch) star nozzle. Pipe 5-cm (2-inch) rings on to lightly greased baking sheets allowing room for spreading. Decorate with a quartered cherry and pieces of angelica. Repeat with the remaining mixture.

Bake at 190°C (375°F) mark 5 for about 20 minutes until pale golden. Allow to firm up slightly on the baking sheets for about 30 seconds before sliding on to a wire rack to cool. Dredge with icing sugar. Store in an airtight container for 2–3 weeks.

To freeze Pack carefully and freeze. To use, thaw at cool room temperature for 30 minutes.

WALNUT COFFEE CAKE

melted lard
4 large eggs
175 g (6 oz) soft dark
  brown sugar
finely grated rind of
  1 lemon
125 g (4 oz) plain flour

150 g (5 oz) walnut pieces,
  finely chopped
275 g (10 oz) icing sugar
150 g (5 oz) softened
  butter
45 ml (3 tbsp) coffee
  essence

Using melted lard, grease and base line a 25.5-cm (10-in), 2.3-litre (4-pint) deep sandwich tin. When the grease has set dust out with caster sugar and flour.

Whisk the eggs, sugar and finely grated lemon rind; preferably with an electric hand mixer, until very thick and mousse like in appearance. Fold in the sifted flour with 50 g (2 oz) of the chopped walnuts. Pour the mixture into the prepared tin and bake at 180°C (350°F) mark 4 for about 40 minutes, or until firm to the touch. Turn out and cool on a wire rack.

Gradually beat the sifted icing sugar into the butter until smooth, work in the coffee essence. Split the gâteau in half and sandwich together again with half the butter cream, dust the top with icing sugar. Spread the remaining butter cream around the sides and press chopped nuts on to the edge. Decorate with a lattice of chopped nuts.

To freeze Open freeze, overwrap when firm. To use, unwrap and thaw at cool room temperature for about 6 hours.

APRICOT CRUNCH
Makes 16 wedges

75 g (3 oz) dried apricots
100 g (4 oz) butter
100 g (4 oz) demerara
  sugar
75 ml (5 level tbsp) golden
  syrup
140 g (5 oz) rolled oats

190 g (7 oz) crunchy
  toasted breakfast cereal
  such as Jordan's
2.5 ml (½ level tsp) mixed
  spice
10 ml (2 tsp) lemon juice

Simmer the apricots gently in 200 ml (7 fl oz) water until softened, about 10 minutes. Liquidise the contents of the pan. Cool.

Slowly melt the butter, sugar and syrup. Stir in the cereal and oats and continue stirring until thoroughly combined. Add the puréed apricots, spice and lemon juice. Mix well. With non-stick paper base line two 18-cm (7-inch) round sandwich tins. Divide the mixture between the tins and spread evenly over the base. Press down well.

Bake at 180°C (350°F) mark 4 for about 35 minutes. Cut each round into 8 wedges. Cool in the tin until firm. Ease out and store in an airtight container for 2–3 weeks.

To freeze Pack and freeze. To use, thaw at cool room temperature for 1 hour.

APPLE PARKIN
Serves 6–8

450 g (1 lb) eating apples
25 g (1 oz) butter or
  margarine
225 g (8 oz) plain flour
10 ml (2 level tsp) baking
  powder
15 ml (3 level tsp) ground
  ginger
50 g (2 oz) lard

125 g (4 oz) medium
  oatmeal
75 g (3 oz) caster sugar
125 g (4 oz) golden syrup
125 g (4 oz) black treacle
1 egg, beaten
30 ml (2 tbsp) milk
cheese wedges

Grease and base line a 1.7-litre (3-pint) loaf tin.

Peel, quarter, core and chop the apples. Melt the butter in a small saucepan, add the apples, cover and cook gently until soft. Beat the apples to a purée, cool.

Sift the flour, baking powder and ginger into a large mixing bowl. Rub in the lard; stir in the oatmeal and sugar. Warm the syrup and treacle together until evenly mixed then stir into the dry ingredients with the apple purée, egg and milk. Stir until evenly blended. Turn into the prepared tin and bake at 180°C (350°F) mark 4 for about 1½ hours; covering lightly with foil after 45 minutes. Turn out of the tin, cool. Wrap and store for 2 days before eating. Serve sliced accompanied by wedges of cheese.

To freeze Freeze after maturing. To use, thaw at cool room temperature for about 8 hours.

Cherry garlands make a special treat to look forward to at teatime

SWISS ROLL
Serves 6–8

lard for greasing
caster sugar and flour for
    dusting
3 large eggs
100 g (4 oz) caster sugar
100 g (4 oz) plain flour

25 g (1 oz) walnut pieces,
    finely chopped
142-ml (5-fl oz) carton
    double cream
plum, raspberry or
    strawberry jam

Cut an oblong of greaseproof paper to fit the base of a 330 × 225 × 15-mm (13 × 9 × ⅝-inches) Swiss roll tin. Brush the inside of the tin with melted lard and fit the paper into the base. Brush over the paper with melted lard. Leave the lard to set then dust out with caster sugar followed by flour, knocking out any excess to give a fine sugar/flour coating.

Place the eggs and caster sugar in a deep mixing bowl which will fit over (not in) a pan of simmering water. Whisk vigorously—if you use a powerful electric whisk you don't need to heat the mixture—until it is very thick and light in colour and when lifted, falls in a thick ribbon and holds its shape. Do not overheat the bowl. Sift the flour directly over the surface of the whisked eggs then sprinkle over the nuts. Using a spatula or large metal spoon, fold by cutting and turning the flour and nuts through the egg mixture. Do this only until no traces of flour remain. Work lightly to avoid knocking air out of the mixture. Fold in 15 ml (1 tbsp) water. Hold the mixing bowl just above the prepared tin and gently pour the mixture into it. Don't pour from a great height or again, air will be knocked out of the mixture. Level the surface in the Swiss roll tin.

Preheat the oven to 200°C (400°F) mark 6. Place the tin in the centre of the oven and bake for 10–12 minutes. When baked the cake mixture should be light golden brown and should spring back, leaving no imprint when pressed with a finger. The Swiss roll should have slightly shrunk away from the sides of the tin. Run a blunt knife all the way around the edges. Sprinkle generously with caster sugar and lay a sheet of greaseproof paper and a large baking sheet on top. Invert the baking sheet and Swiss roll tin together and carefully ease off the tin.

Using a large knife, trim the crusty edges off the Swiss roll. Make a shallow cut across one narrow end of the roll—this helps to start the rolling. From this end gently, and not too tightly, roll up the sponge mixture keeping the paper inside. When completed, twist the ends of the paper to prevent it unrolling. Cool in the paper. As soon as the roll is cool, lightly whip the cream. Carefully unroll the Swiss roll and ease the paper off the inside. Spread this side with jam, then top with cream. Roll up again, without the paper. Lift, using two fish or pastry slices and place seam side down on a serving plate. Dust the surface with sugar for serving.

To freeze Place the completed Swiss roll on a baking sheet lined with non-stick paper. Open freeze until firm, then label and overwrap the roll in freezer film or polythene bags. Pack in a rigid container if there is any danger of the Swiss roll being squashed in the freezer. When required, unwrap the roll, place on a serving plate and leave to thaw at cool room temperature for about 4 hours.

BRANDY SNAP BASKETS

50 g (2 oz) butter or block
    margarine
50 g (2 oz) caster sugar
50 g (2 oz) golden syrup

50 g (2 oz) plain flour
2.5 ml (½ level tsp) ground
    ginger
5 ml (1 tsp) brandy

Cut up the fat and place in a small saucepan with the caster sugar and golden syrup. Warm gently until the sugar dissolves and the ingredients are evenly blended. Remove from the heat and stir in the flour and ginger sifted together. Lastly stir in the brandy. Line 2 large baking sheets with non-stick paper. Spoon on the brandy snap mixture, making 6 circles in all, allowing plenty of room for spreading. Bake at 180°C (350°F) mark 4 for about 12 minutes, or until the 'snaps' are golden brown. (It is best to place the baking sheets in the oven with a 5-minute interval so that you have time to shape one batch before the second is cooked.) Leave the baked brandy snaps on the baking sheets for about 45 seconds to firm up slightly. Ease them off the paper using a fish slice and mould over upturned ramekin dishes. Once they're set, twist the brandy snap baskets off their moulds and complete the cooling on a wire rack. Store in an airtight container until required.

To freeze Pack into a rigid container and freeze. To thaw, unwrap, place on a wire rack and leave to thaw for 1 hour before serving.

GUINNESS CAKE

175 g (6 oz) glacé cherries,
    roughly chopped
175 g (6 oz) sultanas
175 g (6 oz) seedless
    raisins
finely grated rind of
    1 lemon
7.5 ml (1½ level tsp) mixed
    spice

175 g (6 oz) currants
275-ml (9.68-fl oz) can
    Guinness
175 g (6 oz) butter or
    block margarine
175 g (6 oz) soft dark
    brown sugar
3 large eggs, beaten
350 g (12 oz) plain flour

Mix the cherries, sultanas, raisins, currants, lemon rind and spice. Pour over the Guinness, stir to mix, cover and leave to marinate overnight.

Grease a 215-mm (8½-inch), 2.3-litre (4-pint) spring form cake tin with a tubular base and dust out with flour.

Beat the fat and sugar together until light in texture. Gradually beat in the eggs. Mix the fruits, creamed ingredients and flour lightly together and spoon into the prepared tin. Bake at 170°C (325°F) mark 3 for about 1¾ hours covering lightly with foil if necessary. Cool a little in the tin, turn out on to a wire rack to complete cooking. Store for 2–3 days in an airtight tin before eating.

To freeze Wrap and freeze after maturing. To use, thaw, wrapped at cool room temperature for about 8 hours.

Swiss roll will be welcome at teatime or as a finale to dinner

FRUIT BRAZIL BUTTER CAKE

175 g (6 oz) butter or
  block margarine
175 g (6 oz) caster sugar
3 large eggs, beaten
125 g (4 oz) Brazil nuts
50 g (2 oz) candied lemon
  peel
125 g (4 oz) dried apricots

125 g (4 oz) sultanas
125 g (4 oz) plain flour
125 g (4 oz) self-raising
  flour
apricot glaze
almond paste and Brazil
  nuts for decoration

Line the bottom and sides of a 20.5-cm (8-inch) round cake tin or 1.7-litre (3-pint) loaf tin with greased greaseproof paper.

Cream the fat and sugar together until pale and fluffy. Add the beaten eggs gradually, beating all the time. Roughly chop or coarsely grate the nuts and finely chop the candied peel. Snip the apricots into small pieces. Mix all the fruit and nuts together.

Fold the sifted flours into the creamed mixture followed by the fruit mixture. Spoon into the prepared tin. Bake at 180°C (350°F) mark 4 for about 1¼ hours, covering if necessary. Cool a little then turn out on to a rack.

To finish, brush the top of the cake with apricot glaze. Cover top with rolled out almond paste. Score in a diamond pattern. Place a slice of soaked, dried Brazil nut in each diamond. Grill cake top until evenly browned.

To freeze Pack and freeze. To use, leave wrapped at room temperature for about 8 hours.

GINGER THINS
Makes 12

50 g (2 oz) block or soft
  tub margarine
15 ml (1 level tbsp) caster
  sugar
60 g (2 oz) golden syrup

15 ml (1 level tbsp) ground
  ginger
40 g (1½ oz) plain flour
40 g (1½ oz) chopped
  mixed nuts

Line 2 baking sheets with non-stick paper or oiled foil.

Over a very gentle heat, melt together the margarine, sugar, golden syrup and ground ginger. Off the heat, stir in the flour and nuts. Immediately place 12 spoonfuls of mixture on to the prepared baking sheets, leaving room for spreading. Spread each one out thinly with an oiled, round-bladed knife to approximately 9-cm (3 -inch) diameter. Don't worry if holes appear in the rounds; these disappear on baking.

Bake the trays of biscuits in rotation at 200°C (400°F) mark 6 for 10–12 minutes or until a deep golden brown all over.

Carefully lift the biscuits with a fish slice and fold over a lightly oiled rolling pin or empty wine bottle to cool into a curled shape. Cool completely then ease off the pin. Store in an airtight container and eat on day of making.

Not suitable for freezing.

MALTED FRUIT LOAF

350 g (12 oz) plain flour
2.5 ml (½ level tsp)
  bicarbonate of soda
5 ml (1 level tsp) baking
  powder
250 g (9 oz) sultanas

30 ml (2 level tbsp)
  demerara sugar
135 ml (9 level tbsp) malt
  extract
2 eggs, beaten
200 ml (7 fl oz) milk

Grease and base line a 1.6-litre (2¾-pint) loaf tin and grease the underside of a baking sheet.

In a bowl combine the flour, bicarbonate of soda and baking powder. Stir in the sultanas. Slowly heat together the demerara sugar, and malt extract—do not boil. Pour the malt mixture on to the dry ingredients. Add the eggs and milk and beat well.

Turn the mixture into the prepared tin. Cover with baking sheet, greased side down. Place a weight on top. Bake at 150°C (300°F) mark 2 for about 1½ hours. Turn out on to a wire rack to cool. Wrap and keep for two days.

To freeze When completely cold, wrap and leave for two days before freezing. To use, thaw at cool room temperature for 5–6 hours.

OATMEAL COOKIES
Makes 12

50 g (2 oz) block or soft
  tub margarine, chilled
40 g (1½ oz) medium
  oatmeal
75 g (3 oz) plain
  wholewheat flour
1 egg, beaten

40 g (1½ oz) light soft
  brown sugar
50 g (2 oz) walnut pieces,
  roughly chopped
75 g (3 oz) eating apple,
  peeled and cored
12 walnut halves

Rub the chilled margarine, oatmeal, flour and sugar together. Stir in the chopped walnuts. Coarsely grate the apple into the mixture. Beat in half the egg and continue beating until the mixture is thoroughly combined and soft.

Drop 12 spoonfuls of mixture on to lightly greased baking sheets. Flatten slightly into rounds. Place a walnut half on each. Glaze with remaining beaten egg. Bake at 190°C (375°F) mark 5 for 15–20 minutes until well browned. Cool on a wire rack. Store in an airtight container for 3–4 days only.

To freeze Pack and freeze. To use, thaw at cool room temperature for 30 minutes.

LEMON FORK BISCUITS

45 ml (3 tbsp) vegetable oil
50 g (2 oz) caster sugar
1 small egg
grated rind ½ lemon
125 g (4 oz) plain flour

2.5 ml (½ level tsp) baking
  powder
pinch of salt
pinch of ground nutmeg
granulated sugar

In a medium-sized mixing bowl whisk together the oil, caster sugar, egg and lemon rind. Sift the flour, baking powder, salt and nutmeg over the oil mixture. Stir to combine, then knead lightly to ensure the ingredients are well mixed. Using floured hands, shape the mixture into 16 balls. Dip the tops of the balls into granulated sugar. Place the balls well apart, sugar side up on lightly greased baking sheets. Flatten them well with a damp fork; they should be about 3 cm (1¼ inch) in diameter. Bake the biscuits at 190°C (375°F) mark 5 for about 12 minutes, or until light golden brown. Cool on a wire rack. Store in an airtight container until required.

To freeze Pack into a rigid container, freeze. Thaw for about 1 hour at cool room temperature.

SOURED CREAM COFFEE CAKE

125 g (4 oz) butter or
  block margarine
200 g (7 oz) caster sugar
2 eggs, beaten
two 141-ml (5-fl oz)
  cartons soured cream
5 ml (1 tsp) vanilla essence

175 g (6 oz) self-raising
  flour
5 ml (1 level tsp)
  bicarbonate of soda
75 g (3 oz) walnut pieces,
  roughly chopped

Grease and line a 18-cm (7-inch) square, 2.3-litre (4-pint) deep baking tin.

Beat the butter until soft and creamy, gradually beat in the sugar. Creaming takes longer than usual due to the high proportion of sugar. Beat in the eggs, soured cream and vanilla essence, a little at a time. Sift in the flour and bicarbonate of soda and using a wooden spoon, beat in lightly with 50 g (2 oz) of the walnuts.

Turn into the prepared tin and bake at 180°C (350°F) mark 4 for about 55 minutes. Half way through cooking time scatter over the rest of the nuts without actually removing the cake from the oven. Allow to cool a little in the tin. Ease out and serve warm in thick slices with coffee.

To freeze Cool, pack and freeze. To use, reheat from frozen wrapped in foil at 180°C (350°F) mark 4 for about 1 hour. Serve warm.

LEMON & NUTMEG SHORTIES
Makes 24

125 g (4 oz) butter,
  softened
50 g (2 oz) caster sugar
175 g (6 oz) plain flour
1.25 ml (½ level tsp)
  ground nutmeg

25 g (1 oz) ground rice
grated rind of 1 lemon
5 ml (1 tsp) lemon juice
caster sugar and nutmeg to
  finish

Cream together the butter and sugar until very pale. Stir in the plain flour, ground rice, nutmeg, lemon rind and juice. Knead very well to form a smooth, workable paste. On a lightly sugared surface, roll out the dough to slightly more than 5-mm (¼-inch) thickness. With a large, sharp knife, cut into 7.5 × 2-cm (3 × ¾-inch) fingers. Place on lightly greased baking sheets and chill for 30 minutes.

Bake at 190°C (375°F) mark 5 for about 25 minutes until just changing colour. Dredge with caster sugar and ground nutmeg while still warm. Leave to cool completely on a wire rack. Store in an airtight container for 2–3 weeks.

To freeze Pack and freeze. To use, thaw at cool room temperature for 30 minutes.

CHOCOLATE CRUMBLE SQUARES
Makes about 15

200 g (7 oz) butter
60 ml (4 level tbsp)
  drinking chocolate
  powder
30 ml (2 level tbsp) golden
  syrup

finely grated rind of
  1 lemon
400-g (14.1-oz) packet
  digestive biscuits
two peppermint chocolate
  Aero bars

Place the butter, chocolate powder, syrup and finely grated lemon rind in a large saucepan. Heat gently until the butter melts. Place the biscuits in a polythene bag and finely crush with a rolling pin. Stir the crumbs into the melted mixture to coat. Spoon the biscuit mixture into a lightly greased 270 × 170-mm (10¾ × 6¾-inch) shallow cake tin, pressing down well. Place in the refrigerator to set, about 1 hour.

Melt the chocolate bars and spread roughly over the biscuit cake. Leave to set before cutting into squares to serve. Store in an airtight container for up to a week.

To freeze Pack and freeze. To use, thaw at cool room temperature for about 3 hours.

COCONUT MACAROONS
Makes 18

2 egg whites
100 g (4 oz) icing sugar,
  sieved
100 g (4 oz) ground
  almonds

almond essence
100 g (4 oz) desiccated
  coconut
30 ml (2 level tbsp)
  premium shred coconut

Whisk the egg whites until stiff but not dry. Lightly fold in the sugar. Gently stir in the almonds, almond essence and desiccated coconut until the mixture forms a sticky dough. Spoon walnut-sized pieces of the mixture on to non-stick paper lined baking sheets. Press a few strands of shredded coconut on to the top of each one.

Bake at 150°C (300°F) mark 2 for about 25 minutes. The outer crust should be pale golden while the inside remains soft. Cool on a wire rack. Store in an airtight container for up to one week.

Not suitable for freezing.

HAZELNUT CRISPS

50 g (2 oz) ground
  hazelnuts
75 g (3 oz) caster sugar

5 ml (1 level tsp) plain
  flour
1 egg white

Preheat the oven to 180°C (350°F) mark 4. Stir together the hazelnuts, sugar and flour. Add the egg white and beat very well. Line a baking sheet with rice paper or non-stick parchment. Place small spoonfuls of mixture well apart on the prepared baking sheet. Bake for 25–30 minutes until golden and crisp. Allow to cool slightly before easing off the sheet with a palette knife or fish slice. Cool completely on a wire rack. Store in an airtight tin.

To freeze Pack, when cold, in a rigid container. To thaw, lay flat on a lined baking sheet and cover loosely with foil. Bake in a hot oven, 200°C (400°F) mark 6, for 5 minutes.

FLORENTINES
Makes 12

25 g (1 oz) hazelnuts,
  finely chopped
25 g (1 oz) blanched
  almonds, finely chopped
3 glacé cherries, chopped
30 ml (2 level tbsp) cut
  mixed peel, chopped

15 ml (1 level tbsp)
  sultanas, chopped
50 g (2 oz) butter
50 g (2 oz) caster sugar
10 ml (2 tsp) top of milk
100 g (4 oz) plain
  chocolate

Mix together the fruit and nuts. Melt the butter in a saucepan. Stir in the sugar and bring slowly to the boil, stirring; take the pan off the heat immediately and then stir in the fruit and nut mixture with the milk. Allow the mixture to cool slightly, stirring occasionally, until evenly blended and no longer oily in appearance. Spoon out on to baking sheets lined with non-stick paper, leaving plenty of space. Bake in the oven at 180°C (350°F) mark 4 for about 12 minutes until golden brown. Neaten the edges with an oiled palette knife, allow them to cool for 1–2 minutes, then using a fish slice, slide them on to a wire rack to cool.

Break up the chocolate and place in a basin. Stand the basin over a pan of simmering water until chocolate melts. Don't let water get in the basin. Remove basin, stir chocolate until cool and of a thick spreading consistency. Spoon a little chocolate on to smooth side of each florentine. Carefully spread out to coat. Leave chocolate to firm slightly. It should be creamy, not set. Draw the prongs of a fork across in a wavy line. Wipe the paper and use a fish slice to replace florentines on lined baking sheet. Refrigerate to set. Store in the fridge interleaved with non-stick paper.

APPLE & WALNUT LOAF
Serves 8

225 g (8 oz) plain flour
225 g (8 oz) block
  margarine
3 eggs
125 g (4 oz) light soft
  brown sugar
125 g (4 oz) self-raising
  flour

2.5 ml (½ level tsp) ground
  cinnamon
175 g (6 oz) walnut pieces,
  chopped
small eating apple, peeled
50 g (2 oz) icing sugar
a few pistachio nuts,
  roughly chopped

Rub together the plain flour and 125 g (4 oz) block margarine. Bind to a dough with 1 egg and a little water if necessary. Knead lightly. Chill.

Grease and base line a 1.4-litre (2½-pint) loaf tin. Line with the pastry, pressing it well into the corners; flute the pastry edges. Chill for at least 1 hour.

Cream together the remaining margarine and sugar. Gradually beat in two whole eggs. Fold in the self-raising flour, cinnamon and chopped walnuts. Spoon the sponge mixture evenly into the prepared tin. Arrange apple slices neatly on top. Bake at 190°C (375°F) mark 5 for about 1¼ hours. Leave to cool a little before turning out on to a wire rack.

Beat the sifted icing sugar to a thin coating consistency with water. Drizzle over the top of the cake. Decorate with chopped pistachios.

To freeze Cool, pack and freeze without icing or pistachios. To use, thaw unwrapped at cool room temperature for 4–5 hours. Finish as above.

CHAPTER EIGHT

DINNER PARTIES

A MONTH-BY-MONTH GUIDE
TO STYLISH ENTERTAINING

JANUARY

Spiced Onions/Hot Veal & Ham Terrine/Grated Vichy Carrots/Fresh Pear Shortcake/Crème Anglaise

SPICED ONIONS

Large onions could be used when shallots or button onions are unobtainable. Skin the onions, cut them into quarters or eighths keeping the root ends intact to prevent the onions falling apart.

700 g (1½ lb) small shallots or button onions	25 g (1 oz) butter
	226-g (8-oz) can tomatoes
1 large green pepper	15 ml (1 tbsp) cider
12 black olives	vinegar
15 ml (1 level tbsp) ground cumin	salt and milled pepper
	watercress to garnish

Skin the shallots or button onions. This is made easier by covering the onions in boiling water and leaving them to stand for 2–3 minutes; the skins will peel away quite easily. Halve, de-seed and dice the pepper. Halve and stone the black olives.

Melt the butter in a medium-sized saucepan and gently fry the cumin for 1–2 minutes. Add the onions and pepper. Cook, stirring for a few minutes before adding the tomatoes, vinegar and olives. Simmer very gently until the onions and pepper are cooked—at least 10 minutes. Season, pour into a bowl and leave to cool. Cover and chill well before serving in individual dishes. Garnish with watercress and serve with melba toast.

HOT VEAL & HAM TERRINE

An interesting combination of flavours; don't be alarmed that the centre remains pink, it's because of the layer of ham.

700 g (1½ lb) minced veal	1 bunch watercress
2 large eggs	40 g (1½ oz) butter
284-ml (10-fl oz) carton single cream	125 g (4 oz) button mushrooms, wiped
salt and milled pepper	100 g (4 oz) sliced cooked
1.25 ml (¼ level tsp) ground nutmeg	ham
	1 bayleaf
30 ml (2 tbsp) dry sherry	5 ml (1 level tsp)
1 clove garlic, skinned and crushed	arrowroot

Liquidise together the veal, eggs, cream, 2.5 ml (½ level tsp) salt, milled pepper, nutmeg and sherry. This will probably have to be done in two batches. Trim any hairy root ends off the watercress and discard. Wash, drain and finely chop remainder, then sauté with the garlic in half the butter until softened, about 2–3 minutes. Set aside to cool.

In the same pan melt the remaining butter and sauté the finely sliced mushrooms until just cooked. Set aside to cool. Cut one slice of ham into fine shreds, cover and reserve. Cut the remaining ham into wide strips.

Base line a 1.4-litre (2½-pint) terrine dish with greaseproof paper. Divide the veal mixture into four. Place alternate layers of veal, watercress, ham and mushrooms in the prepared dish, beginning and ending with a layer of veal. Place the bayleaf on top. Cover tightly with foil.

Bake in a roasting tin half filled with water at 180°C (350°F) mark 4 for about 1½ hours, until just firm to the touch. When cooked, drain the juices into a saucepan through a sieve lined with muslin. Turn the terrine on a serving dish and gently scrape away the creamy curd from the sides. Rub this through the strainer and add to the juices. Re-cover the terrine and keep warm in a low oven. Bring the juices to the boil, stir in the arrowroot mixed to a smooth paste with a little water. Simmer, whisking all the time until slightly thickened. Add the reserved shreds of ham and spoon over the terrine. Serve with the carrots and creamed potatoes.

GRATED VICHY CARROTS

900 g (2 lb) carrots, pared	salt and milled pepper
90 ml (6 tbsp) light stock	chopped parsley to garnish
25 g (1 oz) butter	

Grate the carrots on the coarsest blade of the grater. Place in a large saucepan of boiling, salted water, bring back to the boil and boil for 1 minute. Drain in a fine colander or sieve. Run under the cold tap to stop them cooking further.

Place in a deep 1.1-litre (2-pint) ovenproof dish. Pour in the stock and dot the butter on top of the carrots. Season, cover tightly and cook at 180°C (350°F) mark 4 for 30 minutes. Stir once during the cooking time. Check seasoning before serving. Garnish with the chopped parsley.

CRÈME ANGLAISE

2 eggs	300 ml (½ pint) milk
5 ml (1 level tsp) caster sugar	pared rind of 1 lemon
	almond essence

Whisk the eggs and sugar lightly. Scald the milk and lemon rind and strain on to the eggs. Stir over a very gentle heat until the sauce thickens and lightly coats the back of the spoon. Do *not* boil. Stir in a few drops of almond essence. Keep warm in a basin over a pan of simmering water.

FRESH PEAR SHORTCAKE

If ripe pears are unavailable the peeled pears should be poached in sugar syrup until softened. Serve Crème Anglaise, single cream or a dessert wine with the shortcake.

150 g (5 oz) self-raising flour	50 g (2 oz) soft dark brown sugar
25 g (1 oz) ground rice grated rind of 1 lemon	125 g (4 oz) full fat soft cheese
150 g (5 oz) butter	1 egg
4 ripe medium, even-sized pears—about 550 g (1¼ lb) in weight	almond essence
	15 g (½ oz) flaked almonds

Lightly grease a 20.5-cm (8-inch) loose-based metal flan tin. In a mixing bowl, stir together the flour, ground rice and lemon rind. Sieve in the dark brown sugar. Rub in the butter and continue lightly kneading the mixture until it forms a dough. Press into the prepared tin with floured fingertips. Mark into eight portions and prick well with a fork. Bake at 190°C (375°F) mark 5 for 30–35 minutes until light brown and cooked through. Leave in the tin to cool slightly.

Peel, halve and scoop the cores out of the pears using a teaspoon. Slice each pear half crosswise, into 3-mm (⅛-inch) thick pieces keeping the slices together. Place a sliced pear half on each portion of shortcake, fan out the slices a little.

Beat together the soft cheese, egg and almond essence, until smooth, then spoon over the pears completely covering both fruit and shortcake. Scatter over the flaked almonds. Bake at 180°C (350°F) mark 4 for 40 minutes until golden. Ease out of the tin and serve warm or cold.

WINES FOR THE FOOD

This is not a meal for great wines, but admirably suited to let younger reds of racy breed show their paces. A *fino* or *amontillado* sherry, or a dry Montilla would complement the spiced onions, but otherwise start as you mean to continue with the terrine, which is more delicate than rustic and thus requires a light and zesty wine rather than anything too robust. Beaujolais is the obvious candidate, Gamay de Haut-Poitou or Ardèche excellent substitutes. Other possibilities include Côtes de Buzet Cuvée Napoleon, red Bergerac, or claret from Fronsac, Bourg or Blaye.

With Fresh Pear Shortcake, take either a glass of chilled Muscat de Beaumes-de-Venise (it keeps well in the fridge after opening), or an eau-de-vie Poire William.

COUNTDOWN

The day before: Prepare the Spiced Onions. Cool, cover with cling film and keep refrigerated. Make the melba toast, store in an airtight container until required. Prepare and bake the base of the Fresh Pear Shortcake. Cool, then foil wrap and store in a cool place. Beat together the cream cheese, egg and almond essence. Cover and keep refrigerated. Poach the pears if necessary. Cover tightly and store in a cool place.

In the morning: Prepare the ingredients for the Veal & Ham Terrine and layer into the dish. Cover and keep refrigerated. Refrigerate the shreds of ham in a polythene bag. Wash watercress, drain, pat dry and refrigerate in a polythene bag. Prepare the carrots, blanch, drain well then spoon into the cooking dish. Don't add the stock yet, cover and refrigerate. Peel 1.4 kg (3 lb) potatoes, cover with cold water and store in a cool place. Make the Crème Anglaise, cover with damp greaseproof paper, and refrigerate.

To serve at 8pm:

About 6pm: Preheat the oven to 180°C (350°F) mark 4.

6.15-ish: Stand the prepared terrine in the roasting tin half filled with water and put into oven to cook. Stir the Spiced Onions and spoon into individual serving dishes. Keep refrigerated. Garnish with watercress before serving.

7pm: Peel, halve and slice pears and arrange on shortcake. Spoon the cream cheese mixture evenly over and scatter with almonds. Place in oven to cook for 40 minutes. When cooked, leave at room temperature.

7.15pm: Add stock, butter and seasoning to carrots. Place in oven below terrine.

7.30-ish: Boil the potatoes until tender. Mash with an egg, a little butter, crushed garlic and seasoning. Cover and keep warm in a low oven.

7.45pm: Drain juices from terrine into saucepan. Turn oven down to low. Turn the terrine on to serving dish and strain the creamy curds into juices. Re-cover terrine and keep warm in oven. Thicken the juices, check seasoning. Stir in shreds of ham. Keep sauce warm over a low heat. Place Crème Anglaise over pan of simmering water to warm.

8-ish: Serve the meal. Serve the wine cool and fresh, but not chilled.

FREEZER NOTES

Prepare and freeze the terrine in its dish before cooking. To use, cook from frozen for about 2½ hours. The Fresh Pear Shortcake can be baked and frozen. Thaw at room temperature for 2 hours before serving cold.

An Italian Inspired Menu: Mixed Salad/Fish Casserole/Crusty Bread/Cheese Board/Orange Water Ice/Italian Sweetmeats

ITALIAN MIXED SALAD (*Antipasti*)

The classic Italian starter of thinly sliced ham, salami and sausage. The meats vary in flavour and texture depending on what part of Italy they originated from. We accompanied the meats with shredded radicchio, which looks like a small purple lettuce. It's sometimes braised or served on its own as a salad in Italy. There's no need to serve a dressing with the radicchio, as the meats are rich enough in themselves.

1 head radicchio or a small lettuce
75 g (3 oz) Mozzarella cheese
75 g (3 oz) Parma ham, thinly sliced
75 g (3 oz) mixed salami and mortadella, thinly sliced
black olives
lemon slices
bread sticks to accompany

Wash the radicchio or lettuce leaves; drain well and pat dry with kitchen paper. Coarsely shred the leaves. Using a swivel peeler or snarp knife, pare the cheese into thin strips. Ease any skin or rind off the salami. Place a bed of radicchio or lettuce on a large serving platter. Arrange the slices of salami, mortadella, ham and cheese on top. Garnish with black olives and lemon slices. Cover tightly with clingfilm and refrigerate for at least 2 hours. Leave at cool room temperature for about 20 minutes before serving. Accompany with bread sticks.

CHUNKY FISH CASSEROLE (*Cassola*)

Italy is renowned for its fish dishes and varieties of *Cassola* or *Buridda* (fish casserole) are found across the country. Nearly every region has access to the sea and there are plenty of fish from the freshwater lakes too. We've avoided last-minute pasta cooking by adding pasta shells to the casserole. It is best to serve the casserole, with its delicious juices, in soup plates.

125 g (4 oz) small pasta shells
1 green pepper
1 yellow pepper
175 g (6 oz) onion
225 g (½ lb) button mushrooms
450 g (1 lb) fillets of sole, skinned
6 scallops
60 ml (4 level tbsp) plain flour
salt and milled pepper
200-g (7-oz) can whole artichoke hearts
75 g (3 oz) butter
clove garlic, skinned
300 ml (½ pint) dry vermouth
150 ml (¼ pint) light stock
5 ml (1 level tsp) dried sage or 15 ml (1 level tbsp) fresh chopped
225 g (½ lb) peeled prawns
crusty bread to accompany

Cook the pasta shells in boiling salted water for three-quarters of the time recommended on the packet. Drain in a colander and run cold water over the pasta. Halve the green and yellow peppers and remove the seeds; cut the flesh into small squares. Skin and slice the onion; wipe the mushrooms, then slice. Cut the sole into finger-sized strips. Ease the black thread and any membrane away from the scallops, cut the flesh into chunks. Toss the prepared fish in the flour, seasoned with salt and milled pepper. Quarter the artichoke hearts. Melt 50 g (2 oz) of the butter in a large frying pan. Add the peppers, onions and mushrooms and fry over a high heat for a few minutes. Remove from the pan using draining spoons and place in a deep 2.8-litre (5-pint) oven-proof dish.

Add the remaining butter to the pan and when frothing add the sole and scallops with the crushed garlic. Fry for a couple of minutes, turning gently to avoid breaking up the fish. Stir in the vermouth, stock, sage and seasoning and bring up to the boil. Pour over the vegetables. Add the artichoke hearts, prawns and pasta shells and stir gently to mix the ingredients. Cover the dish and bake at 180°C (350°F) mark 4 for about 40 minutes. Adjust seasoning and serve in shallow soup plates with plenty of hot crusty bread.

THE CHEESEBOARD

Choose a selection of Italian cheese such as:
Gorgonzola—a slightly soft blue veined cheese made from cow's milk. It's one of the best known Italian cheeses to be found in this country and is named after a village near Milan.
Fontina—a delicious semi-hard cheese produced in the Aosta Valley in Northern Italy.
Pecorino—a firm, strongly flavoured cheese made from ewe's milk. Allowed to mature until it is hard enough to grate, it can then be used as an alternative to Parmesan.

Orange Water Ice (*Granita di Arancia*)

Water ices (*Granite*) are light tangy mixtures which provide the perfect end to a rich Italian meal. Allow the water ice plenty of time to soften in the refrigerator before serving it.

175 g (6 oz) caster sugar
10 large oranges
1½ lemons
2 egg whites

Place the caster sugar and 450 ml (¾ pint) water in a medium-sized saucepan. Heat gently until the sugar dissolves then boil gently for 10 minutes.

Meanwhile, using a potato peeler, thinly pare off the rind from four of the oranges and the lemons and place them in a bowl. Pour over the syrup and leave to go quite cold. Squeeze the juice from the four oranges and the lemons. Strain them into a measuring jug; there should be about 450 ml (¾ pint). Strain the cold syrup into a shallow freezer container and stir in the fruit juices. Mix well, cover and freeze until mushy; about 4 hours.

Remove from the freezer and turn the frozen mixture into a bowl. Beat well with a fork to break down the ice crystals. Stiffly whisk the egg whites and fold into the orange mixture until evenly blended. Return to the freezer container and freeze until firm; at least 8 hours.

Meanwhile, using a serrated knife, cut away the peel and pith from the remaining oranges. Slice the oranges down into thin rings, ease out and discard any pips. Place the oranges in a serving bowl; cover tightly with cling film and refrigerate. Place the water ice in the refrigerator for 45 minutes before serving. Serve with the fresh orange slices.

Italian Sweetmeats (*Dolce Italiana*)

These small sweet slices of fruit and nuts are delicious served with coffee. Add a few glacé cherries for a change.

50 g (2 oz) shelled
* hazelnuts*
50 g (2 oz) dried apricots
50 g (2 oz) dried figs
50 g (2 oz) stoned dates
10 ml (2 tsp) brandy

Toast the nuts under a hot grill then rub off their skins; cool. Roughly chop the apricots, figs and dates. Mince the fruits and cold nuts and place in a small bowl. Gradually beat in the brandy and continue stirring until the mixture comes together. Divide in two and form each piece, between the palms of your hands, into a roll about 10 cm (4 inch) long. Do not overwork or the mixture will become very oily. Roll up each piece inside clingfilm, place on a plate and chill for at least 2 hours. Slice the rolls into rings about 5 mm (¼ inch) thick and arrange on serving plates. Cover with clingfilm and refrigerate until required. Serve with the coffee.

Countdown

The day before: Prepare and freeze the Orange Water Ice. Make the Sweetmeats, wrap and refrigerate.

The morning: Wash the radicchio or lettuce leaves, dry and refrigerate in a polythene bag. Part-cook the pasta shells as directed, drain, cover with cold water and store in a cool place. Cut up the peppers into small squares, slice the onion and mushrooms; refrigerate the vegetables in polythene bags. Cut up the fish, don't toss in flour yet, cover tightly and refrigerate. Quarter the artichoke hearts, cover and refrigerate. Prepare and slice the oranges, place in the serving bowl, cover, refrigerate.

To serve at 8pm:

About 5.30: Cut up the Mozzarella cheese and arrange on a serving platter with the radicchio and meats. Garnish with black olives and lemon slices. Cover and refrigerate.

7-ish: Preheat the oven to 180°C (350°F) mark 4, start the fish casserole then put in the oven to bake—remember to drain the pasta shells before adding to the casserole. Place white wine in fridge to chill, open red wines and stand in cool place to serve slightly below room temperature.

About 7.45: Take the Italian Mixed Salad out of the refrigerator. Check casserole.

8-ish: Place the water ice in the refrigerator to soften. Bring white wines to table in buckets of iced water.

Serve the meal.

Freezer Notes

The fish casserole does not freeze well. Freeze the Orange Water Ice as directed. Do not freeze the orange slices. The Sweetmeats can be prepared and formed into rolls then wrapped and frozen. Leave the rolls to thaw at cool room temperature for about 2 hours, chill before slicing for serving.

Wines with the Food

It would be possible to accompany the *antipasti* with a light young Italian red—Valpolicella or try a Bardolino—but this is really an occasion for Italian whites. To start, try Verdicchio dei Castelli de Jesi. The fish casserole requires a generously flavoured white, such as Montecarlo Bianco '77 by Mazzini Franca, Vermentino '80, or a Vernaccia di San Gimignano.

The same wines may accompany the cheeseboard, but take none with the *granita*. With the sweetmeats the authentic Italian touch should be a Moscata Passito.

Chicory & Melon Salad/Chicken with Saffron/Duchesse Potatoes/Steamed Green Beans/Apricot Flan

CHICORY & MELON SALAD

Shredded endive would be a good alternative to chicory.

2 heads chicory
30 ml (2 tbsp) olive oil
15 ml (1 tbsp) vegetable oil
15 ml (1 tbsp) lemon juice
salt and milled pepper
pinch of sugar

medium-sized melon —
about 1.1 kg (2½ lb)
50 g (2 oz) walnut pieces
brown bread and butter to
accompany

Trim off the root end of the chicory; separate out the leaves. Wash and drain well then dry the leaves and place in a large polythene bag. Refrigerate for at least 2 hours to crisp up the leaves. Place the oils, lemon juice, seasoning and sugar in a large mixing bowl and whisk together. Halve the melon and discard the seeds. Using a melon baller scoop out the flesh and place in the bowl with the dressing. Cover tightly with cling film and refrigerate.

Roughly chop the nuts then toast under the grill until well browned. Cool. Just before serving, arrange the chicory leaves on individual serving plates and spoon the melon salad into the centre. Scatter the toasted nuts over the melon to garnish. Serve the salad with thin slices of brown bread and butter.

CHICKEN WITH SAFFRON

Be sure to strain the sauce after cooking or the saffron flavour will continue to infuse and could become too strong.

six chicken breasts on the
bone, about 175 g (6 oz)
each
30 ml (2 level tbsp) flour
salt and milled pepper
40 g (1½ oz) butter
200 ml (7 fl oz) chicken
stock

30 ml (2 tbsp) dry white
wine
sachet of saffron (large
pinch)
2 egg yolks
60 ml (4 tbsp) single cream
chopped parsley

Skin the chicken breasts and remove any fat. Lightly coat the chicken in the flour, seasoned with salt and milled pepper. Melt the butter in a medium-sized flameproof casserole. Fry the chicken pieces, half at a time, until golden brown. Replace all the chicken pieces with any remaining flour and pour in the stock and wine. Sprinkle in the saffron, pushing it down under the liquid. Bring up to the boil, cover tightly, and bake on the lower shelf of the oven set at 180°C (350°F) mark 4 for about 50 minutes until cooked. Lift the chicken out of the juices and place in an edged serving dish. Cover and keep warm in a low oven.

Strain the cooking juices into a small saucepan. Mix the egg yolks and cream together and off the heat stir into the cooking juices. Cook gently, stirring all the time until the juices thicken slightly. Do *NOT* boil. Adjust seasoning, spoon over the chicken and garnish with chopped parsley.

STEAMED GREEN BEANS

Steaming the beans helps to prevent them over-cooking and keeps them crisp.

700 g (1½ lb) French beans
salt and milled pepper
knob of butter

Top and tail the beans and cut into 2.5-cm (1-inch) lengths. Wash and drain well. Steam over boiling salted water for about 15 minutes. Place in a serving dish and add a good knob of butter and plenty of seasoning. Cover and keep warm.

DUCHESSE POTATOES

These can be spooned rather than piped out, but the finish won't be so professional.

900 g (2 lb) potatoes
50 g (2 oz) butter or
margarine

salt and milled pepper
grated nutmeg
2 eggs, beaten

Boil the potatoes. Drain *well*, then sieve or mash. Beat in the butter with plenty of seasoning and a dash of nutmeg. Gradually beat in most of the eggs, reserving a little for glazing. Cool the potato mixture then spoon into a piping bag fitted with a large star nozzle. Pipe the mixture in pyramids on to a greased baking sheet. Brush carefully with the remaining egg to which a pinch of salt has been added. Bake on the top shelf of the oven set at 180°C (350°F) mark 4 for about 40 minutes, or until golden brown and set. Place in a serving dish. Keep warm uncovered.

APRICOT FLAN

The fresh apricots could be replaced with two 420-g (14.8-oz) cans of apricot halves. Do not poach the canned apricots, but drain off the syrup and reduce slightly before thickening with arrowroot.

175 g (6 oz) plain flour
5 ml (1 level tsp) ground cinnamon
75 g (3 oz) caster sugar
3 egg yolks
50 g (2 oz) granulated sugar

75 g (3 oz) softened butter
15 ml (1 tbsp) lemon juice
700 g (1½ lb) fresh apricots
15 ml (1 level tbsp) arrowroot
30 ml (2 tbsp) Amaretto di Saronno

Sift the flour and cinnamon on to a clean dry work surface. Make a well in the centre of the dry ingredients and in it place the caster sugar, egg yolks and butter. With the fingertips of one hand only, pinch the well ingredients together until blended. With the help of a palette knife gradually draw in the flour and knead lightly until just smooth. Wrap the pastry and chill for 30 minutes. On a lightly floured surface roll out the pastry and use to line a 24-cm (9½-inch) loose based fluted flan tin. Refrigerate for about 20 minutes to firm up the pastry. Prick the pastry base with a fork and fit a sheet of greaseproof paper into the flan case. Fill with baking beans. Bake at 200°C (400°F) mark 6 for about 12 minutes. Remove the beans and paper and return to the oven for a further 12 minutes, or until the pastry is golden brown and the base dried out. Cool the flan case then ease out of the tin and place on a serving plate.

Place granulated sugar in a stainless frying or sauté pan with the lemon juice and 300 ml (½ pint) water. Heat gently until the sugar dissolves then bring to the boil and bubble for 2 minutes, take off the heat. Halve and stone the apricots and add to the syrup. Bring slowly up to the boil and simmer gently until the fruit is *just* tender. Carefully lift the apricots out of the syrup using draining spoons; cool. Strain the juices into a small pan. Mix the arrowroot with a little water to form a smooth paste. Stir into the apricot juices with the Amaretto di Saronno. Bring slowly up to the boil, stirring all the time, and cook for 1 minute. Remove from the heat and allow to cool a little. Brush a little syrup over the base and sides of the cold flan case. Arrange the poached apricots in the flan case and spoon over the remaining cool syrup. When cold refrigerate the flan for up to 3 hours before serving. Serve with cream.

FREEZER NOTES

Do not freeze the salad or the chicken dish.

To freeze the Apricot Flan prepare the pastry case, bake blind then cool. Pack it into a rigid container and freeze until required. Leave to thaw for about 1 hour before completing as in Apricot Flan recipe.

COUNTDOWN

The day before: Prepare and bake the flan case, cool, then store in an airtight container until required.
The morning: Wash the chicory leaves, drain, dry and refrigerate in a polythene bag. Prepare the dressing, scoop out the melon balls, mix together then refrigerate tightly covered. Toast the nuts, cool, store in an airtight container. Cut wafer thin slices of brown bread and butter; arrange on a serving plate and cover tightly with cling film. Refrigerate.

Skin the chicken breasts and remove any fat; cover and refrigerate. Peel the potatoes, boil and mash. Complete the Duchesse Potatoes and pipe on to the baking sheet. Don't glaze or bake yet. Cover loosely and store in a cool place. Top and tail the French beans and cut into 2.5-cm (1-inch) lengths. Wash and drain well then refrigerate in a polythene bag. Prepare the syrup and poach the apricots. When tender, lift out of the syrup and lay flat on a large plate. Pour the syrup into a jug. Store both lightly covered in a cool place.
To serve at 8pm:
About 5pm: Complete the Apricot Flan, cool, then refrigerate until required. Place sherry in fridge.
6.45-ish: Preheat the oven to 180°C (350°F) mark 4. Brown the chicken pieces and complete the chicken dish. Put in the oven, on the lower shelf. Place white wines in fridge.
About 7.15: Glaze the potatoes and put in the oven to bake. Take the bread and butter out of the refrigerator.
7.45-ish: Steam the beans. Check the chicken, lower the oven temperature and keep chicken warm, covered. Thicken the chicken juices, cover and leave beside the stove; *don't* spoon over the chicken yet. Place Duchesse Potatoes in a serving dish and keep them warm uncovered.
8-ish: Spoon the Chicory & Melon Salad on to individual serving dishes. Warm the saffron sauce and spoon over the chicken at serving time. Serve the meal. Bring wines to table.

WINES FOR THE FOOD

White wine is more and more popular as an apéritif, and it would be possible to start with a crisp, dry white rioja. Otherwise start with *fino* sherry.

For the chicken dry Spanish white at its best will complement the saffron much loved in Spanish cooking. Ideal, both in colour and flavour, is Viña Tondonia yellowish with a full, smooth and fragrant vanilla nose to match the sweetness of the dish. Should you wish to maintain the Spanish theme, the best Spanish sweet white is Masia Bach's Extrisimo. Otherwise serve Amaretto di Saronno with the flan.

Prawn & Apple Salad/Kidneys Flamed with Brandy/Steamed Broccoli/Buttered New Carrots/Iced Lemon Mousse

PRAWN & APPLE SALAD

A crunchy refreshing salad. Once fresh mint is available, chop some and add to the salad with a little vinegar in place of the bottled variety.

150 ml (¼ pint)
unsweetened apple juice
5 ml (1 level tsp) fresh
garden mint in vinegar
salt and milled pepper
225 g (½ lb) peeled prawns

225 g (½ lb) crisp eating
apples
lettuce leaves
paprika pepper
hot toast to accompany

In a medium-sized mixing bowl whisk together the apple juice, mint and seasoning. Dry the prawns with kitchen paper. Polish the skins of the apples with a clean tea towel. Quarter, core and roughly chop the apples. Stir the prawns and apple into the dressing until well mixed. Cover tightly with cling film and refrigerate for several hours.

Wash the lettuce leaves, dry and shred finely. Place a little lettuce in six individual serving dishes. Spoon the prawn salad on top and dust with paprika. Serve with fingers of hot toast.

KIDNEYS FLAMED WITH BRANDY

If you're not sure whether your guests are kidney lovers, replace all or half the kidneys with strips of rump steak.

1.4 kg (3 lb) old potatoes
salt and milled pepper
90–120 (6–8 tbsp) milk
75 g (3 oz) butter
2 eggs
1.1 kg (2½ lb) lambs'
kidneys
225 g (½ lb) onion
225 g (½ lb) button
mushrooms

90 ml (6 tbsp) brandy
20 ml (4 level tsp)
wholegrain mustard
300 ml (½ pint) stock
2 bayleaves
10 ml (2 level tsp)
arrowroot
25 g (1 oz) fresh brown
breadcrumbs

Peel the potatoes and cut them into large chunks. Cover with cold salted water and bring to the boil; cover and boil until tender. Drain the potatoes well then mash with the milk, 25 g (1 oz) butter, one egg and seasoning. Beat well until smooth then cool slightly. Spoon into a piping bag fitted with a large star nozzle. Pipe the potato around the edge of a 2.3-litre (4-pint) shallow ovenproof dish.

Halve, skin and core the kidneys. Cut each kidney half into two or three pieces. Skin and roughly chop the onion; wipe the mushrooms and halve if large. Melt the remaining butter in a large frying pan. Add the onion and fry gently for 4–5 minutes. Increase the heat, add the kidneys and

brown quickly. Lower the heat, add the brandy and when it is slightly warm, ignite it with a match. Shake the pan gently until the flames subside. Stir in the mustard with the stock, bayleaves, seasoning and mushrooms. Bring to the boil.

Mix the arrowroot to a smooth paste with a little water. Off the heat stir this into the kidney mixture then bring up to the boil, stirring all the time; cook for 1 minute. Adjust seasoning; then carefully pour the kidney mixture into the centre of the potato lined dish. Sprinkle the crumbs over the kidneys. Lightly whisk the remaining egg with a little salt and brush over the potato. Stand the dish on a baking sheet and cook at 220°C (425°F) mark 7 for about 25 minutes. Serve with sliced buttered carrots and steamed broccoli.

STEAMED BROCCOLI

Lightly cooked broccoli perfectly offsets the richness of the kidneys.

900 g (2 lb) broccoli
salt and milled pepper

Trim off any thick tough stalks; divide the broccoli into florets then wash and drain well. Place a large metal sieve or colander over a pan of boiling salted water—neither should touch the water. Place the broccoli in the sieve or colander, stalks downward—the stalks will take longer to cook than the heads so they need to be closest to the source of heat. Cover with a tightly fitting lid or cover closely with foil. Steam for about 15 minutes or until the stalks are just tender. Season with salt and pepper. Arrange in a warmed serving dish, cover and keep warm.

BUTTERED NEW CARROTS

900 g (2 lb) small new
carrots
25 g (1 oz) butter

5 ml (1 level tsp) sugar
salt and milled pepper
chopped parsley

Scrub the carrots, trimming off the roots and tops. Place the carrots in a medium-sized saucepan and *just* cover with cold water. Add the butter, sugar and seasoning and bring to the boil. Cover the pan and simmer until the carrots are nearly tender: about 8 minutes. Uncover and boil rapidly until all the liquid evaporates and the carrots are glazed with a light butter/sugar coating. Shake the pan frequently to prevent the carrots sticking to the base. Spoon the carrots into a serving dish; sprinkle with parsley. Cover the dish and keep warm in a low oven.

ICED LEMON MOUSSE

A combination of mousse and ice cream, this tangy dessert needs only 10 minutes to soften in the refrigerator before serving.

5 ml (1 level tsp)
  powdered gelatine
3 eggs
125 g (4 oz) caster sugar
2 lemons

141-g (5-oz) carton
  natural yogurt
lemon twists
chopped pistachio nuts

Spoon 30 ml (2 tbsp) water in a small basin and sprinkle the gelatine over the surface. Leave to stand until the gelatine swells and becomes spongelike in texture.

Meanwhile separate the eggs and place the yolks in a deep mixing bowl; stir in the caster sugar. Finely grate the lemon rinds and add to the bowl. Whisk the egg yolks and sugar until really thick—it's best to use an electric whisk. Squeeze the juice from the lemons—there should be about 90 ml (6 tbsp)—and add a little at a time to the egg yolk mixture. Whisk well between each addition of lemon juice, keeping the mixture as thick as possible.

Dissolve the gelatine by standing the basin in which it is soaking in a pan of simmering water. When the gelatine is clear and liquid stir it into the lemon mixture. Stand the basin in a roasting tin of iced water and stir occasionally until the lemon mixture begins to set. Stir in the yogurt with one stiffly whisked egg white. Gently pour the mixture into six small ramekin dishes and freeze. When firm overwrap and return to the freezer. Ten minutes *only* before serving transfer the lemon mousse to the refrigerator. Decorate with lemon twists and chopped pistachio nuts for serving.

FREEZER NOTES

The Prawn & Apple Salad will not freeze satisfactorily. Cook and mash the potato for the kidney dish. Pipe around the baking dish, but don't glaze; freeze. Overwrap when firm and return to the freezer. When required, unwrap and leave to thaw at cool room temperature for 2 hours. Prepare the kidney mixture, glaze the potato and cook as before.

Freeze the Iced Lemon Mousse for up to 3 months.

COUNTDOWN

The day before: Prepare and freeze the Iced Lemon Mousse. When firm overwrap and return to the freezer. Place red wine upright in warm room to acclimatise.

The morning: Prepare the Prawn and Apple Salad, cover tightly and refrigerate. Wash the lettuce leaves, dry with kitchen paper and refrigerate in a polythene bag. Peel, cook and mash the potatoes; spoon or pipe around their baking dish. Prepare the kidney mixture and spoon into the centre of the dish. Cool slightly, sprinkle the crumbs over the kidneys but do not glaze the potato yet. When quite cold cover loosely and refrigerate until required. Scrub the carrots, trim; cover with cold water and store in a cool place. Chop a little parsley, refrigerate covered. Trim the broccoli, divide into florets then wash and drain well, refrigerate in polythene bags. Skin and chop pistachios; cover tightly.

To serve at 8pm:

About 7.20: Preheat the oven to 220°C (425°F) mark 7. Glaze the potatoes and put the kidneys into the oven to bake. Open red wine and decant to let it breathe. Place white and dessert wines in fridge to chill.

7.30-ish: Put the carrots on to cook; when nearly tender uncover and allow liquid to evaporate. Spoon into a serving dish, sprinkle with parsley, cover and keep warm. Put the broccoli on to steam; when cooked keep warm in a covered dish. Check the kidney dish.

Just before 8pm: Shred the lettuce leaves and arrange in individual serving dishes. Spoon the prawn salad on top and dust with paprika. Make the toast and serve the meal. Transfer the Iced Lemon Mousse to the refrigerator 10 minutes before serving. Decorate with lemon twists and pistachios.

WINES WITH THE FOOD

The starter is not an easy partner to wine, but if you make the attempt a flavoursome southern white would suit best. The Marqués de Murrieta '76 white rioja or Vernaccia di San Gimignano '80 are two which are not to be undermined.

Kidneys are an excellent foil for red wines of quality. A Côtes du Rhone or Mastroberardino's strapping Taurasi '77 would admirably complement the dish. Other options would include Australian, Californian or Chilean Cabernet Sauvignon, or red rioja.

Iced Lemon Mousse is a disincentive to wine, but do not deprive yourself of a luscious dessert wine to follow. Choose a Sauternes or Ruster Gewürztraminer Trockenbeerenauslese 1981 from Austria.

Asparagus Soup/Lamb with Rosemary & Garlic/Steamed Mange-tout/ Sliced Potatoes with Gruyère/
Pineapple & Kiwifruit Compote

CHILLED ASPARAGUS SOUP

Make this delicate soup from blanched asparagus or use green for a better finished appearance. The very thin stalks ('sprew') are excellent for soup making—you'll need to put several of the heads in each of the accompanying rolls.

700 g (1½ lb) stalks of asparagus	butter or margarine
salt and milled pepper	142-ml (5-fl oz) carton single cream
225 g (½ lb) onion	small brown uncut loaf
1.4 litres (2½ pints) chicken stock	lemon slices to garnish

Rinse each asparagus stalk. Cut off the heads and simmer very gently in salted water until just tender. Drain carefully and cool; cover and refrigerate until required. Scrape the remaining stalks with a potato peeler or knife to remove any scales; cut off the woody ends. Thinly slice the stalks and the onion.

Melt 50 g (2 oz) butter or margarine in a large saucepan. Add the asparagus and onion, cover and cook over a moderate heat for 5–10 minutes, or until beginning to soften. Add the stock and seasoning and bring to the boil. Cover and simmer for 30–40 minutes, or until the asparagus and onion are quite tender. Cool slightly then purée in an electric blender until smooth. Sieve if necessary. Cool, then stir in the cream and adjust seasoning. Cover and chill well before serving.

Cut thin slices of brown bread; butter, cut off the crusts and halve lengthwise. Roll asparagus heads inside each piece of bread; place on a serving plate, cover with cling film and refrigerate until required. Serve the soup well chilled, garnished with wafer thin lemon slices and accompanied by the asparagus rolls.

LAMB WITH ROSEMARY & GARLIC

Now is the time to enjoy young English lamb, simply roasted with garlic and rosemary. Choose a joint with only a thin covering of fat.

2 kg (4½ lb) leg lamb	50 g (2 oz) butter, softened
2 large cloves garlic	salt and milled pepper
15 ml (1 level tbsp) fresh chopped rosemary or 5 ml (1 level tsp) dried	30 ml (2 level tbsp) flour 400 ml (¾ pint) stock watercress sprigs to garnish

Score the surface of the lamb into a diamond pattern to the depth of about 3 mm (⅛ inch). Skin the cloves of garlic and cut them into wafer thin slices. Push the slices into the scored surface of the lamb. Mix the butter with the rosemary and seasoning and then spread all over the lamb. Place the joint in a shallow dish, cover tightly with cling film and refrigerate for at least 12 hours.

Uncover the lamb and transfer it to a medium-sized roasting tin. Place on the middle shelf in the oven and cook at 180°C (350°F) mark 4 for about 2¼ hours; baste occasionally as the fat begins to run. Pierce the joint with a fine skewer; when done the juices should run clear at first, then with a hint of red. Place the joint on a serving plate, cover loosely and keep warm in a low oven. Pour all excess fat out of the roasting tin leaving about 45 ml (3 tbsp) fat with the meat juices. Sprinkle the flour into the roasting tin and stir until evenly mixed. Cook over a gentle heat until well browned, stirring frequently. Add the stock and seasoning and bring to the boil, stirring. Simmer for 3–4 minutes, adjust seasoning. Serve the gravy separately and garnish the lamb with watercress.

STEAMED MANGE-TOUT

700 g (1½ lb) mange-tout
salt and milled pepper

Top and tail the pods and remove any side strings. Wash in cold water. Place in a colander or steamer placed over a pan of boiling, salted water. Cover and steam gently for about 5 minutes, or until they are just tender. Do not overcook or they will lose their colour and texture. Spoon into a serving dish, toss gently with salt and milled pepper. Cover and keep warm in a low oven.

SLICED POTATOES WITH GRUYÈRE

900 g (2 lb) old potatoes	nutmeg
25 g (1 oz) butter	568 ml (1 pint) milk, preferably not homogenised
125 g (4 oz) Gruyère cheese, grated	
salt and milled pepper	

Peel the potatoes then thinly slice. Do not soak them in cold water. Use a little of the butter to lightly grease a 1.4-litre (2½-pint) shallow ovenproof dish. In this, layer the potatoes and most of the cheese; season, adding a generous grating of nutmeg. Top with cheese and then pour over the milk which should just cover the potatoes. Dot the surface with the remaining butter. Stand the dish on a baking sheet and then place on the lower shelf in the oven. Cook at 180°C (350°F) mark 4 for about 2 hours, or until the potatoes are tender and most of the milk absorbed, the top golden brown.

Pineapple & Kiwifruit Compote

Pineapple and kiwifruit make a refreshing compote to end the meal. The natural sweetness of the dates and Grand Marnier should be sufficient, but have a bowl of sugar on the table for those with a sweet tooth.

1 medium-sized pineapple
4 ripe kiwifruit
12 fresh dates
60 ml (4 tbsp) Grand Marnier
toasted coconut to decorate

Cut the pineapple into 1-cm (½-inch) thick slices. Trim away the skin and stamp out the pineapple core; cut the flesh into large chunks. With a sharp knife trim the ends off the kiwifruit, then peel. Halve the fruits lengthwise and slice the flesh into half-moon shaped pieces. Halve and stone the dates and cut them into thick slices. In a large bowl mix the pineapple, kiwifruit and dates together and spoon over the Grand Marnier. Cover tightly with cling film and refrigerate for several hours. Sprinkle with coconut for serving.

Freezer Notes

Prepare and purée the soup. Freeze without the addition of cream. When required thaw at cool room temperature overnight, stir in the cream and refrigerate until required. Prepare the asparagus and brown bread rolls. Pack into a polythene bag or rigid container and freeze. Thaw, wrapped, at cool room temperature for about 2 hours.

When mange-tout are in season, prepare and blanch them in boiling water for 1 minute. Drain well then pack into polythene bags and freeze. Steam from frozen for about 5 minutes. The Sliced Potatoes with Gruyère, and Pineapple & Kiwifruit Compote will not freeze satisfactorily.

Countdown

The day before: Prepare the Asparagus Soup, cool, cover and chill. Cook the asparagus heads, cover and refrigerate. Score the lamb, push the sliced garlic into the surface and spread with the butter and rosemary mixture. Cover the joint tightly and refrigerate. Stand red wine to bring to room temperature.

In the morning: Cut the brown bread and butter; roll up with the asparagus heads inside. Place on a serving plate, cover tightly with cling film and refrigerate. Wash some watercress sprigs, dry on a kitchen paper, refrigerate in a polythene bag. Top and tail the mange-tout and remove any side strings. Wash and drain well, refrigerate in a polythene bag. Grate the Gruyère cheese, keep covered. Don't peel the potatoes yet. Prepare the Pineapple & Kiwifruit Compote; cover tightly with cling film and refrigerate. Toast the coconut, cool then store in an airtight container.

To serve at 8pm:
About 5.30: Preheat the oven to 180°C (350°F) mark 4. Put the lamb in the oven to cook; baste occasionally as the fat begins to run. Peel and slice the potatoes and layer with the milk and cheese in the baking dish. Stand the dish on a baking sheet and place on the lower shelf in the oven.
About 6pm: Place white wines in fridge to chill, open red wine and preferably decant.
7.45-ish: Take the asparagus rolls out of the refrigerator. Test the lamb. When cooked, place on a serving plate loosely covered; keep warm. Make the gravy, leave on the side of the stove. Check the potatoes.
8-ish: Ladle the soup into serving bowls and garnish with lemon slices. Serve with the asparagus rolls. Steam the mange-tout over a pan of salted water while serving the first course. Decorate the compote with the toasted coconut at serving time.

Wines with the Food

Aperitifs for this meal could suitably come from asparagus growing areas—the Loire or lower Rhineland. Most supermarkets now have reliable Kabinett or Landwein from Rheinhessen or Rheinpfalz. From the Loire Château Moncontour demisec Vouvray is particularly enjoyable.

With the lamb, choose flavourful claret or its equivalents like St Emilion or Pomerol of the 1973, 1976 or 1978 vintages; or the widely available blended clarets, Sandeman's, Harvey's No 1 or Mouton-Cadet. From other countries Franzia Cabernet Sauvignon or Christian Bros are excellent value from California, or from Italy, Villa Antinori Chianti Classico 1971 or Pio Cesare Barbaresco.

For dessert wine try sweet Vouvray.

JUNE

Serves 6

Fennel & Tomato Salad/Fresh Trout Mousse/Steamed Runner Beans/New Potatoes/Raspberry & Apple Torte/
Hazelnut Truffles (see page 92)

FENNEL & TOMATO SALAD

Blanch the fennel quickly to mellow the flavour and keep it crisp. The dressing will be absorbed better if it is added while the fennel is still warm. Walnut oil is expensive, but worth buying for its distinctive flavour.

90 ml (6 tbsp) vegetable oil or half vegetable, half walnut oil	12 black olives
	450 g (1 lb) Florence fennel
45 ml (3 tbsp) lemon juice	450 g (1 lb) ripe tomatoes
salt and milled pepper	

In a medium-sized mixing bowl, whisk the oils, lemon juice and seasoning together. Halve and stone the olives and add to the dressing. Snip off the feathery ends of the fennel and refrigerate them in a polythene bag. Thinly slice the fennel, discarding the roots. Blanch in boiling salted water for 2–3 minutes then drain. While it is still warm, stir into the dressing. Cool, cover tightly with cling film and refrigerate.

Skin and thinly slice the tomatoes; refrigerate covered. Just before serving, arrange the tomatoes and fennel mixture on individual serving plates. Snip the fennel tops over the tomatoes. Serve with the Scone Fingers.

WHOLEWHEAT SCONE FINGERS

The essence of good scone dough is speed and lightness of hand—never over-knead. The salad dressing is quite rich, so it is best to leave the fingers unbuttered.

125 g (4 oz) plain wholewheat flour	25 g (1 oz) butter or block margarine
5 ml (1 level tsp) baking powder	75 ml (5 level tbsp) natural yogurt
milk	grated Parmesan cheese

Mix the flour and baking powder well together. Cut and rub in the fat until the mixture resembles fine breadcrumbs. Stir in the yogurt and 15 ml (1 tbsp) water and knead lightly until just smooth. On a lightly floured surface, roll out the dough to an 18 × 10-cm (7 × 4-inch) oblong. Divide into strips about 5 × 2 cm (2 × ¾ inch). Place the dough strips on a lightly greased baking sheet, brush with milk and sprinkle lightly with Parmesan cheese. Bake at 230°C (450°F) mark 8 for 10–12 minutes, or until well risen and brown. Ease off the baking sheet and serve warm.

FRESH TROUT MOUSSE

These individual mousses are more substantial and richer than the light-as-air cold varieties, so the portions are not as small as they may seem. They are turned out on to croûtes to mop up all the delicious juices. Allow yourself plenty of time to make them—to get a fine enough texture you may need to mince the fish twice.

900 g (2 lb) fresh trout	salt and milled pepper
100 g (4 oz) onion	6 single fillets plaice—
1 clove garlic	about 450 g (1 lb) total
142-ml (5-fl oz) carton double cream	weight, ie fillets from 1½ fish
2 whole eggs	100 g (4 oz) butter
3 egg yolks	6 large slices brown bread
60 ml (4 tbsp) fresh chopped coriander	125 g (4 oz) carrots
	175 g (6 oz) peeled prawns

Cut off the heads and tails of the trout, open out along the underside, wash under running water and dry with kitchen paper. Place on a board fleshside down and press firmly along the backbone to completely flatten. The trout can then be turned over and the loosened bone gently eased out. Snip off any remaining fins and divide each fish into two fillets; skin and rinse each.

Roughly chop the onion; skin the garlic. Finely mince the trout, onion and garlic together and place in a bowl. Beat in the cream, whole eggs, egg yolks, 30 ml (2 tbsp) coriander and seasoning. Skin, rinse and dry the plaice fillets. Lightly butter six large, about 175 ml (6 fl oz), ramekin dishes. Push a plaice fillet into the base and up the sides of each dish. Fill with the trout mixture and fold the ends of the plaice over the top. Cover each dish with well-buttered foil and place in a roasting tin with water to come halfway up the sides. Bake at 170°C (325°F) mark 3 for about 40 minutes, or until just firm to the touch. Meanwhile, using a 9-cm (3½-inch) plain cutter, stamp out six rounds from the slices of bread. Place on a dry baking sheet and then bake on the top shelf of the oven for about 20 minutes. Cut the carrots into matchstick-sized pieces.

Five minutes before serving, melt the butter in a medium-sized saucepan, add the carrots, prawns and remaining coriander and cook gently for 3–4 minutes, stirring occasionally. Run a blunt-edged knife around the mousses to loosen them. Turn out each mousse on to a croûte and spoon over the butter mixture. Serve with runner beans and new potatoes.

STEAMED RUNNER BEANS

900 g (2 lb) runner beans
salt and milled pepper

Top and tail the beans and trim away the stringy sides. Slice into diagonal pieces, wash and drain. Steam over a pan of rapidly boiling salted water for about 12 minutes, or until just tender. Season.

RASPBERRY & APPLE TORTE

450 g (1 lb) eating apples
150 g (5 oz) butter or
  block margarine
450 g (1 lb) fresh
  raspberries
65 g (2½ oz) demerara
  sugar
5 ml (1 tsp) lemon juice

225 g (8 oz) plain flour
10 ml (2 level tsp) ground
  cinnamon
25 g (1 oz) icing sugar
1 egg, separated
natural yogurt to
  accompany

Peel, quarter, core and roughly chop apples. Melt 25 g (1 oz) butter in a medium-sized saucepan, then add the apples, raspberries and 50 g (2 oz) demerara sugar. Heat gently until the sugar dissolves. Increase the heat and cook, stirring, for about 10 minutes, or until the apples are soft and any excess moisture has been driven off. Turn the mixture into a bowl, stir in the lemon juice and cool.

Meanwhile, sift the flour and cinnamon into a mixing bowl. Cut and rub in the remaining fat until the mixture resembles fine breadcrumbs. Stir in the icing sugar. Mix the egg yolk with 45 ml (3 tbsp) water and stir into the pastry mixture; knead lightly until just smooth. Roll out two-thirds of the pastry and use to line a 24.5-cm (9½-inch) loose-based fluted flan tin.

Spoon in the cold raspberry and apple mixture and lattice with remaining pastry. Place on a baking sheet and bake at 200°C (400°F) mark 6 for about 15 minutes, or until the pastry is set but not browned.

Lightly whisk the egg white, brush over the pastry lattice and sprinkle with remaining demerara sugar. Return to the oven for a further 15–20 minutes, or until well browned. Cool slightly, then ease out of the tin and place on a serving plate. Serve well chilled with a little natural yogurt if wished.

FREEZER NOTES

Do not freeze the Fennel & Tomato Salad. Freeze the baked scones; thaw and reheat for serving. The raw trout mixture can be frozen; thaw for about 4 hours then bake. Pack and freeze the torte; thaw and chill before serving.

COUNTDOWN

The day before: Prepare the pastry for the torte, wrap in cling film and refrigerate. Prepare the raspberry and apple filling and refrigerate. Make the Hazelnut Truffles and when they are firm, overwrap and refrigerate.

The morning: Take the pastry out of the refrigerator to soften. Make the dressing for the Fennel & Tomato Salad; blanch the fennel and stir into the dressing. Cool, cover and refrigerate. Skin and slice the tomatoes; refrigerate covered. Make the Wholewheat Scone Fingers: cool and store in an airtight container. Prepare the Fresh Trout Mousse, spoon into their cooking dishes, cover and refrigerate. Stamp out the bread rounds and wrap in cling film. Pare the carrots and cut into matchsticks; cover with cold water and store in a cool place. Prepare the runner beans; wash, drain and refrigerate in a polythene bag. Scrub 900 g (2 lb) small new potatoes; cover with cold water. Make the Raspberry & Apple Torte; bake then cool slightly before removing from the tin; chill.

To serve at 8pm:
7-ish: Preheat the oven to 170°C (325°F) mark 3. Place the scones on a baking sheet, loosely covered with foil, ready to reheat. Arrange the Fennel & Tomato Salad on serving plates; cover. Chill white wine in fridge.

About 7.15: Put the fish mousses into the oven to cook. A little later, put the bread into the oven to brown.

About 7.30: Put the new potatoes on to boil. When cooked, drain, keep warm, covered, in a low oven. Put the beans on to steam. When tender, season, keep warm, covered, in a low oven. Reheat the scones for 5–10 minutes on the bottom shelf in the oven. Check the mousses. When they are set, leave in the low oven to keep warm, but don't turn out.

8-ish: Bring wine to table in bucket of iced water. Serve the first course. While eating the salad, leave the butter, carrot and prawn mixture to cook over a low heat. Turn out the mousses on to the croûtes at serving time. Spoon over the butter and prawn mixture. Remember to take the truffles out of the refrigerator about 30 minutes before serving to serve with coffee.

WINES WITH THE FOOD

For the first two courses, choose a dry white with more than crispness to it: Savennières, Sancerre or Pouilly Fumé, or, perhaps best of all, Alsatian Riesling. It would be possible to maintain the Alsatian theme with the sweet. An adventurous talking point would be a Gewürztraminer Vendange Tardive. Otherwise take a nip of Alsatian framboise eau-de-vie.

One other more modest but nonetheless interesting possibility would be to offer a sweetish variation on kir as a palate-cleaning finish to the meal—liqueur crème de framboise in sparkling Vouvray.

Cauliflower & Courgette Tartlets/Duckling Roulades with Peaches/Minted Peas/Sliced New Potatoes/Currant Kisel

CAULIFLOWER & COURGETTE TARTLETS

This refreshing blend of cauliflower and courgette marinaded in a tarragon dressing perfectly offsets the slight richness of the duckling that follows. The pastry can be baked in a 20.5-cm (8-inch) flan tin, although it takes a little longer to cook. Cut into wedges, though, this starter is not so impressive as it is served in individual pastry shells.

75 ml (5 tbsp) dry white wine	225 g (½ lb) trimmed cauliflower
30 ml (2 tbsp) vegetable oil	175 g (6 oz) baby courgettes
5 ml (1 level tsp) chopped fresh tarragon or 1.25 ml (¼ level tsp) dried	75 g (3 oz) plain flour 25 g (1 oz) plain wholemeal flour
1 clove garlic	75 g (3 oz) butter
salt and milled pepper	

In a medium-sized bowl whisk together the wine, oil, tarragon, crushed garlic and seasoning. Cut the cauliflower into small florets. Blanch it in boiling salted water for 1 minute only. Drain well, then while still hot stir into the dressing. Slice the courgettes into thin rings and add to the bowl, stirring gently to mix. When cold cover with clingfilm and refrigerate for several hours or overnight.

Mix the flours together with a pinch of salt. Rub in the butter until the mixture resembles fine breadcrumbs then bind to a dough with 15–30 ml (1–2 tbsp) water. Knead the pastry lightly until just smooth then roll out and use to line six 7.5-cm (3-inch) individual flan cases. Bake blind at 200°C (400°F) mark 6 for about 15 minutes until just set and tinged with colour. Remove the paper and baking beans and return to the oven for a further 8–10 minutes or until well browned. Cool slightly, ease cases out of tins and leave until completely cool. Store in an airtight container until required. Just before serving place the pastry cases on individual plates and spoon in the cauliflower and courgette salad.

DUCKLING ROULADES WITH PEACHES

Boning the duckling and removing the fat and skin before cooking does away with the problem of carving the birds. Serve the fat in crisply grilled fingers with drinks. Don't keep these for more than 2–3 days. Duckling portions can be found in most supermarkets and many butchers' shops. Alternatively, you could joint three duckling yourself, using the breast portions for this recipe and the legs for a pâté or casserole. Bat out the flesh thinly otherwise it's hard to make neat roulades. The stuffing will ooze out a little during the cooking and the crumbs help to thicken the juices in the dish.

6 duckling wing portions, about 350 g (12 oz) each	25 g (1 oz) hazelnuts 2 firm ripe peaches
slices onion, carrot, bayleaf for flavouring	65 g (2½ oz) butter 30 ml (2 tbsp) brandy
salt and milled pepper	50 g (2 oz) fresh brown breadcrumbs
50 g (2 oz) onion	30 ml (2 level tbsp) flour

Ease the skin and fat together off each duckling portion. Snip the fat into thin fingers and grill until golden and crisp. Cool, then store in an airtight container in the refrigerator for 2–3 days. Serve with drinks.

Carefully fillet the duckling flesh in one piece away from the breast bone. Place the breast meat between sheets of clingfilm and bat out *thinly*; cover and refrigerate. Cut any remaining duckling flesh off the wing bones and chop finely. Place the bones in a saucepan with the flavourings and seasoning. *Just* cover with water, bring to the boil. Simmer uncovered for 30–40 minutes, or until about 300 ml (½ pint) stock remains. Strain off the stock and reserve.

Meanwhile finely chop the onion, roughly chop the hazelnuts, skin and chop the peaches. Melt 25 g (1 oz) butter and fry the onion, chopped duckling flesh and hazelnuts for 3–4 minutes, turning frequently. Stir in the peaches and fry for a few minutes longer or until the peaches are beginning to soften. Remove from the heat and stir in the brandy, breadcrumbs and seasoning, cool. Divide the cold stuffing between the duckling fillets and roll them up tightly. Secure each one with the two wooden cocktail sticks and then halve each roll. Sprinkle the flour over the rolls. Melt the remaining butter in a large shallow flameproof casserole. Add the duckling rolls and brown lightly all over. Sprinkle in any remaining flour and then pour in 300 ml (½ pint) duckling stock. Season. Bring to the boil, cover and bake at 180°C (350°F) mark 4 for about 40 minutes, or until the duckling is tender. Adjust seasoning and skim the juices before serving with sliced new potatoes and fresh peas.

MINTED PEAS

Mint grows in abundance now and is the perfect accompaniment for fresh peas—a little more trouble to prepare than frozen, but worth it for their superior flavour and crispness.

1.4–1.8 kg (3–4 lb) fresh peas in the pod	salt and milled pepper large sprig of mint

Pod the peas; wash in cold water then drain. Bring a large pan of salted water to the boil. Add the mint and peas and boil for about 10 minutes, or until the peas are just tender. Drain; season and keep warm in a covered dish.

SLICED NEW POTATOES

Steaming is a sadly neglected method of cooking—potatoes can be cooked to perfection this way with little danger of disintegration. Make sure that the colander is tightly covered with foil to prevent the steam escaping.

900 g (2 lb) medium-sized	*salt and milled pepper*
new potatoes	*40 g (1½ oz) butter*

Scrape or peel the potatoes; wash. Place the potatoes in a colander over a pan of steaming salted water. Cover and steam until tender—about 20 minutes. Thickly slice the potatoes and place in a serving dish. Dot with butter, season with black pepper. Cover the potatoes and keep warm.

CURRANT KISEL

450 g (1 lb) blackcurrants	*finely grated rind ½ lemon*
450 g (1 lb) redcurrants	*15 ml (3 level tsp)*
125–175 g (4–6 oz) soft	*arrowroot*
light brown sugar	*single cream to accompany*

Use a fork to strip the blackcurrants and redcurrants off their stalks. Place the fruit in a saucepan with the lemon rind and 300 ml (½ pint) water. Bring slowly to the boil and then simmer gently until the fruits pop. Stir in the sugar until dissolved—taste for sweetness—then remove the pan from the heat. Mix the arrowroot to a smooth paste with a little water, stir into the fruit mixture. Return to the heat and bring to the boil, stirring all the time. Cook for 1 minute only, then pour out into a bowl and leave to cool. When cold cover with clingfilm and refrigerate for several hours before serving. Serve with cream.

FREEZER NOTES

Make and bake the tartlet cases; cool then pack into rigid container and freeze. When required place the frozen pastry cases on a baking sheet; cover loosely with foil and refresh in the oven set at 180°C (350°F) mark 4 for about 10 minutes, cool. The cauliflower and courgette mixture will not freeze satisfactorily. Using fresh duckling portions only, bone the wing portions. Prepare the roulades as directed, brown, add the stock but don't bake yet. Cool quickly; pack and freeze. When required thaw at cool room temperature overnight. Place in the refrigerator until required, then bake as directed. Make the Currant Kisel, cool, pack and freeze. Leave to thaw at cool room temperature for about 6 hours; stir lightly then cover and refrigerate until required.

COUNTDOWN

The day before: Prepare the pastry, then roll it out and use to line the tartlet cases. Bake blind as directed. Make and bake the tartlet cases. When quite cold store in an airtight container. Prepare the cauliflower and courgette salad for the tartlets; cover and refrigerate. Prepare the Currant Kisel; cool, cover with clingfilm and refrigerate.
The morning: Fillet the duckling flesh off the bone; bat out thinly. Prepare the stock, strain, cool and refrigerate. Prepare the stuffing for the roulades, cool. Roll up the stuffing inside the duckling pieces and secure with wooden cocktail sticks—don't sprinkle with flour yet. Cover and refrigerate. Pod the peas, wash, drain and refrigerate in a polythene bag. Scrape the potatoes, cover with cold water and store in a cool place.
To serve at 8pm:
7-ish: Preheat the oven to 180°C (350°F) mark 4. Sprinkle the duckling roulades with flour then brown them. Complete the duckling dish, put into the oven to bake. Take the cauliflower and courgette mixture out of the refrigerator. Put white and apéritif wines in fridge to chill. Open red wine and set in dining room.
About 7.30: Put the potatoes on to steam. When tender, slice and keep warm, covered. Boil the peas until tender, drain, keep warm, covered. Check the duckling roulades, skim the juices.
8-ish: Spoon the cauliflower and courgette mixture into the flan cases.
    Serve the meal.

WINES WITH THE FOOD

The fashion is for crisp white wine as an apéritif, but if you wish the wine also to accompany this first course it will need to be fruity, though dry. Nothing too sharp or austere will suit the flavours of the tartlets. That would usually suggest, for example, Sauvignon from the Bordeaux region or from California rather than from the Loire. There are also fruity and gulpable young red wines to serve cool or chilled which are attractive too. The classic light young red for cool drinking is Beaujolais. For the Duckling Roulades, which are neither fatty nor too strongly flavoured a perfect accompaniment is expensive.

A classy Alsatian Tokay would be successful with the sweet. The Currant Kisel is an occasion for a small glass of Crème de Cassis blackcurrant liqueur rather than wine. The bottle is a good investment: at other times it can be used to flavour dry white or sparkling wine to make those delicious summer apéritifs, Kir and Kir Royal.

AUGUST

Serves 6

Seafood Tomatoes/Veal Chops with Spinach Purée/New Potatoes/ Radicchio & Alfalfa Salad/Almond Peach Brûlée/ Hazelnut Crisps (see page 100)

SEAFOOD TOMATOES

Smoked mackerel or trout fillets make a good alternative filling.

6 medium-sized tomatoes, about 125 g (4 oz) each	salt and milled pepper
50 g (2 oz) long grain rice	20 ml (4 level tsp) creamed horseradish or mayonnaise
50 g (2 oz) smoked salmon pieces	30 ml (2 level tbsp) chopped parsley
50 g (2 oz) cooked, peeled prawns	pinch sugar

Peel the tomatoes by plunging them into boiling water for 10–15 seconds (depending on ripeness). Lift them out immediately and place in a bowl of cold water. Carefully peel off the skins. If some skins are more difficult to remove, repeat the process. Cut a thin slice from the base (opposite stalk end) of each tomato, and reserve. With a small teaspoon or grapefruit knife, and taking care not to pierce the outer shell, scoop out the tomato centres leaving them completely hollow. Push the tomato pulp through a nylon sieve to extract the juices. Reserve.

Cook the rice in plenty of boiling, salted water for 10 minutes, or until just tender. Drain well, running cold water over the rice to stop it cooking further. Cool. Roughly chop the smoked salmon and prawns. Mix together with the rice, 10 ml (2 level tsp) creamed horseradish, 15 ml (1 level tbsp) parsley and seasoning. Season the tomato shells on the inside with salt and pepper. Pack the rice mixture into the tomatoes, piling it up well. Whisk the remaining horseradish or mayonnaise into the reserved tomato juice. Season with salt and pepper and a pinch of sugar. To serve the tomatoes, place on individual serving plates. Spoon over the dressing and garnish with remaining chopped parsley and reserved tomato tops.

VEAL CHOPS WITH SPINACH PURÉE

Pork chops, boned then batted out lightly, would be an excellent substitute for the veal. When available, sorrel could be used as an alternative to the spinach: 50 g (2 oz) chopped and liquidised with the veal juices will produce a delicate sweet/sour sauce for the chops.

6 veal chops, about 175 g (6 oz) each	100 g (4 oz) butter
2 lemons	2.5 ml ($\frac{1}{2}$ level tsp) grated nutmeg
150 ml ($\frac{1}{4}$ pint) dry Vermouth	75 g (3 oz) leek or a small bunch spring onions
1 large clove garlic	1 egg
salt and milled pepper	30 ml (2 tbsp) vegetable oil
225 g (8 oz) fresh spinach	

Place trimmed chops in a large, shallow dish. Whisk together the finely grated rind of both lemons with 90 ml (6 tbsp) strained juice, the Vermouth, crushed garlic and seasoning. Pour over the chops. Cover and marinate in a cool place overnight. Pull off any tough stalks from the spinach. Wash well in several changes of cold water. Drain. Cook covered in a large saucepan without any extra water for 3–4 minutes. Press well between two plates to extract as much liquid as possible. Finely chop. Sauté the spinach with 25 g (1 oz) butter and nutmeg for 1–2 minutes to drive off any excess moisture. Transfer to a bowl. Cool and cover.

Prepare the garnish. Wash and trim the leeks or spring onions. Cut in half lengthwise. With cut surface downwards cut the leeks or spring onions into very thin shreds. Cut across into matchstick lengths. Blanch in boiling water for 1 minute. Drain into a sieve and run cold water over the leeks to refresh them. Drain well. Cover and refrigerate. Boil the egg for 10 minutes. Cool quickly under running cold water to prevent a black line forming round the yolk. Shell and chop finely. Cover and refrigerate. Remove chops from marinade. Drain well. Pat dry with kitchen paper. Heat the oil with 50 g (2 oz) butter in a large sauté pan till foaming. Brown the chops well on both sides, one or two at a time. Place in a single layer in one or two shallow ovenproof dishes. Pour the marinade into the sauté pan. Bring to the boil, stirring any sediment from the base. Strain over the chops. Cover tightly and cook at 180°C (350°F) mark 4 for about 50 minutes, or until chops are tender. Remove veal from oven and skim off fat. Pour off the pan juices into a blender goblet. Return veal, tightly covered, to a lower oven — 150°C (300°F) mark 2. Purée the spinach mixture with reserved pan juices until smooth. Simmer gently in a small saucepan, whisking in the remaining butter. Season. Pour a third of the purée on to the base of a large serving plate. Arrange the veal chops on top. Garnish with the chopped egg and shredded leek or spring onion. Serve the remaining purée separately. Serve with Sliced New Potatoes (page 115).

RADICCHIO AND ALFALFA SALAD

If radicchio is unobtainable use 350 g (12 oz) thinly shredded red cabbage.

2 heads radicchio	1 small clove garlic, crushed
50–75 g (2–3 oz) alfalfa sprouts	1.25 ml ($\frac{1}{4}$ level tsp) sugar
90 ml (6 tbsp) salad oil	15 ml (1 tbsp) single cream, optional
30 ml (2 tbsp) white wine vinegar	salt and milled pepper

Tear the radicchio into bite-sized pieces. Wash, drain and pat dry on kitchen paper. Wash and dry the alfalfa sprouts. Mix the alfalfa and radicchio together and refrigerate in a large polythene bag. Whisk together the remaining ingredients. Season well. Toss with the radicchio and alfalfa. Serve.

ALMOND PEACH BRÛLÉE

If the peaches are under-ripe poach them gently in sugar syrup for 10–12 minutes until tender. Skin and cool.

6 large, ripe peaches	*30 ml (2 level tbsp) icing*
30 ml (2 tbsp) lemon juice	*sugar*
142-ml (5-fl oz) carton	*142-ml (5-fl oz) carton*
double cream	*soured cream*
30 ml (2 tbsp) Amaretto di	*90–120 ml (6–8 level*
Saronno or few drops	*tbsp) demerara sugar*
almond essence	

Peel the peaches by dipping them in boiling water for 30 seconds. Plunge immediately into cold water. Carefully peel off skins. Cut the peaches in half. Twist to separate, remove stones. Thinly slice the flesh. Toss in lemon juice. Whip the double cream with the icing sugar until it just holds its shape. Gradually whisk in the liqueur or almond essence. Fold in the soured cream and peach slices. Divide this mixture between six 150-ml ($\frac{1}{4}$-pint) ramekin dishes. Cover and chill overnight.

Sprinkle the demerara sugar on top, enough to form a complete covering. Place under a hot grill for 3–4 minutes until the sugar has caramelised. Chill thoroughly for about 1 hour before serving with Hazelnut Crisps (see page 100).

FREEZER NOTES

If the prawns and smoked salmon are fresh (ie not previously frozen) then the filling for the Seafood Tomatoes may be frozen. Defrost overnight in the refrigerator. Stir well before spooning into prepared tomatoes.

The veal chops with spinach purée will not freeze well when completed. Spinach may be frozen separately before being puréed. Boil as directed, press to extract moisture, then freeze. Thaw before use.

Blanch new potatoes in boiling, salted water for 5 minutes. Cool, drain well and freeze. Defrost for 1–2 hours, steam over a pan of simmering water.

COUNTDOWN

The day before: Skin and hollow out the tomatoes. Place upside down on a flat plate with reserved tops. Cover tightly and refrigerate. Prepare the filling. Keep refrigerated in a polythene bag. Make the dressing. Keep in a cool place. Place the chops in the marinade. Cover and keep in a cool place. Prepare, cook and sauté the spinach. Cool, cover and refrigerate. Prepare the egg and leek garnish. Refrigerate in a polythene bag. Prepare the peach and soured cream mixture. Spoon into ramekin dishes. Cover and chill overnight. Make and bake the Hazelnut Crisps; when cold store in an airtight container.

On the day: Wash the potatoes well. Pat dry. Cover and keep in a cool place. Wash and dry the radicchio and alfalfa sprouts. Keep refrigerated in polythene bags. Make the salad dressing.

To serve at 8pm:

6.30pm: Caramelise the Almond Peach Brûlées, return to the refrigerator.

6.45pm: Brown the chops. Place in oven with marinade.

7pm: Fill the tomatoes. Do not spoon dressing over yet. Cover and keep in a cool place. Do not refrigerate again.

7.30-ish: Put a pan of salted water on to boil for the potatoes.

7.45pm: Strain juices from veal. Cover dish tightly and return veal to oven reset at 150°C (300°F) mark 2. Purée juices with spinach. Reheat gently with remaining butter.

Keep warm, tightly covered, in a low oven.

8pm: Place the tomatoes on individual serving plates. Spoon dressing over tomatoes. Garnish with parsley and reserved tops to serve. Toss Radicchio and Alfalfa Salad with the well-whisked dressing at serving time.

WINES FOR THE FOOD

This meal has a predominantly Italian flavour and so provides an opportunity to sample some first class Italians. Italian apéritif wines which will certainly not offend with the starter are the widely available Frascati and less common but very similar Marino. Romans drink them with everything, and most high street shops will be able to supply them. For a little more character and fuller body I would suggest the rather soft and bland Soave—the widely stocked Bolla is very fair. The veal chops are originally a Florentine dish, so the wine preferred is a Tuscan chianti. Lemon is quite strong in the dish, so one wants a wine with the guts to put up a fight. Your chianti should at least be a *classico* — 1977, 1978, 1979 or 1981 vintages.

The perfect accompaniment to the dessert would be for a glass of Amaretto di Saronno liqueur, or Prunelle de Bourgogne, which has been likened to liquid marzipan.

SEPTEMBER

Serves 6

Okra Vinaigrette/Pigeon with Juniper/Braised Celery/Crumbed Potatoes/
Hot Blackberry Soufflés/Lemon Fork Biscuits (see page 99)

OKRA VINAIGRETTE

When buying okra, look for small, clean dark green pods. Quickly blanched courgettes or leeks can also be used.

450 g (1 lb) small okra
1 small red pepper about 75 g (3 oz)
75 ml (5 tbsp) white wine vinegar
100 ml (4 fl oz) vegetable oil

2.5 ml (½ level tsp) sugar
2.5 ml (½ level tsp) each chopped parsley, chives and thyme
salt and milled pepper
lettuce to garnish

Top and tail the okra. Trim any damaged pods. Halve, remove the seeds and finely chop the pepper. Cook the vegetables in boiling, salted water for about 3 minutes or until *just* tender. Drain well. In a large bowl, whisk together the remaining ingredients. While the okra and pepper are still warm, stir in the dressing. Cool, cover tightly with clingfilm and chill. To serve, check seasoning, toss well and spoon on to lettuce-lined plates.

PIGEON WITH JUNIPER

20 ml (4 level tsp) juniper berries
125 g (4 oz) unsalted butter
6 wood pigeons
slices of onion and carrot
bayleaf
6 peppercorns

salt and milled pepper
125 g (4 oz) thinly sliced streaky bacon, rinded
700 g (1½ lb) button onions
45 ml (3 level tbsp) flour
15 ml (1 level tbsp) tomato paste
1 large clove garlic

Finely crush the juniper berries in a mortar and pestle or in a sturdy mixing bowl with the end of a rolling pin, then beat with the butter until well mixed. With poultry shears or sharp scissors, remove the wings and backbone from each pigeon, in one piece if possible. Rub the juniper butter over the pigeon breasts, cover and marinate for 30 minutes. Place the wings and backbones in a saucepan with just enough cold water to cover. Add the carrot, onion, bayleaf and peppercorns with a little salt. Bring to the boil and simmer, covered, for at least 30 minutes; strain. Return to uncovered saucepan and reduce by boiling to 300 ml (½ pint).

Halve six rashers of bacon and roll up tightly; reserve. Roughly chop the remainder. Soak the onions in warm water for about 20 minutes, then peel and trim the hairy root ends. In a large, deep flameproof casserole, brown the pigeon breasts well on all sides; remove from the casserole

and set aside. In the same pan, sauté the onions and chopped bacon until browned. Lift out with draining spoons; reserve. Stir in the flour and tomato paste. Cook, stirring, for 1–2 minutes, until coloured. Add 300 ml (½ pint) reserved stock and the crushed garlic. Bring to the boil, stirring. Return the pigeon breasts to the casserole, cover tightly and cook at 170°C (325°F) mark 3 for 1 hour. Add the bacon rolls, onions and chopped bacon. Baste well with the juices, re-cover and cook for a further 45 minutes. Test the pigeon with a skewer; it should slide into the flesh easily. When cooked, place with the onions and bacon rolls in a large serving dish. Keep warm, covered, in a low oven. Sieve the casserole juices into a small saucepan, stir in the juices from the braised celery (see below) and reduce by boiling until syrupy; adjust seasoning. Spoon some of the juices over the pigeon breasts and garnish with snipped celery tops. Serve the remaining juices separately.

BRAISED CELERY

1.1 kg (2½ lb) celery (with tops)
30 ml (2 tbsp) vegetable oil

1 bayleaf
300 ml (½ pint) light stock
salt and milled pepper

Wash the celery well. Cut into 5-cm (2-inch) lengths and reserve the leafy green tops for garnish. Heat the oil in a large flameproof casserole. Sauté the celery and bayleaf for 2–3 minutes, add the stock and seasoning, and bring to the boil. Cover tightly and cook at 170°C (325°F) mark 3 for 25–30 minutes; it should retain some bite. Strain the juices and add to the pigeon juices. Adjust seasoning to serve.

CRUMBED POTATOES

1.4 kg (3 lb) old potatoes
salt and milled pepper
45 ml (3 level tbsp) flour
2 eggs, beaten

100 g (4 oz) dried white breadcrumbs
45 ml (3 tbsp) oil

Wash and peel the potatoes. Cut into 2-cm (1-inch) dice. Cook in boiling salted water for 2 minutes only. Drain well. Have ready two large bowls, one containing flour, the other, the beaten eggs. Spread the breadcrumbs out on a large shallow dish. Toss the potatoes in the flour until well coated; lift out with a slotted spoon. Coat well with beaten egg and finally toss in the breadcrumbs. Shake in a colander to remove excess crumbs. Heat the oil in a large roasting tin, add the potatoes and stir over a high heat until beginning to brown. Transfer to the oven. Cook at 170°C (325°F) mark 3 for about 1½ hours, stirring occasionally.

HOT BLACKBERRY SOUFFLÉS

350 g (12 oz) blackberries
75 g (3 oz) caster sugar
Kirsch
20 ml (4 level tsp)
  cornflour
200 ml (7 fl oz) milk

few drops vanilla essence
15 g (½ oz) butter
3 eggs, separated
icing sugar
single cream to serve

Place the blackberries in a saucepan with 50 g (2 oz) sugar. Cover and cook over a gentle heat until very soft, about 10–15 minutes. Pour into a blender goblet with 30 ml (2 tbsp) Kirsch and purée until smooth. Push through a nylon sieve to remove pips. Spoon into six 150 ml (5 fl oz) ramekin dishes; cool. Mix the cornflour to a smooth paste with 30 ml (2 tbsp) milk. Bring the remaining milk, sugar and vanilla essence to the boil. Stir in the cornflour paste. Return to the boil, stirring all the time. Cook for 1–2 minutes. Off the heat, beat in the butter and egg yolks. Turn into a bowl, cover with damp greaseproof paper and cool.

Whisk the egg whites until stiff but not dry. Stir one small spoonful of egg white into the custard mixture, then gently fold in the remainder. Divide the soufflé mixture between the ramekins. Cover, and freeze at once until solid, preferably overnight. Unwrap, cook from frozen at 190°C (375°F) mark 5 for about 35 minutes, until well risen, golden brown and just firm to the touch. Dust with icing sugar, and serve immediately. The soufflés can be served with single cream to which 5 ml (1 tsp) icing sugar and 30 ml (2 tbsp) Kirsch have been added.

Serve with Lemon Fork Biscuits (page 99).

WINES WITH THE FOOD

Wine is seldom recommended with vinaigrette salads, but it is always possible to substitute wine for wine vinegar in mixing the dressing, and to drink on unperturbed. Okra is another challenge. One solution would be very inexpensive red—Moroccan Tarik, a deep purple wine with a spicy bouquet and rich fruity flavour which would drink easily with okra, and probably go on satisfactorily with the pigeons as well.

Pigeons, being rather fiddly to eat, require easy drinking. Most of the classic red wines would suit well—claret, Chianti Classico, Cabernet Sauvignon wines from the New World and equivalents.

The blackberry soufflés, if they are to be accompanied by a dessert wine, need a full-flavoured and powerful one. Try the 1964 Moulin Touchais from Anjou or Apetloner Gewürztraminer Beerenauslese 1981 from Austria. Either is better served lightly chilled.

An alternative is to finish with port: not necessarily traditional vintage which is expensive and requires decanting. Late-bottled (1978) vintage ports at not too great a price are available and are rich, ripe and fruity.

COUNTDOWN

The day before: Top and tail the okra, de-seed and finely chop the red pepper; refrigerate in polythene bags. Whisk together the dressing ingredients; keep in a cool place. Soak and peel the onions, pat dry with absorbent kitchen paper and refrigerate in a polythene bag. Prepare the potatoes and coat in breadcrumbs. Place on a flat baking sheet in a single layer. Cover loosely with clingfilm and keep in a cool place. Make the soufflés and freeze. Prepare the biscuits. When cold pack into an airtight container.

On the day: Cook the okra and pepper. Toss in the dressing, cover and refrigerate; stir occasionally. Wash lettuce and dry with absorbent kitchen paper; refrigerate in a polythene bag. Make the stock. Brown the breasts, and prepare, but don't cook the casserole. Cover tightly and keep refrigerated. Sauté the celery in oil, add the stock and seasoning; cover and keep in a cool place. Mix the single cream, icing sugar and Kirsch together; cover and refrigerate. Place red wine in warm room to come to serving temperature.

To serve at 8pm:
5.30pm: Heat oven to 170°C (325°F) mark 3.
5.45pm: Bring pigeon casserole to the boil. Place in the preheated oven.
About 6.15pm: Brown the potatoes in the oil. Place in top of oven. Open red wines and decant if you wish.
About 6.45pm: Add bacon rolls, onions and chopped bacon to the casserole. Take okra out of fridge.
7pm: Bring the braised celery to the boil. Place in oven below the casserole.
7.45pm: Place the pigeon breasts, onion and bacon rolls on a large serving dish. Keep warm, covered, in a low oven. Strain juices into saucepan, stir in the juices from the celery, cover and keep warm. Reduce all the liquid by boiling. Keep warm over a low heat; adjust seasoning. Place dessert wines in the fridge to chill.
8pm: Spoon Okra Vinaigrette on to lettuce-lined plates and serve. Don't forget to turn the oven up to 190°C (375°F) mark 5 after the main course has been served. Unwrap the soufflés and bake for about 30 minutes. Serve at once.

FREEZER NOTES

The Okra Vinaigrette will not freeze satisfactorily. Pigeons can be frozen for up to 8 months. Make sure that they haven't been previously frozen when you buy them. When required, unwrap and thaw in the refrigerator overnight. Cook within 24 hours. Open freeze the Crumbed Potatoes before frying and baking. Pack into polythene bags. Cook from frozen. The frozen blackberry soufflés will keep, frozen, for 4–6 months.

OCTOBER

Ramekins of Baked Crab/Marinated Beef with Mushrooms/Cauliflower with Tomato/Brown Rice Pilaff/
Apricot & Orange Fool/Brandy Snap Baskets (see page 97)

RAMEKINS OF BAKED CRAB

The yogurt and mustard perfectly offset the richness of the crabmeat. Serve only small portions, as we have here, to stimulate the appetite for the courses to follow.

50 g (2 oz) onion	*10 ml (2 level tsp) French*
25 g (1 oz) butter or	*mustard*
margarine	*141-g (5-oz) carton*
225 g (½ lb) white	*natural yogurt*
crabmeat or white and	*45 ml (3 tbsp) single cream*
brown mixed	*or milk*
50 g (2 oz) fresh brown	*salt*
breadcrumbs	*about 40 g (1½ oz)*
cayenne pepper	*Cheddar cheese*

Finely chop the onion and fry in the butter or margarine until golden brown. Flake the crabmeat, taking care to remove any membranes or shell particles. Mix the onion, crabmeat and breadcrumbs well together. Stir in the mustard with the yogurt and cream. Sprinkle generously with cayenne pepper, then add salt to taste. Spoon the mixture into 6 individual ramekin dishes. Grate the cheese thinly over the surface of each dish. Stand the dishes on a baking sheet. Place on the top shelf in the oven and cook at 170°C (325°F) mark 3 for 25–30 minutes, or until really hot. Serve with crispbreads.

MARINATED BEEF WITH MUSHROOMS

For a cheaper alternative to rump steak use good quality braising steak. It'll need longer cooking—about 1 hour—so if the juices reduce too much add 150 ml (¼ pint) brown stock.

900 g (2 lb) rump steak	*400 ml (¾ pint) red wine*
225 g (½ lb) onion, skinned	*60 ml (4 tbsp) oil*
and sliced	*salt and milled pepper*
45 ml (3 tbsp) fresh	*225 g (½ lb) button*
chopped mint	*mushrooms*
1 large clove garlic,	*25 g (1 oz) butter*
skinned	*10 ml (2 level tsp)*
15 ml (1 tbsp) wine	*cornflour*
vinegar	*fresh mint leaves to garnish*

Cut the meat into strips about 5 cm (2 inch) long and 5 mm (¼ inch) thick, discarding any excess fat. Place the onions in a deep bowl with the meat, chopped mint and crushed garlic. Pour over the wine with the vinegar and half the oil. Season with plenty of milled pepper. Stir the ingredients to mix well, then cover tightly and marinate in the refrigerator for at least 24 hours. Stir occasionally during the marinating time.

Strain off the marinade and reserve. Wash the mushrooms by rinsing them quickly in cold water. Drain straight away— don't leave them soaking in water—then thickly slice. Heat the remaining oil in a large flameproof casserole. Add the butter and when it is frothing, brown the meat and onions a little at a time. Replace all the meat and onions, stir in the marinade and seasoning and bring to the boil, scraping any sediment off the base of the pan. Add the sliced mushrooms and stir well to mix. Bring the contents of the casserole to the boil; cover. Bake at 170°C (325°F) mark 3 for 20–25 minutes or until the meat is just tender.

Mix the cornflour to a smooth paste with a little water. Stir into the pan juices and bring up to the boil, stirring all the time. Boil for 1 minute. Adjust seasoning and serve the casserole, garnished with fresh mint leaves.

CAULIFLOWER WITH TOMATO

Cooking the cauliflower whole gives an attractive appearance to the final dish. Don't overboil the cauliflower as it should retain a hint of crispness.

30 ml (2 tbsp) oil	*salt and milled pepper*
450 g (1 lb) tomatoes,	*bayleaf*
skinned and chopped	*1 large cauliflower, about*
50 g (2 oz) onion, chopped	*900 g (2 lb) trimmed*
30 ml (2 level tbsp) tomato	*weight*
paste	*snipped parsley*
pinch sugar	

Heat the oil; add the onion and lightly brown. Stir in the tomatoes with the tomato paste, sugar, seasoning and bayleaf. Simmer gently until the tomatoes are broken down and the sauce thick and mushy, about 10–15 minutes. Adjust seasoning and remove the bayleaf.

Meanwhile trim the cauliflower, leaving on some of the tender leaves; rinse under running water. Place the cauliflower, stem side down, in a large pan of boiling salted water; the water should just cover the cauliflower. Cover the pan and gently boil the cauliflower for 10–12 minutes, or until just tender. Drain well and place the whole cauliflower in a serving dish. Spoon over the tomato sauce and garnish with snipped parsley. Cover and keep warm in a low oven.

BROWN RICE PILAFF

450 g (1 lb) long grain brown rice	*30 ml (2 level tbsp) sesame seeds*
50 g (2 oz) butter or margarine	*about 750 ml (1¼ pints) beef stock*
salt and milled pepper	

Wash the brown rice; drain well. Heat the butter or margarine in a flameproof casserole. Add the rice and half the sesame seeds and fry for 1–2 minutes, stirring frequently. Pour in the stock, season and bring to the boil. Cover tightly and bake at 170°C (325°F) mark 3 for about 50 minutes until crunchy-tender and all the stock absorbed. Check after 35–40 minutes: it may require a little more stock. Meanwhile toast the remaining sesame seeds until golden. Scatter over the rice before serving.

APRICOT & ORANGE FOOL

225 g (½ lb) dried apricots	*142-ml (5-fl oz) carton whipping cream*
2 large juicy oranges	
2 egg whites	

Cut up the apricots into small pieces; place in a medium-sized bowl. Finely grate the orange rind and add to the bowl. Squeeze the orange juice and measure it—there should be about 200 ml (7 fl oz). Pour the juice and 300 ml (½ pint) water over the apricots. Stir well, cover and leave to soak overnight. Bring the apricots and juice to the boil, cover and simmer for about 20 minutes, or until the apricots are tender. Cool slightly then purée in an electric blender until quite smooth. Add a little extra water, if dry. The apricot purée must remain fairly thick. Turn out the purée into a large bowl and cook.

Lightly whip the cream and stir through the cold apricot purée. Stiffly whisk the egg whites and fold into the apricot mixture. Cover and refrigerate for at least 2 hours. Place the Brandy Snap Baskets on individual serving plates. Spoon in the apricot mixture and refrigerate for about 2 hours.

FREEZER NOTES

The crab mixture can be frozen, unbaked, provided that the crabmeat hasn't been previously frozen. Thaw at cool room temperature for about 8 hours before baking. Prepare the Marinated Beef with Mushrooms, cook for 20 minutes only without juices. Pack and freeze. Thaw overnight at cool room temperature. Reheat and thicken as directed. Don't freeze the Brown Rice Pilaff. The tomato sauce can be prepared then frozen. Thaw at cool room temperature for about 8 hours.

Freeze the Apricot & Orange Fool without the addition of egg whites. Thaw overnight at cool room temperature, add the whisked egg whites and refrigerate before serving.

COUNTDOWN

The day before: Cut up the meat and onions; marinate overnight as directed. Prepare the Apricot & Orange Fool; cover tightly and refrigerate. Make the Brandy Snap Baskets; when quite cold store in an airtight container.

The morning: Prepare the Ramekins of Baked Crab but don't cook yet. Cover with clingfilm and refrigerate. Strain the marinade off the meat; reserve. Prepare the mushrooms. Brown the meat and onions; add the marinade and mushrooms, don't cook yet. Cool, cover and store in a cool place. Skin and roughly chop the tomatoes, finely chop the onion. Prepare the tomato sauce, simmer for 10–15 minutes, adjust seasoning and remove the bayleaf. Pour into a bowl, cool, cover and refrigerate. Trim the cauliflower, rinse under cold water. Drain, then refrigerate in a polythene bag. Toast 15 ml (1 level tbsp) sesame seeds, cool, then store in an airtight container.

To serve at 8pm:

About 6pm: Spoon the Apricot & Orange Fool into the Brandy Snap Baskets; refrigerate until required.

7-ish: Preheat the oven to 170°C (325°F) mark 3. Take the crab ramekins out of the refrigerator. Wash the rice, drain, complete the pilaff and place in the oven to cook. Place white wine in fridge to cool; open red and place in dining room to come to room temperature.

Just before 7.30: Bring the beef mixture up to the boil, cover and place in the oven to cook. Bake the crab ramekins on the top shelf in the oven. Boil the cauliflower. Reheat the tomato sauce. Drain the cauliflower; spoon over the sauce; keep warm, covered, in a low oven. Thicken the meat juices; cover and keep warm.

8pm: Serve the meal. Remember to scatter the toasted sesame seeds over the pilaff for serving.

WINES FOR THE FOOD

With the ramekins the requirement is for something full bodied and with a generous flavour. If choosing champagne for the dinner party opt for vintage, if Chablis, *premier cru* rather than ordinary, if German wine, Spätlese rather than Kabinett, and if Graves, *cru classé* rather than unclassified wine.

The marinated beef bears a resemblance to beef Stroganoff and calls for a dramatic red such as Tedeschi's Capitel San Rocco 1978, a *vino da tavola* that has left many a Valpolicella Superiore trailing in blind tastings, or a Côtes du Rhône.

The apricot and orange fool is not too acid, but the sweet brandy snap tulips dictate quite a determined dessert wine. Perhaps the ideal solution would be Gewürztraminer Vendange Tardive, Sélection des Grains Nobles, 1976, the Alsatian equivalent of a Beerenauslese.

NOVEMBER

Sliced Pears in Cider/Pork Fillets & Celeriac/Carrot & Cucumber Sticks/Chilled Coffee Custards

SLICED PEARS IN CIDER

Buy the pears a few days ahead to ensure that they're ripe. If they're still a little hard, slice and poach in the cider for a few minutes only. Cool the cooking juices to use in the dressing.

3 large ripe dessert pears	salt and milled pepper
150 ml ($\frac{1}{4}$ pint) dry cider	1 small lettuce
15 ml (1 tbsp) lemon juice	toasted flaked almonds to
1.25 ml ($\frac{1}{4}$ level tsp)	garnish
ground cumin	brown bread rolls to
45 ml (3 level tbsp) ground	accompany
almonds	

Peel the pears, quarter, core and cut into neat slices. Place them in a deep bowl with the cider, lemon juice, cumin, ground almonds and seasoning. Stir gently to mix. Cover tightly with clingfilm and refrigerate for several hours.

Meanwhile, wash the lettuce. Drain, pat dry with kitchen paper and shred. Refrigerate in a polythene bag. Just before serving arrange the lettuce and pears on individual serving plates, spooning over the dressing. Garnish with flaked almonds and serve with warm brown bread rolls.

PORK FILLETS & CELERIAC

Celeriac is a rough-skinned root vegetable with a mild celery flavour, which makes an excellent stuffing for these pork rolls. Bat out the pork tenderloins as thinly as possible with a rolling pin or heavy pan. It's important not to puncture the flesh or the stuffing may ooze out during cooking.

175 g (6 oz) streaky bacon	75 g (3 oz) shredded suet
175 g (6 oz) onion, skinned	salt and milled pepper
75 ml (5 tbsp) vegetable oil	3 pork fillets (tenderloins)
700 g (1$\frac{1}{2}$ lb) celeriac	about 350 g (12 oz)
1 clove garlic, skinned	each
lemon juice	50 g (2 oz) butter or
125 g (4 oz) fresh brown	margarine
breadcrumbs	200 ml (7 fl oz) stock

Snip the bacon into small pieces, discarding the rind and gristle. Chop the onion. Heat 45 ml (3 tbsp) oil in a frying pan. Add the bacon and half the onion and cook gently until the fat begins to run out of the bacon. Increase the heat and fry the ingredients until lightly browned.

Meanwhile cut the celeriac into wedges, peel with a sharp knife, and finely grate two-thirds of it. Roughly chop the remainder; cover this with water to which a few drops of lemon juice or vinegar have been added. Add the grated celeriac and crushed garlic to the frying pan and stir over a moderate heat for 2–3 minutes. Remove from the heat and stir in the breadcrumbs, suet, 15 ml (1 tbsp) lemon juice and seasoning. Turn out into a large bowl and cool.

Meanwhile trim the pork fillets of all transparent skin and excess fat. Split each one lengthwise, leaving a hinge at the base, and open out like a book. Place one fillet at a time between two sheets of cling film and bat out very thinly, carefully keeping it all in one piece. Divide the cold celeriac stuffing between the fillets and fold in the narrow ends very securely. Roll up each fillet separately and tie at regular intervals.

Heat the remaining oil in a roasting tin (it should be just large enough for the three stuffed fillets). Put the butter in with the hot oil and when it is frothing, add the pork fillets and brown well. Lift out of the tin, add the drained, chopped celeriac and remaining onion and lightly brown. Replace the pork fillets and pour on the stock; season well. Cover the tin tightly with a double layer of kitchen foil. Bake at 170°C (325°F) mark 3 for about 1 hour, or until the meat is tender.

Lift the fillets out of the roasting tin, cut off the string and carve into thick slices. Cover and keep warm in a low oven. Pour the cooking juices into a blender goblet or food processor and whirl until almost smooth. Reheat in a saucepan, adjust seasoning and spoon a little over the pork. Serve the rest separately.

CARROT & CUCUMBER STICKS

For a change replace the cucumber with thin strips of courgettes, leaving the skin on to provide colour for the finished dish.

900 g (2 lb) carrots	2.5 ml ($\frac{1}{2}$ level tsp) dried
25 g (1 oz) butter or	sage
margarine	salt and milled pepper
15 ml (1 tbsp) lemon juice	1 large cucumber

Pare the carrots and cut into thin finger-sized pieces. Melt the fat in a flameproof casserole. Add the carrots and stir over a moderate heat for 1–2 minutes. Stir in the lemon juice, sage and seasoning, mixing well. Cover tightly and bake at 170°C (325°F) mark 3 for 25 minutes. Meanwhile wipe the cucumber and cut into pieces similar in size to the carrots. Uncover the carrot dish, stir in the cucumber. Re-cover and return to the oven for 15 minutes, or until the vegetables are just tender. Adjust seasoning if necessary.

CHILLED COFFEE CUSTARDS

These delicately flavoured custards make the lightest of desserts. When kiwifruit are ripe you should be able to peel the skins off gently rather than cut them away.

25 g (1 oz) butter or margarine	*12.5 ml (2½ level tsp) powdered gelatine*
100 g (4 oz) coffee beans	*3 egg yolks*
568 ml (1 pint) milk	*75 g (3 oz) caster sugar*
142-ml (5-fl oz) carton single cream	*4 ripe kiwifruit Irish cream liqueur*

Melt the fat in a medium-sized saucepan, add the coffee beans and stir over a moderate heat for 1–2 minutes. Pour in the milk and cream and bring to the boil. Remove the pan from the heat, cover and leave to infuse for 30 minutes.

Meanwhile measure 45 ml (3 tbsp) water into a small basin. Sprinkle over the gelatine and leave to soak until sponge-like in texture. Beat the egg yolks and caster sugar together. Strain the milk on to the yolks, stirring well. Rinse out the pan then return the milk mixture. Cook over a gentle heat, stirring all the time, until the mixture thickens very slightly—do *not* boil or the mixture will curdle. Pour the custard out into a large bowl, stir in the gelatine until dissolved then leave to cool.

When the mixture is quite cold and beginning to thicken slightly, divide between six ramekin dishes. Refrigerate the mixture to set—at least 3 hours.

Meanwhile halve the kiwifruit lengthwise, then trim away the skin and cut the flesh into half-moon shaped slices. Cover with clingfilm and refrigerate. Turn out the coffee custards; using a damp finger gently ease the custard away from the sides of the ramekins to loosen. Place an individual serving plate over the ramekin and turn it over. Hold the plate and ramekin firmly together and give them a few sharp sideways shakes until the custard is released. Lift off the ramekin dish. Arrange the slices of kiwifruit around the custards. Cover with cling film and return to the refrigerator until required. At serving time spoon a little liqueur over each custard.

FREEZER NOTES

The Sliced Pears in Cider will not freeze satisfactorily. For the Pork Fillets & Celeriac, prepare the stuffing, fill the pork fillets and tie, wrap and freeze. (The pork fillets must not have been previously frozen.) When required thaw loosely wrapped, at cool room temperature overnight. Refrigerate until cooking time. Do not freeze the Carrot & Cucumber Sticks or the Chilled Coffee Custards.

COUNTDOWN

The day before: Prepare the Chilled Coffee Custards; leaving them in the ramekins, cover and refrigerate.
The morning: Prepare the Sliced Pears in Cider; cover tightly with cling film and refrigerate. Wash and dry the lettuce; shred and then refrigerate in a polythene bag. Toast some flaked almonds for garnish, cool, store in an airtight container. Make the stuffing for the pork fillets, cool. Bat out the pork fillets and fill with the stuffing, tie. Refrigerate, covered. Roughly chop the remaining celeriac, as directed. Cut the carrot and cucumber strips, place in separate polythene bags and refrigerate. Peel the potatoes, cover with cold water and store in a cool place. Cut up the kiwifruit, cover with cling film and refrigerate.
To serve at 8pm:
6.30-ish: Preheat the oven to 170°C (325°F) mark 3. Brown the pork fillets, complete and put in the oven to cook. Turn out the coffee custards, decorate with kiwifruit, cover and return to the refrigerator.
About 7pm: Fry the carrots, add the lemon juice, sage and seasoning; cover and place in the oven to cook. Put the potatoes on to boil. Stir the cucumber into the carrots after 25 minutes cooking time. Re-cover and return to the oven for a further 15 minutes.
7.45-ish: Loosely wrap brown rolls in foil and place in the oven to warm. Mash the potatoes, cover and keep warm in a low oven. Slice the meat, cover and keep warm. Purée the cooking juices; pour into a saucepan ready to reheat. Chill cider or wine in refrigerator door.
About 8pm: Arrange the lettuce and pears on serving plates and garnish with flaked almonds. Spoon a little liqueur over each coffee custard.

WINES FOR THE FOOD

Cider is obvious here, since it is in the starter and apples are a traditional and pleasing accompaniment to pork. The most appropriate choice of cider should be Bulmers' Special Reserve Fine Dry, since it is actually made with a mixture of perry (fermented pear juice) in the blend. It is not the cleanest of cider flavours, though, and you might prefer dry, sparkling La Cidraie Brut from Normandy or Bulmers' excellent full-flavoured dry still No 7. Gewürztraminers will also go with both the first two dishes.

The obvious accompaniment to the coffee custards is coffee cream liqueur, such as Kahlúa or Tia Maria coffee liqueur; for the richness of the dessert, I would be tempted to cut the liqueur sweetness by mixing it half and half with brandy (the drier B&B formula can be applied to any liqueur). Or one could even mix coffee liqueur with Calvados apple brandy, or finish off with a rich dessert Gewürztraminer wine—Hugel 1976 Selection des Grains Nobles.

DECEMBER

Serves 6

Chestnut & Orange Soup/Salmon Escalopes with Dill & Cucumber/Whisky Marinaded Grapes/Crème Fraîche

CHESTNUT & ORANGE SOUP

If fresh chestnuts are unavailable, use a 283-g (10-oz) can (drained weight) of whole chestnuts.

450 g (1 lb) whole chestnuts	40 g (1½ oz) butter
125 g (4 oz) carrots	1.4 litre (2½ pint) beef stock
225 g (8 oz) onions	salt and milled pepper
125 g (4 oz) mushrooms	10 ml (2 level tsp) finely grated orange rind
5 ml (1 level tsp) plain flour	parsley to garnish

Nick the brown outer skins of the chestnuts with a pair of scissors, or the tip of a sharp knife. Cook the chestnuts in boiling water for 3–5 minutes, then lift out using a draining spoon, a few at a time. Peel off both the brown and inner skins and discard. Pare the carrots, skin the onions and finely chop both; wipe the mushrooms, then finely chop. Melt the butter in a large saucepan, add the vegetables and fry together until lightly browned. Mix in the flour and cook, stirring for a further 3–4 minutes, or until the flour begins to colour. Off the heat, stir in the stock, prepared chestnuts and seasoning. Bring slowly to the boil, stirring. Simmer, covered, for 40–45 minutes, or until the chestnuts are quite tender. Cool a little, then liquidise a small quantity at a time. Add the orange rind and reheat for serving. Adjust seasoning and garnish with snipped parsley.

SALMON ESCALOPES WITH DILL & CUCUMBER

Frozen imported salmon is readily available at this time of the year and is good value. We used a salmon tail which is even less expensive.

400 g (14 oz) cucumber, peeled	dill seeds or sesame seeds
salt and milled pepper	125 g (5 oz) butter
397-g (14-oz) packet puff pastry	10 ml (2 level tsp) plain flour
beaten egg	200 ml (7 fl oz) rosé wine
700 g (1½ lb) salmon, thawed	5 ml (1 level tsp) dried dill weed

Dice the cucumber finely. Place in a stainless steel colander, sprinkle generously with salt and leave for 1 hour to let the juices run out. Rinse well, then pat dry with kitchen paper. Meanwhile, on a floured surface, roll the puff pastry to a rectangle 38 × 12.5 cm (15 × 5 inch). Halve lengthwise then cut across at 12.5-cm (5-inch) intervals to give six rectangles. Lightly mark an inner rectangle 5 mm (¼ inch) in from the edges of each one. Place on a baking sheet and brush the tops lightly with beaten egg, taking care not to brush any egg down the sides as this will prevent the pastry from rising. Sprinkle with dill or sesame seeds. Bake at 220°C (425°F) mark 7 for 10–15 minutes, until a deep golden brown and well risen. Remove from oven, carefully cut out 'lids' and scoop any uncooked dough from the centre. Return cases to oven (without lids) for 2–3 minutes.

To prepare the fish escalopes, first fillet the salmon flesh off the bone: with a small, sharp knife, make an incision straight along the centre of the back of the salmon right down to the bone. Starting from the thicker end of the fish, ease the knife under the flesh of the top left-hand fillet. Working with long, clean strokes and keeping the blade as close to the bone as possible, gradually remove the fillet. Turn the fish around and cut off the second top fillet. Fillet the underside in the same way. No flesh should be left on the bone. Place the fillets skin side down and hold at one end. Using the same knife, keep the blade almost parallel to the flesh and slice off 5-mm (¼-inch) thick escalopes about 7.5–10-cm (3–4-inch) long until all the flesh has been removed.

In a large, preferably non-stick, frying pan, melt 50 g (2 oz) butter. When foaming, quickly sauté the escalopes a few at a time until just coloured on both sides. Using slotted spoons, remove to a 1.4-litre (2½-pint) shallow oven-proof dish. In the same pan, sauté the well-dried cucumber with a further 25 g (1 oz) butter until softened—about 3–4 minutes. Spoon half the cucumber over the salmon. Stir the flour into the remaining cucumber, cook for 2–3 minutes, then remove from the heat, cover and set aside. Add the wine, dill weed and seasoning to the salmon. Cover tightly with buttered foil and bake at 200°C (400°F) mark 6 for about 25 minutes. Five minutes before end of cooking time, put pastry cases on a baking sheet, cover loosely with foil and place in low oven to reheat.

Strain juices from salmon and reserve. Return salmon, still covered, to oven to keep warm. Gently reheat reserved cucumber mixture, stir in juices and bring to the boil, stirring. Simmer for 2 minutes, whisking in the remaining butter. Check seasoning. Spoon escalopes into warmed pastry cases and pour over the sauce to serve. Replace lids.

124

Whisky Marinaded Grapes

Adjust the amount of honey and lemon juice according to the sweetness of the grapes.

350 g (12 oz) black grapes
350 g (12 oz) green grapes
30 ml (2 tbsp) whisky

45 ml (3 tbsp) runny
honey
5 ml (1 tsp) lemon juice

Wash the grapes, drain well and dry with kitchen paper. Carefully halve lengthwise and ease out the pips with the point of a knife. In a large mixing bowl, stir together the whisky, honey and lemon juice. Add the grapes and stir well. Cover with cling film and leave in a cool place (not the refrigerator) to marinade for at least 4 hours, preferably oovernight. Chill in the refrigerator for 30 minutes before serving. Spoon into a serving dish and serve with Crème Fraîche and shortbread fingers.

Crème Fraîche

Not quite the same as continental crème fraîche, but it goes very well with the Marinaded Grapes.

113-ml (4-fl oz) carton
extra thick cream
pinch sugar (optional)

141-g (5-oz) carton
natural yogurt

Lightly whip the cream, then fold together with the yogurt and sugar. Spoon into a serving dish, cover and chill well.

Freezer Notes

Prepare and liquidise the soup, don't add the orange rind yet. When cold, pack and freeze. When required, leave the soup to thaw at cool, room temperature over-night; refrigerate until serving time. Reheat, adding the orange rind and then complete.

The salmon recipe and Whisky Marinaded Grapes do not freeze well. Make and bake the shortbread fingers. When cold, pack them in a rigid container and freeze. When required, thaw, place them on baking sheets, refresh in the oven loosely covered at 180°C (350°F) mark 4 for 1–2 minutes, then cool on wire racks.

Countdown

The day before: Prepare and liquidise the soup. Pour into a mixing bowl, add the orange rind and when cold, cover and refrigerate. Shape and cook the pastry cases for the fish dish, cool then store in an airtight container. Prepare the grapes and the marinade. Mix together, cover and leave in a cool place. Make some shortbread fingers using your favourite recipe. Cool on a wire rack, then store in an airtight container.

The morning: Wash some parsley sprigs, dry, then refrigerate in a polythene bag. Dice and salt the cucumber. Fillet the fish and slice off the escalopes. Sauté the fish and arrange in the baking dish. Add half the sautéed cucumber, the wine, dill weed and seasoning; cover and refrigerate. Add flour to remaining cucumber, cook for 2–3 minutes, then store, covered, in a cool place. Trim, cut into small florets, wash and drain 900 g (2 lb) broccoli; refrigerate in a polythene bag. Skin and thinly slice 700 g (1½ lb) tomatoes, layer in a shallow serving dish, then cover and refrigerate. In a lidded jar, shake together 75 ml (5 tbsp) olive oil, 30 ml (2 tbsp) white wine vinegar, 5 ml (1 level tsp) French mustard, pinch of sugar, salt and milled pepper; refrigerate. Prepare the Crème Fraîche, cover and refrigerate. Place apéritif in fridge to chill.

To serve at 8pm:

About 7.10: Preheat the oven to 200°C (400°F) mark 6. Place pastry cases on baking sheet ready to reheat.

7.20-ish: Put soup in a pan ready to reheat. Put the fish in the oven to bake. Five minutes before end of cooking time, reheat pastry cases. Chill the rosé wine.

About 7.30: Put on a large pan of water, then steam the broccoli over this.

About 7.45: Test the broccoli. Turn the oven down to low. Place the broccoli in a serving dish, season, cover and keep warm. Pour liquid off fish, reserve. Keep fish covered in a low oven. Prepare the sauce for the fish, keep warm covered on the side of the stove. Reheat the soup. Season and garnish.

8-ish: Chill the Whisky Marinaded Grapes. Serve the meal. Spoon the prepared dressing over the tomatoes. Fill the pastry cases with salmon, whisk the sauce and pour over just before serving the main course. Serve apéritif and bring rosé to table.

Wines for the Food

The soup is an occasion for a classic apéritif wine—chilled dry oloroso sherry or dry port. For the salmon you must seek that rarity, a dry and distinguished rosé. The most suitable would be a Sancerre rosé—every bit as serious as red or white Sancerre, though prettier. The whisky-marinaded grapes seem to dictate a whisky-based liqueur—Drambuie or Glayva, but many people prefer the dry taste of malt whisky even to cognac to round off dinner.

INDEX